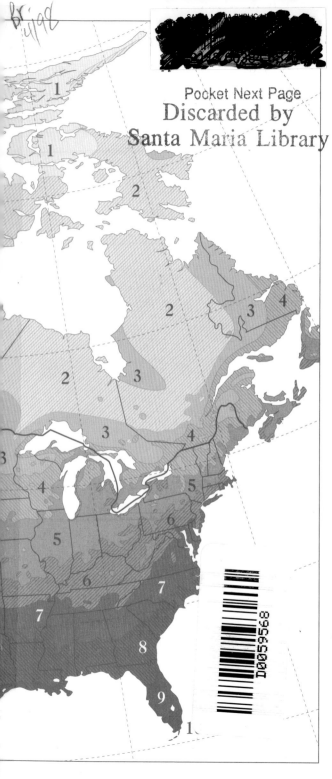

KEY TO HARDINESS ZONES

This map shows eleven geographical zones based on the average annual minimum temperatures recorded for the years 1974 to 1986. The zone numbers accompanying the plants in this book indicate their lower limits of winter cold hardiness. Extreme summer heat and humidity also play a part in a plant's adaptability; many plants hardy in colder zones grow poorly in warmer, wetter ones.

1	BELOW −50°F BELOW −46°C
2	−50° TO −40°F −46° TO −40°C
3	−40° TO −30°F −40° TO −34°C
4	−30° TO −20°F −34° TO −29°C
5	−20° TO −10°F −29° TO −23°C
6	−10° TO 0°F −23° TO −18°C
7	0° TO 10°F −18° TO −12°C
8	10° TO 20°F −12° TO −7°C
9	20° TO 30°F −7° TO −1°C
10	30° TO 40°F −1° TO 4°C
11	ABOVE 40°F ABOVE 4°C

 EYEWITNESS

GARDEN HANDBOOKS

635.931

Annuals & Biennials.   c1997.

EYEWITNESS

GARDEN HANDBOOKS

ANNUALS
&BIENNIALS

DK PUBLISHING, INC

A DK PUBLISHING BOOK

Produced for DK Publishing by PAGE*One*
Cairn House, Elgiva Lane, Chesham,
Buckinghamshire HP5 2JD

PROJECT DIRECTORS Bob Gordon and Helen Parker
EDITOR Neil Kelly
SENIOR EDITOR Charlotte Stock
DESIGNER Matthew Cook

MANAGING EDITOR Louise Abbott
MANAGING ART EDITOR Lee Griffiths
PRODUCTION Silvia La Greca
PICTURE RESEARCH Mollie Gillard, Christine Rista

First American Edition, 1997
2 4 6 8 10 9 7 5 3 1

Published in the United States by
DK Publishing, Inc., 95 Madison Avenue,
New York, New York 10016
Visit us on the World Wide Web at http://www.dk.com

Copyright © 1997
Dorling Kindersley Limited, London

Library of Congress Cataloging-in-Publication Data
Annuals and biennials.
     p.   cm. — (Eyewitness garden handbooks)
   Includes index.
   ISBN 0-7894-1983-1
   1. Annuals (Plants) 2. Biennials (Plants) I. DK Publishing.
   Inc. II. Series.
   SB422.A5745   1997
   635.9'31— dc21   97-19526
                                                         CIP

Color reproduction by Colourscan, Singapore
Printed and bound by Star Standard Industries, Singapore

CONTENTS

CONTRIBUTORS

ALAN TOOGOOD
Consultant

LINDEN HAWTHORNE
Writer

HOW TO USE THIS BOOK

THIS BOOK PROVIDES the ideal quick reference guide to selecting and identifying plants for the garden.

The ANNUALS AND BIENNIALS IN THE GARDEN section is a helpful introduction to annuals and biennials and advises on choosing a suitable plant for a particular site or purpose, such as in borders and containers, or simply as a specimen.

To choose or identify a plant, turn to the CATALOG OF ANNUALS AND BIENNIALS, where color photographs are accompanied by concise plant descriptions and useful tips on cultivation and propagation. The entries are grouped by size and color (see the color wheel below) to make selection easier.

For additional information on plant cultivation, routine care, and propagation, turn to the GUIDE TO ANNUALS AND BIENNIALS CARE, where general advice on all aspects of caring for your plants can be found.

At the end of the book, a useful two-page glossary explains key terms, and a comprehensive index allows quick and easy access to the book by plant name.

The color wheel

All the plants in the book are grouped according to the color of their main feature of interest. They are always arranged in the same order, indicated by the color wheel below, from white through to yellow and orange.

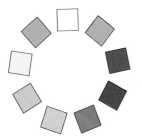

THE SYMBOLS

The symbols below are used throughout the CATALOG OF ANNUALS AND BIENNIALS to indicate a plant's preferred growing conditions and hardiness. However, the climate and soil conditions of your particular site should also be taken into account, as they may affect a plant's growth.

☼ Prefers full sun

☽ Prefers partial shade

☀ Tolerates full shade

pH Needs acid soil

◯ Prefers well-drained soil

◗ Prefers moist soil

◆ Prefers wet soil

HARDINESS

The range of winter temperatures that each plant is able to withstand is shown by the USDA plant hardiness zone numbers that are given in each entry. The temperature ranges for each zone are shown on the endpaper map in this book.

The plants featured in the CATALOG OF ANNUALS AND BIENNIALS are divided according to the average height of a mature plant for the greater part of the year. The specific height measurement given in each individual entry reflects the plant's maximum height. Please note that heights may vary from the ones given, according to site, growing conditions, climate, and age.

The categories are as follows:

LARGE More than 18in (45cm)

MEDIUM 6–18in (15–45cm)

SMALL Up to 6in (15cm)

HOW TO USE THE CATALOG OF ANNUALS AND BIENNIALS

HEADINGS
The Catalog is subdivided into sections, according to the average size of the plants.

The plant's *family name* appears here.

The plant's *common name(s)* appear here.

The plant's *botanical name* appears here.

PLANT PORTRAITS
The color photographs show each plant's main features and color (see the color wheel on previous page).

ENTRIES
A brief plant description giving details of growing habit, flowers, fruits, and leaves, followed by information on native habitat, tips on cultivation and propagation, and a list of other botanical names.

FEATURE PAGES
Plant groups or genera of special interest to the gardener are presented on separate feature pages. A brief introduction giving general information on appearance, use, cultivation, and propagation is followed by concise plant entries.

---

48 • LARGE

| Compositae/Asteraceae | CHINA ASTER |

CALLISTEPHUS CHINENSIS
'Compliment Light Blue'
Habit Erect, fast-growing, bushy annual. *Flowers* Quill-petaled, double, from summer to early autumn. Light blue. *Leaves* Oval. Mid-green.
• NATIVE HABITAT Garden origin. Species occurs on slopes and wasteland. China.
• CULTIVATION Grow in a sheltered site in fertile, neutral to alkaline, moist but well-drained soil, in full sun. Good for cut flowers.
• PROPAGATION Sow seed at 61°F (16°C) in early spring, or *in situ* in mid-spring.

HEIGHT 28in (70cm)
SPREAD 8in (20cm)

| Malvaceae |

ANODA CRISTATA **'Opal Cup'**
Habit Vigorous, upright, bushy annual. *Flowers* Saucer-shaped, 2in (5cm) across, from summer to autumn. Clear silvery-lilac, with dark veins. *Leaves* Hand-shaped, lobed or unlobed, entire, or toothed. Mid-green, with purple marks.
• NATIVE HABITAT Garden origin.
• CULTIVATION Grow in moist but well-drained soil, in sun. Provide support. Deadhead regularly. Good for bedding, mixed or annual borders.
• PROPAGATION Sow seed at 55–59°F (13–15°C) in early spring to spring.

HEIGHT to 5ft (1.5m)
SPREAD 24in (60cm)

| Leguminosae/Papilionaceae |

LUPINUS NANUS **'Pixie Delight'**
Habit Upright or branching annual. *Flowers* Pea-like, in clusters to 8in (20cm) tall, borne in summer. White, pink, blue, or lavender, with some bicolors. *Leaves* Hand-shaped, hairy, divided into leaflets. Mid-green.
• NATIVE HABITAT Garden origin.
• CULTIVATION Grow in light, sandy, slightly acid soil, in sun or part-shade. Suitable for bedding or an annual border.
• PROPAGATION Sow nicked or pre-soaked seed in a seed bed in spring.

HEIGHT 20in (50cm)
SPREAD 9in (23cm)

| Convolvulaceae | MORNING GLORY |

IPOMOEA TRICOLOR **'Heavenly Blue'**
Habit Climbing annual. *Flowers* Funnel-shaped, 3in (8cm) across, borne in summer, or year-round in the tropics. Deep azure, with a white throat. *Leaves* Oval to heart-shaped. Light to mid-green.
• NATIVE HABITAT Garden origin. Species occurs in tropical forest, C. and S. America.
• CULTIVATION Grow in fertile, moist but well-drained soil, in a warm, sunny, and sheltered site.
• PROPAGATION Sow chipped or pre-soaked seed singly at 64°F (18°C). Grow on in warmth, as sudden temperature drops can cause failure.

Min. 45°F (7°C)
HEIGHT 10–12ft (3–4m)

---

26 • HELIANTHUS

HELIANTHUS

The genus *Helianthus* includes some 70–80 species of annuals and perennials. The annual sunflowers described here are grown for their showy, daisy-like flowerheads, which are typically 2–4in (5–10cm) in diameter, but can grow up to 12in (30cm) across in the giant-flowered cultivars. The flowers are available in warm shades of mahogany-red, yellow, or orange, surrounding a brown, purple, or dark yellow central disk. These handsome and dramatic flowers are strong-stemmed and make ideal cut flowers. They are also suitable for a mixed or annual border, or for in-filling in a herbaceous border. The flowers are very attractive to bees and other beneficial insects and, when cut and dried, the seedheads attract birds, especially finches, into the garden in autumn and winter. Small cultivars, such as *H. annuus* 'Teddy Bear', are ideally suited for container plantings.

The rapid growth and spectacular size of the tall and giant-flowered cultivars make them ideal in children's gardens. Like all sunflowers, they flower most reliably in long, hot summers.

Grow in fertile to moderately fertile, neutral to alkaline, well-drained soil that is rich in organic matter. Provide a warm, sheltered position in full sun. Tall cultivars need the support of stakes or strong canes.

Sow seed under glass in late winter at 61°F (16°C), in individual pots. Harden off and set out in their flowering position in spring or early summer. Alternatively, sow *in situ* in early spring.

Slugs may be a problem, especially when plants are young. The cultivars are particularly susceptible to attack from powdery mildew, especially in dry summers, so keep their roots moist and avoid overhead watering.

H. DEBILIS subsp. *CUCUMERIFOLIUS* **'Italian White'**
Habit Vigorous annual. *Flowers* To 4in (10cm) across, borne in summer. Creamy-white or pale lemon-yellow, with a black central disk. *Leaves* Oval to lance-shaped, coarsely hairy, toothed. Mid-green.
• HEIGHT 5ft (1.5m)
• SPREAD 18in (45cm)

H. ANNUUS **'Music Box'**
Habit Well-branched, fast-growing annual. *Flowers* To 4½in (12cm) across, from summer. Dark red to creamy-yellow, with a brown central disk. Also available in bicolors. *Leaves* Oval to heart-shaped. Dark green.
• HEIGHT 28in (70cm)
• SPREAD to 18in (45cm)

H. annuus 'Music Box'

H. DEBILIS subsp. *CUCUMERIFOLIUS*
Habit Stout-stemmed, well-branched annual. *Flowers* To 4in (10cm) wide, borne in summer. Bright yellow, sometimes flushed red, on purple-mottled stems. *Leaves* Oval to lance-shaped. Mid-green.
• OTHER NAME *H. cucumerifolius.*
• HEIGHT 3ft (1m)
• SPREAD 12in (30cm)

H. debilis subsp. *cucumerifolius*

H. debilis subsp. *cucumerifolius* 'Italian White'

SYMBOLS
The symbols indicate the sun, soil, and hardiness requirements (see THE SYMBOLS on previous page). Minimum temperatures are given for plants that cannot survive below 32°F (0°C).

SIZES
The height and spread measurements reflect the maximum dimensions of a mature plant, where applicable in flower.

FEATURE PLANT DESCRIPTIONS
As with the main Catalog entries, a brief plant description is followed by useful tips on cultivation and propagation where these are not already given in the general introduction.

ANNUALS AND BIENNIALS IN THE GARDEN

THE PLANT TYPES known as annuals and biennials are among the most easily grown and inexpensive of all garden plants, with enormous potential for adding color, texture, and fragrance to a wide diversity of garden situations. Most annuals and biennials bloom in profusion throughout summer, with many continuing to provide a brilliant display until autumn.

What are annuals and biennials?

True annuals are short-term plants, in that they grow, bloom, set seed, and die within a single season. Hardy annuals are capable of withstanding frost and may be sown *in situ* in spring or early autumn for earlier blooms the following year. Half-hardy and frost-tender annuals are sown under glass between late winter and early spring, to be set out in the garden when the danger of frost has passed. A few half-hardy annuals may also be sown directly in their flowering site later in spring, when the soil has warmed up. Biennials are sown in summer and produce leaves in their first year, then flower, set seed, and die in their second. A number of tender perennials, such as pelargoniums or busy lizzies (*Impatiens*), bloom in their first year from seed. They can be treated as half-hardy or tender annuals and often produce more flowers and are more vigorous if grown in this way. Annuals and biennials are available in a wide range of heights and habits, from the neat, low mounds of *Ageratum houstonianum* to the towering spires of the hollyhocks (*Alcea rosea*).

Summer-flowering annuals

*Small areas can be transformed by exuberant displays of vividly colored annuals, including busy lizzies (*Impatiens), *cascading lobelias, petunias, and* Schizanthus.

A tapestry of summer color
Irregular patches of hardy and half-hardy annuals are sown in naturalistic and informal drifts to provide a beautiful and long-lived display of brilliant color.

Designing with annuals and biennials

Annuals and biennials are traditionally grown in beds and borders devoted entirely to them, and can be used as a rapid means of achieving a brilliant display of vibrant color. Using them in this way is ideal in new gardens, where they will provide interest while longer-term plants become established. Their versatility also makes them ideally suited for use alongside other plant types in more mature gardens.

Many annuals come in a dazzling, varied range of hot colors that provide an exuberant display when sited appropriately. They are harder to place in planting schemes of more muted tones, but the availability of many modern seed series in a range of single colors, including pastel tints, makes it possible to select harmonious shades whatever the color scheme. Drifts of pure white flowers, or blocks of fresh green foliage, can be used to counterbalance strong hues of scarlet, magenta, and orange, and prevent these shades from appearing dominant or overpowering. Plants with leaves in cool shades of gray or gray-green, such as *Gypsophila elegans* or *Euphorbia marginata*, contrast with – and greatly enhance – the warmth of deep reds, crimsons, or rich velvety-purples.

The key to creating attractive border compositions is an equal balance of leaf-texture combinations, plant forms, and harmonious color associations. Cypress-like columns of *Bassia scoparia* f. *trichophylla*, for example, with their feathery, emerald-green foliage, or the bold, red-purple leaves of *Ricinus communis* 'Impala', both provide bold textural contrasts as well as a foil for bright colors.

The varied height and habit of annuals and biennials provides ample material to create variations in form and shape in the border. Many hybrid seed

Formal bedding scheme
A knot of box and lavender is filled with uniform blocks of strong color to create vivid monochrome panels of scarlet and gold, using compact cultivars of Calendula *and* Pelargonium.

series offer both dwarf and tall cultivars that can be selected according to requirements. Many mat- and mound-formers are equally at home whether softening the edges at the front of the border, or filling patio pots. Plants of a trailing or climbing habit, such as sweet peas (*Lathyrus*), lend a strong, vertical element to a design when covering a wall or trellis, or cascading over the top of walls and banks. To create striking focal points in a planting scheme, use the tall flower-spikes of species like the foxglove (*Digitalis purpurea*), or plants of architectural habit, such as *Onopordum acanthium*.

Annual borders

Whole beds or borders devoted to annuals can be used to create colorful effects in a range of garden styles. The winter-flowering pansies, cultivars of *Viola* x *wittrockiana*, are specially bred to provide color to brighten the darker months between winter and spring. As spring progresses, their display can be complemented with wallflowers (*Erysimum*), forget-me-nots (*Myosotis*), and primulas, with primrose and polyanthus cultivars available in a range of jewel-bright colors. As the

primulas begin to fade, they can be replaced with a varied selection from the vast range of annuals and biennials that flower during the months of summer and early autumn.

The scope for creating attractive plant compositions is limitless, but when planting an annual border, the most successful schemes are often those that use a restricted range of harmonious color. This can be achieved by careful blending of colors at the same end of the spectrum, such as combining dazzling oranges with warm yellows and hot scarlets, or muted pinks with soft mauves and cool blues. The simple theme of combining complementary colors, such as blues and yellows, is also highly effective. Most schemes work best if the plants are used in substantial, interlocking drifts to give bold blocks of color. Single plants, unless large specimens, can easily become isolated and will weaken the overall structure of the design.

Formal bedding

The use of formal bedding, which originally had its heyday during the Victorian era, is currently enjoying a resurgence. Bedding styles common

A mixed border
Annuals and biennials can be used to great effect when planted to form a tapestry of color woven around more permanent plantings of perennials. Many, including marigolds and cornflowers, will self-seed to create a natural cottage-garden style.

to this period, such as knots and parterres, are increasingly used, and contemporary interpretations of Victorian bedding techniques are being adapted to suit small, modern gardens. The uniformity of size and habit, improved vigor, and intense, consistent color of many modern cultivars make them ideal for use in formal bedding. Their dense, uniform growth and continuous flowering are ideal for creating complex patterns, whether set against a permanent framework of living plants, like a box hedge or lavender, or when used in designs defined by bricks, gravel, or other architectural materials.

Mixed and herbaceous borders
Annuals and biennials can play an important role when used to create a range of color highlights among more permanent plantings of shrubs, perennials, and bulbs. They increase the diversity of color and texture in a design, and help to create an interesting floral display that extends beyond the season of the other plantings. Unlike many shrubs and perennials that have a short, albeit glorious, burst of color, most annuals and biennials are noted for their long period

A carpet of color
The cool shade provided by the canopy of trees and shrubs is an ideal situation for busy lizzies (Impatiens) *grown here en masse to create a living carpet of intense color.*

of bloom. If sown annually, they can be carefully placed to co-ordinate existing color themes. If allowed to self-sow, they can become a regular feature, and are especially effective where the designer's intention is to create informal and natural effects. Using plants selected for their color and form, this technique adds charming unpredictability to a scheme, and is ideal for weaving together blocks of color formed by neighboring blooms. The pale, delicately divided leaves and soft blue flowers of love-in-a-mist (*Nigella damascena*) are ideally suited to this technique. Plants such as night-scented stock (*Matthiola longipetala* subsp. *bicornis*) can also be used to add another dimension to a design. The small flowers of this slim annual are intensely fragrant at night, and thrive when scattered randomly among other,

more permanent plantings. Annuals and biennials are particularly useful as temporary fillers in mixed and herbaceous borders. Gaps in the border may occur for a number of reasons; they can be caused by the occasional failure of a plant or, more commonly, during the immature phase of permanent plantings. In some cases, as with the perennial poppy (*Papaver croceum*), plants die back untidily after flowering, leaving a gap that can be filled admirably with airy annuals like *Gypsophila elegans*. Sow seed where the plants are to flower, and select cultivars in a height and color range that will suit the permanent scheme.

Planting in containers

There is a wide range of containers available to the gardener, including pots, tubs, window boxes, and hanging baskets. All of these can be planted up

Planting in the vertical plane

Hanging baskets, wall planters, and window boxes filled with colorful annuals of both upright and trailing habit are used imaginatively here to transform a bare wall. The continuous curtain of color lends strong horizontal and vertical lines to the composition.

to produce eye-catching features for a variety of sites in the garden. Most annuals thrive in containers, either on their own, or to complement longer-term plantings. The uniform habit, long flowering period, and color consistency of modern F1 and F2 seed series make them ideal for long-lasting displays.

Plants with a trailing habit are well suited for hanging baskets and window boxes, and can be particularly useful for disguising containers that would otherwise have a plain and functional appearance. Reliable trailing plants that are ideal for this role include petunias, *Lobelia erinus* Cascade series, *Verbena* x *hybrida* cultivars, and ivy-leaved pelargoniums. All of these are available in a wide range of colors, and compositions in containers are limited only by the imagination of the designer. The use of trailing plants in containers such as hanging baskets, half-baskets, and window boxes can also add height and a strong vertical element to a composition. This is especially useful in small courtyards, on patios, and in other areas where space is limited.

Extending the range

A wide range of annuals may be grown in containers in areas adjacent to a house. Warm, sheltered niches around the house allow plants that would be too tender for more open and exposed garden areas to grow freely. House walls should be checked to ensure that they do not create wind tunnels or areas of turbulence. The requirements of the plants should also be matched to the amount of light and shade available. Displays of annuals in containers are not restricted to the summer months. Although few annuals and biennials bloom through the winter, flowering pansies, polyanthus, and primulas provide color from early spring to early summer, and may remain in flower almost continuously if placed in a sheltered spot.

Annuals for cutting and drying

Many annuals provide excellent, and often unusual, cut flowers. In gardens with ample space, it is well worth devoting a border solely to cut flowers to produce an abundance of material for arranging. Sweet peas are unrivaled as cut flowers, especially the intensely fragranced old-fashioned cultivars. Sunflowers are ideal for displaying in the garden, and make gloriously colorful arrangements at relatively little cost. Everlasting flowers, as well as plants such as *Consolida*, *Amaranthus*, *Bracteantha*, and *Limonium*, are also well suited for cutting and drying. If kept out of direct sunlight, dried arrangements retain their color right through until the following year's harvest.

Window box compositions

The framework of cascading ivies makes a foil for a subtle, restrained color scheme using pale yellow begonias and blue-mauve pansies. These colors are enhanced by the richer shades of blue provided by the trailing lobelias.

Scrophulariaceae	

DIGITALIS PURPUREA f. *ALBIFLORA*

Habit Rosette-forming biennial. *Flowers*
Tubular, 2-lipped, in tall, one-sided clusters,
borne in summer. White. *Leaves* Lance-shaped,
coarse, toothed, and hairy. Bright green.
• NATIVE HABITAT Woods and hedgerows, Europe.
• CULTIVATION Grow in moist but well-drained,
leaf-rich soil, in sun or partial shade. Tolerates dry
soil. Ideal in mixed borders and woodland gardens.
• PROPAGATION Sow seed in containers in a cold
frame in late spring. Remove any seedlings with
red-flushed leaf veins; these bear purple flowers.

Z 4–8

HEIGHT
3–6ft
(1–2m)

SPREAD
24in (60cm)

Caryophyllaceae	

GYPSOPHILA ELEGANS

Habit Upright, slender, well-branched annual.
Flowers Tiny, star-shaped, to ⅜in (1cm) across,
in airy, open heads, borne in summer. White
or pink, sometimes with pink-purple veins.
Leaves Narrowly lance-shaped. Gray-green.
• NATIVE HABITAT Stony or sandy places,
southern Ukraine, Turkey.
• CULTIVATION Grow in deep, light, sharply
drained, slightly alkaline soil, in sun. Ideal
for cutting or for a mixed or annual border.
• PROPAGATION Sow seed *in situ* in spring.

HEIGHT
24in (60cm)

SPREAD
12in (30cm)

Malvaceae	

LAVATERA TRIMESTRIS 'Mont Blanc'

Habit Compact, hairy annual. *Flowers* Funnel-
shaped, 2¼–1⅞in (7–10cm) across, satiny, borne
singly in the upper leaf axils, from summer.
Pure white. *Leaves* Rounded, divided into
5–7 lobes. Dark green.
• NATIVE HABITAT Garden origin.
• CULTIVATION Grow in a sunny, sheltered site
in light, well-drained soil. Ideal as cut flowers
and well suited for annual borders and bedding.
• PROPAGATION Sow seed *in situ* in mid- to late
spring, or in autumn.

HEIGHT
20in (50cm)

SPREAD
18in (45cm)

Papaveraceae	

ARGEMONE GRANDIFLORA

Habit Clump-forming, short-lived perennial or annual. **Flowers** Poppy-like, satiny, to 4in (10cm) across, single or in clusters, borne throughout summer. White or yellow. **Leaves** Deeply lobed, prickly. Blue-green, with white veins.
• NATIVE HABITAT Scrub, waste ground, Mexico.
• CULTIVATION Grow in poor, gritty, drained soil. Well suited for dry, sunny banks or gravel plantings. Deadhead regularly. May self-seed.
• PROPAGATION Sow at 64°F (18°C) in early spring, in modules or individual pots.

☀ ◌

Z 8–11

HEIGHT
to 5ft
(1.5m)

SPREAD
to 16in
(40cm)

Compositae/Asteraceae	BLUE-EYED AFRICAN DAISY

ARCTOTIS VENUSTA

Habit Spreading perennial, grown as an annual. **Flowers** Daisy-like, on slender stems, from summer to autumn. White, with blue disks. **Leaves** Lobed. Dark green with silver-green underside.
• NATIVE HABITAT Dry, stony soils, S. Africa.
• CULTIVATION Grow in light, sharply drained but moisture-retentive soil. In cool climates, grow as a house- or conservatory plant. Ideal for cutting.
• PROPAGATION Sow seed at 61–64°F (16–18°C) in early spring, or in autumn. Overwinter under glass.
• OTHER NAME A. stoechadifolia.

☀ ◌

Min. 41°F
(5°C)

HEIGHT
24in (60cm)

SPREAD
16in (40cm)

Compositae/Asteraceae	FEVERFEW

TANACETUM PARTHENIUM

Habit Bushy, short-lived perennial or annual. **Flowers** Daisy-like, aromatic, to 1in (2.5cm) across, borne throughout summer. White, with a yellow disk. **Leaves** Cut into paired, scalloped, or entire segments. Bright green.
• NATIVE HABITAT Meadows, Europe.
• CULTIVATION Grow in well-drained soil. Ideal for a herb garden, or border edging. Self-sows freely.
• PROPAGATION Sow seed *in situ* in spring.
• OTHER NAMES *Chrysanthemum parthenium*, *Pyrethrum parthenium*.

☀ ◌

Z 5–8

HEIGHT
18–24in
(45–60cm)

SPREAD
12in (30cm)

Campanulaceae	CHIMNEY BELLFLOWER

CAMPANULA PYRAMIDALIS

Habit Upright, rosette-forming perennial, grown as a biennial. **Flowers** Scented, cup-shaped, in clusters. From late spring to summer. White or pale blue. **Leaves** Oval to lance-shaped. Fresh green.
• NATIVE HABITAT Northern Italy, north-western Balkans.
• CULTIVATION Grow in fertile, moist but well-drained, neutral to alkaline soil, in sun. Tolerates dry soils. Needs staking.
• PROPAGATION Sow seed in containers in a cold frame in late spring.

☀ ◌

Z 6–8

HEIGHT
to 10ft (3m)

SPREAD
24in (60cm)

Graminae/Poaceae	VARIEGATED CORN

ZEA MAYS 'Variegata'

Habit Sturdy, upright annual grass. *Flowers*
Male flowers, borne in spike-like clusters, in
terminal plumes, from mid-summer. Straw-
colored. Female flowers, borne in long, silky styles,
enclosed in a papery bract, in the lower leaf axils,
from mid-summer. Straw-colored. *Leaves* Lance-
shaped, pointed, and arching. Mid-green, with
broad, creamy-white stripes. *Fruits* A cob,
composed of flat, fleshy, edible grains. Yellow.
• NATIVE HABITAT Garden origin. The species
occurs at field margins and on disturbed ground

in Mexico. It has been cultivated as a cereal
crop for several thousand years.
• CULTIVATION Grow in fertile, moist but well-
drained soil, in a warm, sunny, and sheltered
site. Needs a long, hot summer to ripen cobs.
In cool regions, plant out in soil prewarmed by
horticultural fleece or similar. Ideal for a mixed
border or interspersed in summer bedding.
• PROPAGATION Sow seed at 64°F (18°C) in
late winter or early spring. In warm regions,
may be sown *in situ* in late spring.

HEIGHT
36in (90cm)

SPREAD
18–24in
(45–60cm)

Gentianaceae	PRAIRIE GENTIAN

EUSTOMA GRANDIFLORUM

Habit Slender annual or biennial. *Flowers*
Bell-shaped, satiny, single or in clusters in the
upper leaf axils, from summer. White, pink, or
blue. *Leaves* Oval to lance-shaped. Gray-green.
• NATIVE HABITAT Damp fields and prairies, US.
• CULTIVATION Grow in well-drained, neutral to
alkaline soil, in a sheltered site. In cool climates,
grow as a house- or conservatory plant.
• PROPAGATION Sow seed at 55–61°F (13–16°C)
in autumn or late winter. Grow on under glass.
• OTHER NAME *E. russellianum.*

☼ ◊

Z 8–10

HEIGHT
24–36in
(60–90cm)

SPREAD
12in (30cm)

Pedaliaceae	COMMON UNICORN PLANT

PROBOSCIDEA LOUISIANICA

Habit Sticky, hairy annual. *Flowers* Foxglove-
like, to 2in (5cm) long, borne in summer. Creamy-
white, with maroon markings. *Leaves* Oval- to
diamond-shaped, lobed, long-stalked. Mid-green.
Fruits Drooping, horn-like seed capsule.
Brown when ripe.
• NATIVE HABITAT C. America, southern US.
• CULTIVATION Grow in fertile, well-drained soil,
in a warm, sheltered site, in full sun.
• PROPAGATION Sow at 70°F (21°C) in early spring.
• OTHER NAMES *P. jussieui, P. proboscidea.*

☼ ◊

HEIGHT
24in (60cm)

SPREAD
12in (30cm)

Malvaceae	FLOWER-OF-AN-HOUR

HIBISCUS TRIONUM

Habit Upright, hairy annual, or short-lived
perennial. *Flowers* Trumpet-shaped, 3in (8cm)
across, from summer to autumn. Pale creamy-
white, with dark chocolate-brown center.
Leaves Lobed, toothed. Dark green.
Fruits Inflated, bladder-like seed capsules.
• NATIVE HABITAT Origin uncertain.
• CULTIVATION Grow in neutral to slightly alkaline
soil. Ideal for an annual border or patio container.
• PROPAGATION Pre-soak seed in hot water for an
hour and sow at 64°F (18°C) in spring.

☼ ◊

Z 10–11

HEIGHT
30in (75cm)

SPREAD
24in (60cm)

Compositae/Asteraceae	CHINA ASTER

CALLISTEPHUS CHINENSIS
Ostrich Plume Series

Habit Bushy, rapid-growing annual. *Flowers*
Daisy-like, from summer to autumn. In pink or
crimson. *Leaves* Oval to triangular. Dark green.
• NATIVE HABITAT Garden origin. Species
occurs on stony slopes and in fields, China.
• CULTIVATION Grow in a warm, sheltered site
in well-drained, neutral to alkaline soil. Ideal in
an annual or wildflower border, or for cutting.
• PROPAGATION Sow seed at 61°F (16°C) in
early spring, or *in situ* later in spring.

☼ ◊

HEIGHT
8–24in
(20–60cm)

SPREAD
10–18in
(25–45cm)

Scrophulariaceae	FOXGLOVE

DIGITALIS PURPUREA 'Apricot Shades'

Habit Rosette-forming biennial. *Flowers* Tubular, 2-lipped, in tall, one-sided clusters, borne from early to mid-summer. Apricot-pink. *Leaves* Lance-shaped, coarse, toothed, and hairy. Mid-green.
• NATIVE HABITAT Garden origin.
• CULTIVATION Grow in moist, well-drained, leaf-rich soil, in sun or partial shade. Tolerates dry soil. Ideal for mixed borders and woodland gardens.
• PROPAGATION Sow seed in containers in a cold frame in late spring.

Z 4–8

HEIGHT
4–5ft
(1.2–1.5m)

SPREAD
24in (60cm)

Malvaceae	HOLLYHOCK

ALCEA ROSEA Majorette Group

Habit Dwarf perennial, grown as an annual or biennial. *Flowers* Funnel-shaped, semi-double, with fringed, rosette-like petals, borne in early summer. In pink, yellow, or apricot. *Leaves* Rounded, lobed, roughly hairy. Mid-green.
• NATIVE HABITAT Garden origin.
• CULTIVATION Grow in well-drained soil in sun. Ideal for a mixed or herbaceous border.
• PROPAGATION Sow seed *in situ* in spring or mid-summer.
• OTHER NAME *Althaea rosea* 'Majorette'.

Z 3–9

HEIGHT
3ft (1m)

SPREAD
12in (30cm)

Compositae/Asteraceae	CHINA ASTER

CALLISTEPHUS CHINENSIS 'Giant Princess'

Habit Bushy, rapid-growing annual. *Flowers* Daisy-like, with quilled ray florets, from late summer to autumn. Pink-purple, with yellow-tipped disk florets. *Leaves* Oval to triangular. Dark green.
• NATIVE HABITAT Garden origin.
• CULTIVATION Grow in a warm site in well-drained, neutral to alkaline soil. Ideal for cutting.
• PROPAGATION Sow seed at 61°F (16°C) in early spring, or *in situ* in mid- to late spring.

HEIGHT
30in (75cm)

SPREAD
8in (20cm)

Compositae/Asteraceae

CHRYSANTHEMUM CARINATUM 'Court Jesters'

Habit Well-branched, upright, rapid-growing annual. *Flowers* Daisy-like, single, strong-stemmed, 3in (8cm) across, borne freely from summer to early autumn. Available in a range of colors, including shades of white, scarlet, maroon, or yellow, with red or orange zones around a purple-brown central disk.
Leaves Narrow, finely divided, fleshy, and feathery. Bright green.
• NATIVE HABITAT Garden origin. Dry fields and waste ground, Morocco.

• CULTIVATION Grow in moderately fertile, well-drained, neutral to slightly acid soil, in full sun. *C. carinatum* 'Court Jesters' are ideal as decorative cut flowers, and are also well suited for use in annual borders, or as fillers in a mixed or herbaceous border.
• PROPAGATION Sow seed in containers in a cold frame in early spring, or *in situ* between spring and early summer. In frost-free areas, seed may be sown *in situ* in autumn for earlier flowers.
• OTHER NAME *C. tricolor* 'Court Jesters'.

HEIGHT
24in (60cm)

SPREAD
12in (30cm)

Malvaceae	

LAVATERA TRIMESTRIS 'Pink Beauty'

Habit Bushy, well-branched, hairy annual.
Flowers Funnel-shaped, 2¼–4in (7–10cm)
across, borne in the upper leaf axils, from
summer. Palest pink, with a purple center and
veining. **Leaves** Rounded, lobed. Mid-green.
• NATIVE HABITAT Garden origin.
• CULTIVATION Grow in light, moderately fertile,
well-drained soil, in sun. Ideal for cutting, annual
borders, and as fillers in a mixed border.
• PROPAGATION Sow seed *in situ* in mid- to late
spring, or under glass at 55°F (13°C) in mid-spring.

☼ ◊

HEIGHT
24in (60cm)

SPREAD
18–24in
(45–60cm)

Compositae/Asteraceae	

BRACTEANTHA BRACTEATA 'Silvery Rose'

Habit Erect annual. **Flowers** Papery, daisy-like,
double, on long stems, from summer to autumn.
Silvery-rose. **Leaves** Lance-shaped. Gray-green.
• NATIVE HABITAT Garden origin.
• CULTIVATION Grow in moist, well-drained soil.
Ideal for drying, and for annual or mixed borders.
• PROPAGATION Sow seed at 64°F (18°C) in early
spring. Sowing in modules is recommended.
• OTHER NAME *Helichrysum bracteatum*
'Silvery Rose'.

☼ ◊

HEIGHT
30in (75cm)

SPREAD
12in (30cm)

Compositae/Asteraceae	

DAHLIA 'Redskin'

Habit Bushy, tuberous perennial, grown as an
annual. **Flowers** Semi-double to double, 2in (5cm)
across, from summer to autumn. Available in lilac-
pink, scarlet, or orange. **Leaves** Oval, toothed,
divided into leaflets. Bronze.
• NATIVE HABITAT Garden origin.
• CULTIVATION Grow in fertile, moist but well-
drained soil that is rich in organic matter, in full
sun. Ideal for bedding, border edges, or containers.
• PROPAGATION Sow seed at 61°F (16°C)
in early spring.

☼ ◊

Z 8–10

HEIGHT
18–24in
(45–60cm)

SPREAD
18–24in
(45–60cm)

Onagraceae	

CLARKIA PULCHELLA Double Mixed

Habit Slender, branching annual. **Flowers**
Double, in slender clusters, 2in (5cm) across,
with lobed petals. White, pink, or lavender,
borne in summer. **Leaves** Lance-shaped,
smooth. Grayish-green.
• NATIVE HABITAT Garden origin. Species occurs
in open sites, in Washington, Oregon, Montana.
• CULTIVATION Grow in moist but well-drained,
moderately fertile soil. Good for cut flowers.
• PROPAGATION Sow seed *in situ* in autumn,
or early spring.

☼ ◊

HEIGHT
18in
(45cm)

SPREAD
9in (23cm)

Malvaceae	HOLLYHOCK

ALCEA ROSEA (single mixed)

Habit Upright perennials, grown as biennials.
Flowers Funnel-shaped, to 4in (10cm) across,
from early to mid-summer. White, cream, pink,
red, yellow, or apricot. *Leaves* Rounded,
lobed. Mid-green.
• NATIVE HABITAT Gardens. Native origin
is probably western Asia.
• CULTIVATION Grow in fertile, well-drained
soil. Good for cottage gardens or mixed borders.
• PROPAGATION Sow seed *in situ* in mid-summer.
• OTHER NAME *Althaea rosea* Mixed.

☼ ◊

Z 3–9

HEIGHT
5–8ft
(1.5–2.5m)

SPREAD
24in (60cm)

Compositae/Asteraceae

RHODANTHE MANGLESII

Habit Slender, slightly fleshy annual. *Flowers*
Daisy-like, with straw-textured bracts, from
summer to early autumn. White, pink, or red, with
a yellow disk. *Leaves* Narrowly oval. Gray-green.
• NATIVE HABITAT Arid areas, Western Australia.
• CULTIVATION Grow in poor, light, well-drained
soil, in full sun. Good for air-drying; cut before
fully open. Ideal for an annual or mixed border.
• PROPAGATION Sow seed at 61°F (16°C) in
early spring.
• OTHER NAME *Helipterum manglesii*.

☼ ◊

HEIGHT
24in (60cm)

SPREAD
6in (15cm)

Compositae/Asteraceae

COSMOS BIPINNATUS 'Sea Shells'

Habit Upright, well-branched annual. *Flowers*
Daisy-like, with fluted ray florets, from summer.
White, pink, or carmine, around a yellow disk.
Leaves Feathery, in fine segments. Bright green.
• NATIVE HABITAT Garden origin.
• CULTIVATION Grow in moderately fertile,
moist but well-drained soil, in full sun. Good
as cut flowers. Ideal for an annual border, or
as fillers in a mixed border.
• PROPAGATION Sow seed at 61°F (16°C) in
mid-spring, or *in situ* in late spring.

☼ ◊

HEIGHT
36in (90cm)

SPREAD
18in (45cm)

HELIANTHUS

The genus *Helianthus* includes some 70–80 species of annuals and perennials. The annual sunflowers described here are grown for their showy, daisy-like flowerheads, which are typically 2–4in (5–10cm) in diameter, but can grow up to 12in (30cm) across in the giant-flowered cultivars. The flowers are available in warm shades of mahogany-red, yellow, or orange, surrounding a brown, purple, or dark yellow central disk. These beautiful and dramatic flowers are strong-stemmed and make ideal cut flowers. They are also suitable for a mixed or annual border, or for in-filling in a herbaceous border. The flowers are very attractive to bees and other beneficial insects and, when cut and dried, the seedheads attract birds, especially finches, into the garden in autumn and winter. Small cultivars, such as *H. annuus* 'Teddy Bear', are ideally suited for container plantings.

The rapid growth and spectacular size of the tall and giant-flowered cultivars make them ideal in childrens' gardens. Like all sunflowers, they flower most reliably in long, hot summers.

Grow in fertile to moderately fertile, neutral to alkaline, well-drained soil that is rich in organic matter. Provide a warm, sheltered position in full sun. Tall cultivars need the support of stakes or strong canes.

Sow seed under glass in late winter at 61°F (16°C), in individual pots. Harden off and set out in their flowering position in spring or early summer. Alternatively, sow *in situ* in early spring.

Slugs may be a problem, especially when plants are young. The cultivars are particularly susceptible to attack from powdery mildew, especially in dry summers, so keep their roots moist and avoid overhead watering.

H. DEBILIS subsp.
CUCUMERIFOLIUS
'Italian White'
Habit Vigorous annual.
Flowers To 4in (10cm) across, borne in summer. Creamy-white or pale lemon-yellow, with a black central disk.
Leaves Oval to lance-shaped, coarsely hairy, toothed. Mid-green.
• HEIGHT 5ft (1.5m).
• SPREAD 18in (45cm).

H. debilis subsp.
cucumerifolius
'Italian White'

☼ ◊

H. ANNUUS
'Music Box'
Habit Well-branched, fast-growing annual.
Flowers To 4½in (12cm) across, from summer. Dark red to creamy-yellow, with a black central disk. Also available in bicolors.
Leaves Oval to heart-shaped. Dark green.
• HEIGHT 28in (70cm).
• SPREAD to 18in (45cm).

H. annuus
'Music Box'

☼ ◊

H. DEBILIS subsp.
CUCUMERIFOLIUS
Habit Stout-stemmed, well-branched annual.
Flowers To 6in (15cm) wide, borne in summer. Bright yellow, sometimes flushed red, on purple-mottled stems. *Leaves* Oval to lance-shaped. Mid-green.
• OTHER NAME
H. cucumerifolius.
• HEIGHT 3ft (1m).
• SPREAD 12in (30cm).

H. debilis subsp.
cucumerifolius

☼ ◊

H. Chrysanthemum-flowered Series

Habit Bushy, upright, fast-growing annual.
Flowers Daisy-like, double, rounded, 6in (15cm) across, borne freely in summer. Golden-yellow.
Leaves Oval, toothed. Mid-green.
• HEIGHT 5ft (1.5m).
• SPREAD 12–18in (30–45cm).

H. Chrysanthemum-flowered Series

H. ANNUUS

Habit Vigorous, fast-growing annual.
Flowers To 12in (30cm) across, borne in summer. Golden-yellow with a brown or purple central disk, sometimes tinted red or purple.
Leaves Heart-shaped to broadly oval, toothed, and roughly hairy. Mid- to dark green.
• HEIGHT to 15ft (5m).
• SPREAD to 2ft (60cm).

H. annuus
Sunflower

H. ANNUUS 'Autumn Beauty'

Habit Robust, fast-growing annual.
Flowers To 6in (15cm) across, borne from summer. Mahogany-red, bronze-red, lemon-yellow, or golden-yellow, with shaded zones.
Leaves Broadly oval, and toothed. Mid-green.
• HEIGHT to 5ft (1.5m).
• SPREAD 12–18in (30–45cm).

H. ANNUUS 'Teddy Bear'

Habit Bushy, compact annual.
Flowers Double, to 5in (13cm) across, borne in summer. Golden-yellow, with a small, greenish-yellow central disk.
Leaves Oval, to heart-shaped. Mid-green.
• HEIGHT to 36in (90cm).
• SPREAD 12in (30cm).

H. annuus
'Teddy Bear'

H. annuus
'Autumn Beauty'

LATHYRUS

The *Lathyrus* genus consists of 150 species of annuals and perennials, many of which are tendril climbers. The many cultivars of the annual *L. odoratus* (sweet pea) have long been valued for their showy, pea-like, often scented flowers, borne throughout summer. The color range excludes pure yellow but includes white, shades of cream, pink, red, purple, and blue, a few picotees and bicolors, and some flushed, rippled, or speckled flowers with contrasting shades. Sweet pea cultivars are classified into distinct horticultural groups.

Old-fashioned The oldest cultivars are noted for their intense colors. Although smaller than most modern cultivars, the flowers are very sweetly scented.

Bush These cultivars, which include the Knee-hi Group, are dwarf, non-climbing, and more or less self-supporting. They can be grown as ground cover, and are invaluable as cut flowers.

Spencer The most commonly grown sweet peas, these cultivars are climbers and may be cordon-grown for exhibition-quality blooms (see pp.174–77). Spencer types bear large, more or less fragrant flowers with waved petals.

Grow in fertile, moist, well-drained soil, in full sun. Incorporate well-rotted organic matter before planting the cultivars, and feed every two weeks when in growth with a balanced liquid fertilizer. Deadhead regularly.

Pre-soak seed and sow in containers in a cold frame in early spring, or *in situ* in spring. In autumn, sow *in situ* in mild-winter areas, or, in frost-prone areas, in containers. Young plants should be overwintered in a cold frame.

Use biological control or insecticides to protect plants against snails, aphids, and thrips. Avoid overhead watering as they are also susceptible to powdery mildew.

L. ODORATUS
Bijou Group
Habit Dwarf, bushy annuals.
Flowers Faintly scented, with small wavy petals, borne from summer to early autumn. White, pink, red, or blue.
Leaves Divided into 2 oval leaflets. Mid-green.
• HEIGHT 18in (45cm).
• SPREAD 18in (45cm).

L. odoratus
Bijou Group
(Dwarf, bush)

L. ODORATUS
'Selana'
Habit Sturdy, vigorous climbing annual.
Flowers Large, fragrant, borne freely from summer to early autumn. White, heavily flushed with soft pink at the petal margins.
Leaves Divided into 2 oval leaflets. Mid-green.
• HEIGHT 6ft (2m).

L. odoratus
'Selana'
(Spencer)

☀ ◊

L. ODORATUS 'Xenia Field'

Habit Slender, moderately fast-growing, climbing annual.
Flowers Large, fragrant, slightly waved petals, borne from summer to early autumn. Available in cream or soft pink.
Leaves Divided into 2 oval leaflets. Mid-green.
• HEIGHT 6ft (2m).

L. odoratus 'Xenia Field' (Spencer)

☼ ◊

L. ODORATUS 'Lady Diana'

Habit Slender, moderately fast-growing, climbing annual.
Flowers Fragrant, with slightly waved petals, borne from summer to early autumn. Pale violet-blue.
Leaves Divided into 2 oval leaflets. Mid-green.
• HEIGHT 6ft (2m).

L. odoratus 'Lady Diana' (Spencer)

☼ ◊

L. ODORATUS 'Old-fashioned Mixed'

Habit Climbing, fast-growing annual.
Flowers Small, delicate, and intensely fragrant, borne from summer to early autumn. White to strong shades of pink, red, or blue.
Leaves Divided into 2 oval leaflets. Mid-green.
• HEIGHT 6ft (2m).

L. odoratus 'Old-fashioned Mixed'

☼ ◊

L. ODORATUS Knee-hi Group

Habit Vigorous, bushy, fast-growing annuals.
Flowers Fragrant, with slightly waved petals, borne from summer to early autumn. White, pink, red, or blue.
Leaves Divided into 2 oval leaflets. Mid-green.
• HEIGHT to 3ft (1m).
• SPREAD to 3ft (1m).

L. odoratus Knee-hi Group (Dwarf, bush)

☼ ◊

L. ODORATUS 'Red Ensign'

Habit Robust, vigorous, climbing annual.
Flowers Large, sweetly scented, borne freely from summer to early autumn. Rich, glossy-scarlet.
Leaves Divided into 2 oval leaflets. Mid-green.
• HEIGHT 6ft (2m).

L. odoratus 'Red Ensign' (Spencer)

☼ ◊

MATTHIOLA

The *Matthiola* genus consists of about
55 species of annuals, perennials, and
a few sub-shrubs. The most commonly
grown are the many cultivars of *M. incana*,
the stocks, or gilliflowers. Valued for their
sweetly scented flowers, they are useful in
spring or summer bedding, or in an annual
border. They also make ideal cut flowers.
The plants fall into five main groups:
Brompton stocks These cultivars bear
tall clusters of single or double flowers.
East Lothian stocks Grown as annuals
or biennials, these plants produce slightly
smaller flowers in spike-like clusters.
Ten-week stocks These annuals
are available as dwarf or tall cultivars.
Column stocks Popular with flower
arrangers, these have tall, spiky clusters
of mostly double flowers. They can be
grown in a cool greenhouse or open garden.
Trysomic stocks These bushy annuals
produce mainly double blooms.

Grow in moderately fertile, moist
but well-drained, neutral to slightly
alkaline soil, in a sheltered site in full sun.
Tall cultivars will need to be supported.

Sow seed of annuals in early spring at
50–64°F (10–18°C). Sow seed of biennials
in mid-summer, in a seed bed, or in
containers in a cold frame. Provide cloche
protection against frost, or overwinter
young plants in a cold frame and set out
in spring. In some seed series, seedlings
listed as "selectable" cultivars can be
selected to produce all double flowers.
On formation of the first pair of seed
leaves, lower the temperature to below
50°F (10°C). Pale-colored or yellow-green
seed leaves will produce double flowers.

Use biological control or insecticides
to protect plants from aphids, flea beetles,
cabbage root fly, and clubroot. Avoid
overhead watering as plants are also
affected by mildew and gray mold.

M. Ten-week Series
Habit Short-lived
perennials or biennials,
grown as annuals.
Flowers Fragrant,
cross-shaped, mainly
double, in dense spikes,
to 6in (15cm) long, from
summer. In shades
of white, pink, crimson,
purple, and lavender.
Leaves Lance-shaped.
Grayish-green.
• HEIGHT 12in (30cm).
• SPREAD 10in (25cm).

M. Ten-week Series

☀ ◊   Z 7–8

M. 'Giant Imperial'
Habit Short-lived
perennial or biennial,
grown as an annual.
Flowers Fragrant,
cross-shaped, mainly
double, in long,
branching spikes,
borne from summer.
White to creamy- or
coppery-yellow.
Leaves Lance-shaped.
Grayish-green.
• HEIGHT 24in (60cm).
• SPREAD 12in (30cm).

M. 'Giant Imperial'
(Trysomic)

☀ ◊   Z 7–8

**M. LONGIPETALA
subsp. BICORNIS**
Habit Upright to
spreading, branching or
single-stemmed annual.
Flowers Scented, cross-
shaped, in dense spikes,
from summer. Pink,
mauve, or purple-violet.
Leaves Lance-shaped.
Grayish-green.
• OTHER NAME
M. bicornis.
• HEIGHT 14in (35cm).
• SPREAD 9in (23cm).

M. longipetala
subsp. *bicornis*
Night-scented stock

☀ ◊

M. 'Giant Excelsior'

Habit Upright, short-lived perennial, grown as an annual or biennial.
Flowers Scented, cross-shaped, mainly double, in dense spikes, to 15in (38cm) long, borne in summer. In shades of white, pink, red, or pale blue.
Leaves Lance-shaped. Grayish-green.
• HEIGHT 30in (75cm).
• SPREAD 12in (30cm).

M. 'Giant Excelsior'
(Column)

☼ ◊　　　Z 7–8

M. Trysomic Group

Habit Compact biennials or short-lived perennials, grown as annuals.
Flowers Fragrant, mainly double, in spikes 6in (15cm) or more long, borne in summer. White, red, yellow, mauve, purple, or violet.
Leaves Lance-shaped. Grayish-green.
• HEIGHT 12in (30cm).
• SPREAD 12in (30cm).

M. Trysomic Group

☼ ◊　　　Z 7–8

M. East Lothian Series

Habit Short-lived perennials, grown as annuals or biennials.
Flowers Fragrant, single or double, from late spring and early summer, or summer to autumn. In shades of white, pink, red, purple, or yellow.
Leaves Lance-shaped. Grayish-green.
• HEIGHT 12in (30cm).
• SPREAD 12in (30cm).

M. East Lothian Series

☼ ◊　　　Z 7–8

M. Brompton Series

Habit Short-lived perennials, grown as biennials or annuals.
Flowers Scented, single or double, borne from late spring to autumn. Available in shades of white, pink, red, purple, or yellow.
Leaves Lance-shaped. Grayish-green.
• HEIGHT 18in (45cm).
• SPREAD 12in (30cm).

M. Brompton Series

☼ ◊　　　Z 7–8

M. Cinderella Series

Habit Short-lived perennials or biennials, grown as annuals.
Flowers Double, 6in (15cm) long, in spikes, borne from late spring or summer. White, pink, red, blue-purple, lavender-blue, or silver-blue.
Leaves Lance-shaped. Grayish-green.
• HEIGHT 10in (25cm).
• SPREAD 10in (25cm).

M. Cinderella Series
(Brompton)

☼ ◊　　　Z 7–8

Malvaceae	HOLLYHOCK

ALCEA ROSEA

Habit Upright perennial, grown as a biennial.
Flowers Funnel-shaped, in terminal plumes,
from early to mid-summer. White, pink, purple,
or yellow. **Leaves** Rounded, lobed. Light green.
• NATIVE HABITAT Native origin western Asia,
introduced to Europe in 1573.
• CULTIVATION Grow in moderately fertile, well-
drained soil. Good for cottage gardens,
wildflower borders, or mixed borders.
• PROPAGATION Sow seed *in situ* in mid-summer.
• OTHER NAME *Althaea rosea*.

☼ ◊

Z 3–9

HEIGHT
5–8ft
(1.5–2.5m)

SPREAD
24in (60cm)

Capparidaceae	

CLEOME HASSLERIANA
'Colour Fountain'

Habit Upright annual. **Flowers** Scented,
4-petaled, in terminal clusters, borne in summer.
White, pink, violet-pink, or rose-red. **Leaves** Oval
to lance-shaped, divided into leaflets. Mid-green.
• NATIVE HABITAT Garden origin.
• CULTIVATION Grow in light, sandy, well-drained
soil, in a sunny, sheltered site. In cool climates,
grow as a house- or conservatory plant. Ideal for
cut flowers, or for an annual or mixed border.
• PROPAGATION Sow seed at 64°F (18°C) in spring.

☼ ◊

Min. 39°F
(4°C)

HEIGHT
to 4ft
(1.2m)

SPREAD
18in (45cm)

Compositae/Asteraceae	

CENTAUREA CYANUS
Standard Tall Group

Habit Upright annual. **Flowers** Hemispherical,
with tubular, lobed florets above fringed bracts,
from spring to autumn. Various colors, including
rose-pink. **Leaves** Lance-shaped. Gray-green.
• NATIVE HABITAT Species native to fields and
hedgerows, northern temperate regions.
• CULTIVATION Grow in well-drained soil, in sun.
Good for cutting, or for annual or mixed borders.
• PROPAGATION Sow seed *in situ* in spring
or autumn.

☼ ◊

HEIGHT
to 36in
(90cm)

SPREAD
6in (15cm)

Caryophyllaceae	CORN COCKLE

AGROSTEMMA GITHAGO 'Milas'

Habit Upright, hairy annual. *Flowers*
Trumpet-shaped, 5-petaled, to 2in (5cm)
across, with long-pointed, hairy sepals, borne
throughout summer. Soft magenta-pink.
Leaves Narrow, lance-shaped. Gray-green.
• NATIVE HABITAT The species is native to the
Mediterranean, but is naturalized elsewhere
in Europe. Once a widespread cornfield weed,
the corn cockle declined because of improved
efficiency in the cleaning of agricultural seed
and the common use of herbicides.

• CULTIVATION Grow in light, low-fertility, well-
drained soil, in sun. Ideal for a wildflower border,
as a filler in a mixed or herbaceous border, or in a
cottage garden. May be used in an annual meadow
mix with cornflowers (*Centaurea cyanus*), corn
marigolds (*Chrysanthemum segetum*), and field poppies
(*Papaver rhoeas*). Deadhead to prolong flowering;
will self-seed if a few flowers are left in place.
• PROPAGATION Sow seed *in situ* in early spring,
or as soon as ripe.
• OTHER NAME *A. githago* 'Rose Queen'.

HEIGHT
24–36in
(60–90cm)

SPREAD
12in (30cm)

Cruciferae	

LUNARIA ANNUA 'Variegata'

Habit Upright annual or biennial. *Flowers* Cross-shaped, in clusters, from late spring to summer. Purple to red-purple. *Leaves* Oval to heart-shaped, variegated. Mid-green, with creamy-white margins. *Fruits* Oval, translucent seed pods.
• NATIVE HABITAT Garden origin.
• CULTIVATION Grow in fertile, moist but well-drained soil, in sun or part-shade. Ideal for a cottage garden, woodland or wildflower garden, or mixed border. Seed pods are good for drying.
• PROPAGATION Sow seed *in situ* in early summer.

Z 7–9

HEIGHT
36in (90cm)

SPREAD
12in (30cm)

Cruciferae	HONESTY, SATIN FLOWER

LUNARIA ANNUA

Habit Upright annual or biennial. *Flowers* Cross-shaped, to ⅜in (1cm) across, in leafy spikes, from late spring to summer. White to pale purple. *Leaves* Heart-shaped to oval, toothed. Mid-green. *Fruits* Oval, translucent seed pods.
• NATIVE HABITAT Woods, waste ground, Europe.
• CULTIVATION Grow in fertile, moist but well-drained soil, in sun or part-shade. Seed pods are good for drying. Suits a cottage garden, woodland or wildflower garden, or mixed border.
• PROPAGATION Sow seed *in situ* in early summer.

Z 7–9

HEIGHT
36in (90cm)

SPREAD
12in (30cm)

Compositae/Asteraceae	

XERANTHEMUM ANNUUM

Habit Slender, upright, branching annual. *Flowers* Papery, daisy-like, on wiry stems, from summer to autumn. Pink, crimson, or chocolate-purple. *Leaves* Oval, woolly. Silver-green.
• NATIVE HABITAT Dry areas, southeast Europe to Iran.
• CULTIVATION Grow in light, well-drained, moderately fertile soil, in sun. Good for cut and dried flowers. Cut before fully open for drying.
• PROPAGATION Sow seed at 61°F (16°C) in early spring.

HEIGHT
10–30in
(25–75cm)

SPREAD
to 18in
(45cm)

Malvaceae	

LAVATERA TRIMESTRIS 'Silver Cup'

Habit Bushy, compact, well-branched, free-flowering annual. *Flowers* Funnel-shaped, with satin-textured petals, borne in the upper leaf axils, from mid-summer to autumn. Bright rose-pink, with dark veins.
Leaves Rounded, heart-shaped at the base, lobed. Mid-green.
• NATIVE HABITAT Garden origin. The species occurs in dry places around the Mediterranean.
• CULTIVATION Grow in light, moderately fertile, well-drained soil, in a sheltered site in full sun.

Growing in too rich a soil will produce leaf growth at the expense of flowers. *L. trimestris* 'Silver Cup' is ideal as decorative cut flowers, and is well suited for use in an annual border, or as a filler plant in a mixed or herbaceous border. The species is also suitable for a cottage garden, or for summer bedding, and is tolerant of coastal conditions.
• PROPAGATION Sow seed *in situ* in mid- to late spring, or under glass at 55°F (13°C) in mid-spring.

HEIGHT
to 30in
(75cm)

SPREAD
18in (45cm)

Scrophulariaceae	

DIGITALIS PURPUREA Foxy Group

Habit Robust, rosette-forming biennials, grown as annuals. **Flowers** Tubular bell-shaped, 2-lipped, in clusters, from early to mid-summer. White, pink, red, creamy-yellow, or spotted maroon. **Leaves** Oval to lance-shaped. Mid-green.
• NATIVE HABITAT Garden origin. Species occurs in woodland and hedgerows, Europe.
• CULTIVATION Grow in leaf-rich, moist but well-drained soil. Good for a border or woodland garden.
• PROPAGATION Sow seed in containers in a cold frame in late spring.

☼ ◐ ◊

Z 4–8

HEIGHT
36in (90cm)

SPREAD
24in (60cm)

Compositae/Asteraceae	

COSMOS BIPINNATUS Sensation Series

Habit Upright, freely branching annual. **Flowers** Saucer-shaped, 3½in (9cm) across. Late spring to late summer. White or pink. **Leaves** Finely cut, in segments. Mid-green.
• NATIVE HABITAT Garden origin.
• CULTIVATION Grow in moist but well-drained, moderately fertile soil, in sun. Ideal as fillers in a mixed or herbaceous border. Well suited for cutting or use in an annual border.
• PROPAGATION Sow seed at 61°F (16°C) in spring, or *in situ* in late spring.

☼ ◊

HEIGHT
36in (90cm)

SPREAD
18in (45cm)

Scrophulariaceae	CHINESE FOXGLOVE

REHMANNIA ELATA

Habit Rosette-forming perennial, grown as a biennial. **Flowers** Half-drooping, tubular bell-shaped, 2¾–4in (7–10cm) long, from summer to autumn. Pink-purple, with a red-spotted throat. **Leaves** Oval, lobed, toothed. Mid-green.
• NATIVE HABITAT Stony places and woods, China.
• CULTIVATION Good for a border or conservatory.
• PROPAGATION Sow seed at 55–61°F (13–16°C) in late winter. In areas where winters are mild and damp, overwinter young plants under glass.
• OTHER NAME *R. angulata*.

☼ ◊

Z 8–10

HEIGHT
to 5ft
(1.5m)

SPREAD
20in (50cm)

Malvaceae	

LAVATERA TRIMESTRIS 'Loveliness'

Habit Robust, well-branched, hairy annual.
Flowers Funnel-shaped, 2¼–4in (7–10cm) across, borne in summer. Deep rose-pink, with pinkish-purple center and veins. *Leaves* Rounded, shallowly lobed. Mid-green.
• NATIVE HABITAT Garden origin. Species occurs in dry, rocky places around the Mediterranean.
• CULTIVATION Grow in light, well-drained soil. Ideal for cutting, bedding, and annual borders.
• PROPAGATION Sow seed *in situ* in mid- to late spring, or at 50–55°F (10–13°C) in early spring.

☀ ◊

HEIGHT
3–4ft
(1–1.2m)

SPREAD
18in (45cm)

Portulacaceae	

CALANDRINIA GRANDIFLORA

Habit Clump-forming, succulent perennial, grown as an annual. *Flowers* Cup-shaped, in clusters, borne in summer. Red-purple to magenta. *Leaves* Oval, flattened. Bright green.
• NATIVE HABITAT Dry, rocky places, Chile.
• CULTIVATION Grow in light, sharply drained, slightly acid soil. In cool climates, grow as a house- or conservatory plant. Good for dry, sunny banks.
• PROPAGATION Sow seed at 61–64°F (16–18°C) in early spring, or sow in autumn and overwinter young plants at 43°F (6°C).

☀ ◊

Min. 43°F
(6°C)

HEIGHT
3ft (1m)

SPREAD
18in (45cm)

Scrophulariaceae	

LINARIA MAROCCANA 'Northern Lights'

Habit Slender, upright, hairy annual.
Flowers Tiny, 2-lipped, ⅝in (1.5cm) long, in loose heads, from summer. Available in white, pink, carmine, lavender, yellow, or orange, with yellow or orange lower lips. *Leaves* Narrow. Pale green.
• NATIVE HABITAT Garden origin. Species occurs in dry, sunny sites in Morocco.
• CULTIVATION Grow in light, sandy, well-drained soil, in sun. Good in an annual border, on dry sunny banks, and in gravel plantings.
• PROPAGATION Sow seed *in situ* in early spring.

☀ ◊

HEIGHT
24in (60cm)

SPREAD
6in (15cm)

Compositae/Asteraceae	CHINA ASTER

CALLISTEPHUS CHINENSIS
Andrella Series (salmon red)

Habit Upright, bushy annual. *Flowers* Single, daisy-like, to 4in (10cm) across, borne from summer to autumn. Salmon-red.
Leaves Oval, coarsely toothed. Mid-green.
• NATIVE HABITAT Garden origin.
• CULTIVATION Grow in fertile, moist but well-drained soil, in a sheltered, sunny site. Ideal for cut flowers, informal or annual borders, and bedding.
• PROPAGATION Sow seed at 61°F (16°C) in early spring or *in situ* in mid-spring.

HEIGHT
24in (60cm)

SPREAD
18in (45cm)

Malvaceae	

MALOPE TRIFIDA 'Vulcan'

Habit Upright, branching annual. *Flowers* Broadly trumpet-shaped, 3in (8cm) across, from summer to autumn. Bright magenta-pink.
Leaves Oval, lobed. Dark green.
• NATIVE HABITAT Garden origin.
• CULTIVATION Grow in moist but well-drained soil, in full sun. Support with pea sticks. Suitable for a cottage garden, in an annual or mixed border. Thrives in coastal gardens and tolerates part-shade.
• PROPAGATION Sow seed at 55–64°F (13–18°C) in early spring, or *in situ* in spring.

HEIGHT
36in (90cm)

SPREAD
9in (23cm)

Nyctaginaceae	

MIRABILIS JALAPA

Habit Bushy, tuberous perennial, grown as an annual. *Flowers* Scented, trumpet-shaped, 2in (5cm) long, in clusters, borne in summer. White, pink, red, magenta, or yellow, often with several colors on one plant. *Leaves* Oval. Mid-green.
• NATIVE HABITAT Dry, open sites, S. America.
• CULTIVATION Grow in fertile, well-drained soil. Water freely when in growth. Lift tubers before first frosts and store in frost-free conditions.
• PROPAGATION Sow seed at 55–64°F (13–18°C) in early spring. Divide tubers in spring.

Z 7–9

HEIGHT
24in (60cm)

SPREAD
24in (60cm)

Boraginaceae	

ECHIUM WILDPRETII

Habit Robust, woody-stemmed biennial. **Flowers** Funnel-shaped, in a dense, column-shaped head, 36in (90cm) or more long, from late spring to summer. Red. **Leaves** Narrowly lance-shaped, silver-hairy, in a basal rosette. Light green.
• NATIVE HABITAT Stony hillsides, Canary Islands.
• CULTIVATION Grow in well-drained soil, in full sun. Makes a statuesque specimen for a border.
• PROPAGATION Sow seed at 55–61°F (13–16°C) in summer, and overwinter at 41–45°F (5–7°C).
• OTHER NAME *E. bourgaeanum.*

☼ ◊

Z 9–10

HEIGHT
6ft (2m)

SPREAD
24in (60cm)

Compositae/Asteraceae	

DAHLIA Unwins Dwarf Group

Habit Dwarf, bushy, tuberous-rooted perennial, grown as an annual. **Flowers** Semi-double or double, to 4in (10cm) across, borne from mid-summer to autumn. White, red, or yellow, some flushed with a second color. **Leaves** Oval, toothed, divided into leaflets. Mid-green.
• NATIVE HABITAT Garden origin.
• CULTIVATION Grow in fertile, moist but well-drained soil. Ideal for bedding or cutting.
• PROPAGATION Sow seed at 61°F (16°C) in early spring.

☼ ◊

Z 8–10

HEIGHT
24in (60cm)

SPREAD
24in (60cm)

Compositae/Asteraceae	CHINA ASTER

CALLISTEPHUS CHINENSIS
Pompon Series

Habit Upright, bushy annual. **Flowers** Small, double, daisy-like, 3in (8cm) across, from summer to autumn. White, pink, red, or blue. **Leaves** Oval, coarsely toothed. Mid-green.
• NATIVE HABITAT Garden origin.
• CULTIVATION Grow in fertile, moist but well-drained soil, in a sunny, sheltered site. Ideal for cutting, an informal or annual border, or bedding.
• PROPAGATION Sow seed at 61°F (16°C) in early spring or *in situ* in mid-spring.

☼ ◊

HEIGHT
24in (60cm)

SPREAD
24in (60cm)

Convolvulaceae	STAR GLORY

IPOMOEA QUAMOCLIT

Habit Twining, climbing annual. **Flowers**
Slender-tubed, with 5 spreading lobes, in clusters,
from summer (year-round in tropics). White or
scarlet. **Leaves** Broadly oval, lobed. Dark green.
• NATIVE HABITAT Forests, tropical America.
• CULTIVATION Grow in moist but well-drained
soil, with shelter from wind, in sun. In cool
climates, grow as a house- or conservatory plant.
• PROPAGATION Sow chipped or pre-soaked seed
at 64°F (18°C) in spring. Grow on in warmth.
• OTHER NAME *Quamoclit pennata.*

☼ ◊

Min.45°F
(7°C)

HEIGHT
6–20ft
(2–6m)

Compositae/Asteraceae	

GAILLARDIA × GRANDIFLORA 'Dazzler'

Habit Bushy, short-lived perennial, grown as
an annual. **Flowers** Daisy-like, 2¼–5½in (7–14cm)
wide, from early summer to autumn. Yellow-
tipped, orange-red ray florets, with maroon central
disk. **Leaves** Lance-shaped, lobed or divided.
Grayish-green.
• NATIVE HABITAT Garden origin.
• CULTIVATION Grow in fertile, well-drained soil,
in sun. Good for mixed borders and for cutting.
• PROPAGATION Sow seed at 55–64°F (13–18°C)
in early spring, or *in situ* in late spring.

☼ ◊

Z 3–8

HEIGHT
24–34in
(60–85cm)

SPREAD
18in (45cm)

Scrophulariaceae	

ALONSOA WARSCEWICZII

Habit Bushy perennial, grown as an annual.
Flowers Spurred, 2-lipped, ⅗–¾in (1.5cm–2cm)
across, in loose clusters, borne from summer to
autumn. White or scarlet. **Leaves** Oval to lance-
shaped, toothed. Dark green.
• NATIVE HABITAT Scrub and stony slopes, Peru.
• CULTIVATION Grow in fertile, well-drained soil,
or in soil-based potting mix under glass.
• PROPAGATION By seed at 64°F (18°C) in early
spring, or autumn for winter-flowering pot plants.
• OTHER NAME *A. grandiflora.*

☼ ◊

Z 10–11

HEIGHT
18–24in
(45–60cm)

SPREAD
12in (30cm)

Convolvulaceae	RED MORNING GLORY

IPOMOEA COCCINEA

Habit Twining, climbing annual. **Flowers** In
clusters, ⅘in (2cm) across, from summer. Scarlet,
with a yellow throat. **Leaves** Heart-shaped,
entire, or toothed. Mid- to deep green.
• NATIVE HABITAT Southeastern US.
• CULTIVATION Grow in moist but well-drained
soil, in a warm, sunny, sheltered site. In cool
climates, grow as a house- or conservatory plant.
• PROPAGATION Sow chipped or pre-soaked seed
at 64°F (18°C) in spring. Grow on in warmth.
• OTHER NAME *Quamoclit coccinea.*

☼ ◊

Min. 45°F
(7°C)

HEIGHT
6–12ft
(2–4m)

Amaranthaceae	GLOBE AMARANTH

GOMPHRENA 'Strawberry Fields'

Habit Bushy, upright annual. *Flowers* Tiny,
2in (5cm) long in clover-like, oval to paddle-
shaped heads, borne freely from summer
to autumn. Bright red.
Leaves Oval to narrow, hairy. Mid-green.
• NATIVE HABITAT Garden origin.
• CULTIVATION Grow in well-drained, moderately
fertile soil, in full sun. Suitable for an annual
border, and ideal for cutting and drying.
• PROPAGATION Sow seed at 59–64°F (15–18°C)
in early spring.

☼ ◊

HEIGHT
30–31in
(75–80cm)

SPREAD
12in (30cm)

Polemoniaceae	SCARLET GILIA, SKYROCKET

IPOMOPSIS AGGREGATA

Habit Slender, upright biennial. *Flowers*
Fragrant, tubular to funnel-shaped, in clusters,
from summer. White, rose, red, yellow, or spotted
yellow. *Leaves* Narrow leaflets. Mid-green.
• NATIVE HABITAT Dry areas, British Columbia
to New Mexico.
• CULTIVATION Grow in fertile, well-drained soil.
Ideal for a conservatory or summer bedding. Under
glass, water moderately and keep well ventilated.
PROPAGATION Sow seed at 55–61°F (13–16°C) in
early spring or early summer.

☼ ◊

Z 7–9

HEIGHT
to 3ft (1m)

SPREAD
12in (30cm)

Malvaceae	HOLLYHOCK

ALCEA ROSEA Summer Carnival Group

Habit Vigorous, upright perennial, grown as an
annual. *Flowers* Funnel-shaped, double, 2–4in
(5–10cm) across, borne throughout summer.
White, rose-pink, red, and yellow. *Leaves*
Rounded, shallowly lobed, hairy. Mid-green.
• NATIVE HABITAT Garden origin.
• CULTIVATION Grow in any moderately fertile,
well-drained soil, in sun. Ideal for a mixed border.
• PROPAGATION Sow seed at 55°F (13°C) in late
winter, or *in situ* in spring.
• OTHER NAME *Althaea rosea* 'Summer Carnival'.

☼ ◊

Z 3–9

HEIGHT
6–8ft
(2–2.5m)

SPREAD
24in (60cm)

Solanaceae	PAINTED TONGUE

SALPIGLOSSIS SINUATA 'Splash'

Habit Upright annual. *Flowers* Funnel-shaped, (2in) 5cm across, borne in the upper leaf axils, from summer to autumn. Pink, red, yellow, and mahogany, with toning or contrasting colors. *Leaves* Lance-shaped. Pale green.
• NATIVE HABITAT Garden origin.
• CULTIVATION Grow in moist, well-drained soil in a sheltered site. Suitable for summer bedding or as houseplants (use a soil-based potting mix).
• PROPAGATION Sow seed at 64–75°F (18–24°C) in spring and autumn, or late winter for pot plants.

☼ ◊

HEIGHT
24in (60cm)

SPREAD
12in (30cm)

Malvaceae	HOLLYHOCK

ALCEA ROSEA 'Chater's Double'

Habit Upright perennial, grown as a biennial. *Flowers* Double, peony-like, 2–4in (5–10cm) across, from summer. In bright or pastel shades of white, pink, red, purple, yellow, or apricot. *Leaves* Rounded, hairy. Mid-green.
• NATIVE HABITAT Garden origin.
• CULTIVATION Grow in any moderately fertile, well-drained soil, in sun. Suitable for a mixed border and cottage gardens.
• PROPAGATION Sow seed *in situ* in mid-summer.
• OTHER NAME *Althaea rosea* 'Chater's Double'.

☼ ◊

Z 3–9

HEIGHT
6–8ft
(2–2.5m)

SPREAD
24in (60cm)

Euphorbiaceae	CASTOR BEAN

RICINUS COMMUNIS 'Impala'

Habit Compact, upright shrub, grown as an annual. *Flowers* In oval spikes, with female flowers borne above males, from summer. Greenish-yellow, female flowers with red stigmas. *Leaves* Lobed, glossy. Red-purple.
• NATIVE HABITAT Garden origin.
• CULTIVATION Good for interplanting in summer bedding. All parts are highly toxic if ingested.
• PROPAGATION Sow pre-soaked seed singly at 70°F (21°C) in late spring. Grow on at 55°F (13°C) and pot on successively until planted out.

☼ ◊

Z 8–10

HEIGHT
4ft (1.2m)

SPREAD
24in (60cm)

Amaranthaceae	PRINCE'S FEATHER

AMARANTHUS HYPOCHONDRIACUS

Habit Upright, bushy annual. *Flowers* Tiny, in plume-like, flattened heads, 6in (15cm) or more in length, from summer to early autumn. Crimson. *Leaves* Narrow to lance-shaped. Dark green to purple-green.
• NATIVE HABITAT Southern US, India, China.
• CULTIVATION Grow in fertile, moist soil that is rich in organic matter, in a warm, sheltered site, in sun. Good for cutting and drying.
• PROPAGATION Sow seed at 68°F (20°C) in mid-spring.

☼ ◊

HEIGHT
4ft (1.2m)

SPREAD
to 18in
(45cm)

Amaranthaceae	LOVE-LIES-BLEEDING

AMARANTHUS CAUDATUS

Habit Upright, bushy annual. **Flowers** Tiny, in drooping clusters, to 24in (60cm) long, from summer to early autumn. Crimson-purple. **Leaves** Oval to paddle-shaped. Pale green.
• NATIVE HABITAT Cultivated fields, waste ground, Africa, India, and Peru.
• CULTIVATION Grow in fertile, moist soil in a warm, sunny, sheltered site. Good for bedding, borders, and for cutting and drying.
• PROPAGATION Sow seed at 68°F (20°C) in spring, or *in situ* in mid-spring.

 ☼ ◌

HEIGHT
3–5ft
(1–1.5m)

SPREAD
18–30in
(45–75cm)

Compositae/Asteraceae	INCENSE PLANT, PLUME PLANT

CALOMERIA AMARANTHOIDES

Habit Upright, aromatic perennial, grown as a biennial. **Flowers** In plumes, from summer to autumn. Brown-pink. **Leaves** Narrow. Dark green.
• NATIVE HABITAT Australia.
• CULTIVATION Grow in fertile, well-drained soil. In cool climates, grow as a house- or conservatory plant. Under glass, use soil-based potting mix. Ensure good ventilation.
• PROPAGATION Sow at 55–64°F (13–18°C) in mid-summer. Keep seedlings frost-free over winter.
• OTHER NAME *Humea elegans*.

 ☼ ◌

Min. 39°F
(4°C)

HEIGHT
4–6ft
(1.2–2m)

SPREAD
3ft (1m)

Chenopodiaceae	

ATRIPLEX HORTENSIS var. RUBRA

Habit Upright annual. **Flowers** Tiny, in terminal plumes, to 8in (20cm) long, borne in summer. Green or red-brown. **Leaves** Lance-shaped, fleshy, edible. Deep blood-red to red-purple.
• NATIVE HABITAT Waste and disturbed ground, Asia. Naturalized in Europe and N. America.
• CULTIVATION Grow in fertile, well-drained soil. Water freely in dry conditions to prevent bolting. Ideal in summer bedding, or in a potager.
• PROPAGATION Sow seed *in situ*, in succession between spring and early summer.

 ☼ ◌

HEIGHT
4ft (1.2m)

SPREAD
12in (30cm)

Convolvulaceae	MORNING GLORY

IPOMOEA TRICOLOR 'Flying Saucers'

Habit Twining, climbing annual. **Flowers** Funnel-shaped, to 4in (10cm) across, borne in summer. Marbled white or purple-blue. **Leaves** Oval to heart-shaped. Light to mid-green.
• NATIVE HABITAT Garden origin. Species occurs in tropical forest, C. and S. America.
• CULTIVATION Grow in fertile, moist but well-drained soil, in a sheltered site, in sun. In cool climates, grow as a house- or conservatory plant.
• PROPAGATION Sow chipped or pre-soaked seed singly at 64°F (18°C). Grow on in warmth.

☀ ◊

Min. 45°F
(7°C)

HEIGHT
10–12ft
(3–4m)

Campanulaceae	BLUE THROATWORT

TRACHELIUM CAERULEUM

Habit Upright perennial, grown as an annual. **Flowers** Tubular, star-shaped, scented, in domed, terminal heads, from summer. White or deep violet-blue. **Leaves** Oval, pointed. Mid-green.
• NATIVE HABITAT Western and central Mediterranean.
• CULTIVATION Grow in well-drained soil in sun. Ideal for cut flowers. Good as a filler in a mixed or herbaceous border.
• PROPAGATION Sow seed at 55–61°F (13–16°C) in early spring.

☀ ◊

Z 7–9

HEIGHT
3–4ft
(1–1.2m)

SPREAD
12in (30cm)

Dipsacaceae	TEASEL

DIPSACUS FULLONUM

Habit Robust, prickly, rosette-forming biennial. **Flowers** Tiny, in narrow to oval heads, 1⅕–3in (3–8cm) long, with prickly bracts underneath, from mid- to late summer. White or mauve. **Leaves** Narrow to lance-shaped, toothed. Dark green.
• NATIVE HABITAT Open woodland, Europe, Asia.
• CULTIVATION Grow in poor to moderately fertile soil. Good in wild or woodland gardens. Flowers attract birds and bees, and are suitable for drying.
• PROPAGATION Sow seed *in situ*; autumn or spring.
• OTHER NAME *D. sylvestris*.

☀ ◊

Z 5–8

HEIGHT
5–6ft
(1.5–2m)

SPREAD
12–31in
(30–80cm)

Scrophulariaceae	

DIGITALIS PURPUREA
Excelsior Hybrids

Habit Robust, rosette-forming biennials. **Flowers** Tubular bell-shaped, in long spikes, borne in early to mid-summer. White, pink, purple, or creamy-yellow. **Leaves** Oval to narrow. Mid-green.
• NATIVE HABITAT Garden origin.
• CULTIVATION Grow in leaf-rich, moist, well-drained soil. Ideal for cut flowers, borders, or woodland gardens.
• PROPAGATION Sow seed in containers in a cold frame or *in situ*, both in late spring.

☀ ◊

Z 4–8

HEIGHT
3–6ft
(1–2m)

SPREAD
60cm (24in)

Compositae/Asteraceae	BASKET FLOWER, STAR THISTLE

CENTAUREA AMERICANA

Habit Vigorous, upright annual. **Flowers** Thistle-like, 3in (8cm) across, from early to mid-summer. Purple or rose-violet, with a pale center. **Leaves** Narrow to lance-shaped, sharp-pointed. Mid-green.
• NATIVE HABITAT Plains of south central to southeast US.
• CULTIVATION Grow in light, well-drained soil, in sun. Good in wildflower gardens, and as a filler in a mixed or herbaceous border.
• PROPAGATION Sow seed *in situ* in spring.

☼ ◊

HEIGHT
3–5ft
(1–1.5m)

SPREAD
12in (30cm)

Dipsacaceae	PINCUSHION FLOWER

SCABIOSA ATROPURPUREA
Cockade Series

Habit Upright biennial or short-lived perennial. **Flowers** Double, pincushion-like, 2in (5cm) across, borne from summer to early autumn. Pink, red, purple, or blue. **Leaves** Basal, lobed. Mid-green.
• NATIVE HABITAT Garden origin.
• CULTIVATION Grow in neutral to alkaline soil. Ideal for cutting, or cottage or wildflower gardens.
• PROPAGATION Sow seed at 43–54°F (6–12°C) in early spring, or *in situ* in mid-spring.

☼ ◊

Z 7–9

HEIGHT
36in (90cm)

SPREAD
8–12in
(20–30cm)

Caryophyllaceae	

AGROSTEMMA GITHAGO 'Purple Queen'

Habit Upright, hairy annual. **Flowers** Trumpet-shaped, 5-petaled, 2in (5cm) across, borne in summer. Deep pink, often with a white eye. **Leaves** Narrow to lance-shaped. Gray-green.
• NATIVE HABITAT Garden origin. Species occurs in cultivated fields, Mediterranean.
• CULTIVATION Grow in poor, light, well-drained soil. Good for cottage or wildflower gardens.
• PROPAGATION Sow seed *in situ* in spring, or as soon as ripe.
• OTHER NAME *A. githago* 'Milas Cerise'.

☼ ◊

HEIGHT
24–36in
(60–90cm)

SPREAD
12in (30cm)

Boraginaceae	CHERRY PIE, HELIOTROPE

HELIOTROPIUM ARBORESCENS

Habit Bushy shrub, grown as an annual. **Flowers** Tiny, fragrant, tubular, in dense, rounded heads, borne in summer. Lavender-blue or deep violet-blue. **Leaves** Oval to lance-shaped. Dark green.
• NATIVE HABITAT Dry, open places, Peru.
• CULTIVATION Grow in moist, well-drained soil, or in soil-based potting mix under glass. Ideal as summer bedding, or as a houseplant.
• PROPAGATION By seed at 61–64°F (16–18°C) in spring. Also by stem-tip cuttings in summer.
• OTHER NAME *H. peruvianum*.

☼ ◊

Z 11

HEIGHT
1½–4ft
(0.5–1.2m)

SPREAD
12–18in
(30–45cm)

Compositae/Asteraceae	MARY'S THISTLE

SILYBUM MARIANUM

Habit Rosette-forming biennial. **Flowers** Slightly fragrant, thistle-like, from summer to autumn. Purplish-pink. **Leaves** Deeply lobed, veined, spined. Dark green, with white markings.
• NATIVE HABITAT Stony slopes, southwest Europe to Afghanistan, N. Africa.
• CULTIVATION Grow in poor to moderately fertile, well-drained soil. Suitable for a cottage or wildflower garden, or as a filler in a mixed border.
• PROPAGATION Sow seed *in situ* in late spring or early summer.

☼ ◊

Z 6–9

HEIGHT
5ft
(to 1.5m)

SPREAD
24–36in
(60–90cm)

Leguminosae/ Papilionaceae	HYACINTH BEAN

LABLAB PURPUREUS

Habit Climbing perennial, grown as an annual. **Flowers** Pea-like, fragrant, to 1in (2.5cm) long, in long plumes, from summer to autumn. White or purple. **Leaves** Oval to triangular. Mid-green.
• NATIVE HABITAT Scrub, tropical Africa.
• CULTIVATION Grow in a warm, sunny, sheltered site, in well-drained soil. Provide support.
• PROPAGATION Sow seed at 66–75°F (19–24°C) in early spring.
• OTHER NAMES *Dolichos lablab, D. niger, D. purpureus.*

☼ ◊

Min. 45°F
(7°C)

HEIGHT
6–20ft
(2–6m)

Compositae/Asteraceae	COTTON THISTLE, SCOTCH THISTLE

ONOPORDUM ACANTHIUM

Habit Rosette-forming, tap-rooted biennial. **Flowers** Thistle-like, 2in (5cm) across, with spiny bracts, borne on hairy, winged, branching stems, from summer. White or pale purple. **Leaves** Divided, spiny-toothed, hairy. Gray-green.
• NATIVE HABITAT Stony slopes, disturbed ground, western Europe to western and central Asia.
• CULTIVATION Grow in fertile, neutral to alkaline soil. Good as a focal point in a mixed border.
• PROPAGATION Sow seed in containers in a cold frame or *in situ* in autumn or spring.

☼ ◊

Z 5–8

HEIGHT
to 10ft (3m)

SPREAD
3ft (1m)

Ranunculaceae	LARKSPUR

CONSOLIDA AJACIS Imperial Series

Habit Bushy, low-branching annuals. **Flowers** Spurred, double, 1⅝in (4cm) across, in long, dense clusters, from summer. White, pink, or blue. **Leaves** Finely cut, feathery. Bright green.
• NATIVE HABITAT Garden origin.
• CULTIVATION Grow in light, fertile, well-drained soil. Ideal for cutting, and suitable as a filler in a mixed border. Provide pea sticks for support.
• PROPAGATION Sow seed *in situ* between spring and early summer.
• OTHER NAME *C. ambigua* Imperial Series.

 ☼ ◊

HEIGHT
4ft (1.2m)

SPREAD
12in (30cm)

Amaranthaceae	

GOMPHRENA GLOBOSA
'Professor Plum'

Habit Bushy, upright annual. *Flowers* Tiny, in clover-like, narrow to oval heads, 2in (5cm) long, from summer to autumn. Deep maroon-purple. *Leaves* Oval to paddle-shaped, hairy. Mid-green.
• NATIVE HABITAT Garden origin.
• CULTIVATION Grow in moderately fertile soil, in full sun. For cutting, grow in rows 6in (15cm) apart. Ideal for drying, an annual border, or for edging.
• PROPAGATION Sow seed at 59–64°F (15–18°C) in early spring.

☼ ◊

HEIGHT
12–24in
(30–60cm)

SPREAD
12in (30cm)

Convolvulaceae	MORNING GLORY

IPOMOEA HEDERACEA

Habit Twining, climbing, hairy-stemmed annual. *Flowers* Slender-tubed, funnel-shaped, in clusters, borne in summer. Purple or blue, with white tubes and long, green sepals. *Leaves* Rounded, divided into 3 lobes. Dark green.
• NATIVE HABITAT Scrub, US to Argentina.
• CULTIVATION Grow in a warm, sunny site, in moist but well-drained soil, with shelter from wind.
• PROPAGATION Sow chipped or pre-soaked seed at 64°F (18°C) in spring. Grow on in warmth.
• OTHER NAME *Pharbitis hederacea*.

☼ ◊

Min. 45°F
(7°C)

HEIGHT
6–10ft
(2–3m)

Polemoniaceae	CATHEDRAL BELL, CUP AND SAUCER VINE

COBAEA SCANDENS

Habit Vigorous, evergreen, climbing perennial, grown as an annual. *Flowers* Fragrant, bell-shaped, 2in (5cm) long, from summer to autumn. Creamy-green, aging to purple. *Leaves* Divided into 4 narrow to oval leaflets. Rich green.
• NATIVE HABITAT Forests and thickets, Mexico.
• CULTIVATION Grow in fertile, moist but well-drained soil, in a sheltered site. Provide support.
• PROPAGATION Sow seed at 64°F (18°C) in spring. Can also be propagated using soft tip cuttings. Overwinter young plants under glass.

 ☼ ◊

Min. 41°F
(5°C)

HEIGHT
30–60ft
(10–20m)

Solanaceae	APPLE OF PERU, SHOO-FLY

NICANDRA PHYSALODES

Habit Vigorous, upright annual. *Flowers* Bell-shaped, 1⅜in (3.5cm) across, from summer to autumn. Violet-blue. *Leaves* Oval or lance-shaped, wavy-margined. Mid-green. *Fruits* Round berries, in papery, lantern-like sepals. Green.
• NATIVE HABITAT Waste ground, open sites, Peru.
• CULTIVATION Grow in fertile, moist but well-drained soil, in sun. Ideal for a wildflower garden or mixed border. Fruiting branches can be dried.
• PROPAGATION Sow seed at 59°F (15°C) in spring, or *in situ* in mid-spring.

☼ ◊

HEIGHT
to 36in
(90cm)

SPREAD
12in (30cm)

Compositae/Asteraceae	CHINA ASTER

CALLISTEPHUS CHINENSIS
'Compliment Light Blue'

Habit Erect, fast-growing, bushy annual. *Flowers* Quill-petaled, double, from summer to early autumn. Light blue. *Leaves* Oval. Mid-green.
• NATIVE HABITAT Garden origin. Species occurs on slopes and wasteland, China.
• CULTIVATION Grow in a sheltered site in fertile, neutral to alkaline, moist but well-drained soil, in full sun. Good for cut flowers.
• PROPAGATION Sow seed at 61°F (16°C) in early spring, or *in situ* in mid-spring.

☼ ◊

HEIGHT
28in (70cm)

SPREAD
8in (20cm)

Malvaceae	

ANODA CRISTATA 'Opal Cup'

Habit Vigorous, upright, bushy annual.
Flowers Saucer-shaped, 2in (5cm) across, from summer to autumn. Clear silvery-lilac, with dark veins. *Leaves* Hand-shaped, lobed or unlobed, entire, or toothed. Mid-green, with purple marks.
• NATIVE HABITAT Garden origin.
• CULTIVATION Grow in moist but well-drained soil, in sun. Provide support. Deadhead regularly. Good for bedding, mixed or annual borders.
• PROPAGATION Sow seed at 55–59°F (13–15°C) in early spring, or *in situ* in spring.

☼ ◊

HEIGHT
to 5ft
(1.5m)

SPREAD
24in (60cm)

Leguminosae/ Papilionaceae	

LUPINUS NANUS 'Pixie Delight'

Habit Upright or branching annual. *Flowers* Pea-like, in clusters to 8in (20cm) tall, borne in summer. White, pink, blue, or lavender, with some bicolors. *Leaves* Hand-shaped, hairy, divided into leaflets. Mid-green.
• NATIVE HABITAT Garden origin.
• CULTIVATION Grow in light, sandy, slightly acid soil, in sun or part-shade. Suitable for bedding or an annual border.
• PROPAGATION Sow nicked or pre-soaked seed in a seed bed in spring.

☼ ◊

HEIGHT
20in (50cm)

SPREAD
9in (23cm)

Convolvulaceae	MORNING GLORY

IPOMOEA TRICOLOR 'Heavenly Blue'

Habit Climbing annual. *Flowers* Funnel-shaped, 3in (8cm) across, borne in summer, or year-round in the tropics. Deep azure, with a white throat.
Leaves Oval to heart-shaped. Light to mid-green.
• NATIVE HABITAT Garden origin. Species occurs in tropical forest, C. and S. America.
• CULTIVATION Grow in fertile, moist but well-drained soil, in a warm, sunny, and sheltered site.
• PROPAGATION Sow chipped or pre-soaked seed singly at 64°F (18°C). Grow on in warmth, as sudden temperature drops can cause failure.

☼ ◊

Min. 45°F
(7°C)

HEIGHT
10–12ft
(3–4m)

Convolvulaceae	MORNING GLORY

IPOMOEA PURPUREA

Habit Twining, climbing annual. **Flowers**
Trumpet-shaped, 2⅜in (6cm) across, from summer.
White, pink, magenta, or blue-purple, sometimes
striped. **Leaves** Oval, entire, or lobed. Mid-green.
• NATIVE HABITAT Uncertain, probably Mexico.
• CULTIVATION Grow in moist but well-drained
soil, in a warm, sunny, sheltered site. In cool
climates, grow as a house or conservatory plant.
• PROPAGATION Sow chipped or pre-soaked seed
at 64°F (18°C) in spring. Grow on in warmth.
• OTHER NAME *Convolvulus purpureus.*

☼ ◊

Min. 45°F
(7°C)

HEIGHT
18ft (5.5m)

SPREAD
10ft (3m)

Convolvulaceae	MORNING GLORY

CONVOLVULUS TRICOLOR 'Major'

Habit Twining, climbing annual. **Flowers**
Funnel-shaped, 4in (10cm) across, from summer.
White, red, or blue. **Leaves** Oval to lance-
shaped. Dark green.
• NATIVE HABITAT Garden origin.
• CULTIVATION Grow in well-drained, poor
to moderately fertile soil, in sun. Deadhead
regularly. Train up a tripod in an annual or
mixed border. Provide support.
• PROPAGATION Sow seed *in situ* in spring.
• OTHER NAME *C. minor* 'Major'.

☼ ◊

HEIGHT
to 10ft (3m)

Labiatae/Lamiaceae	

PERILLA FRUTESCENS var. CRISPA

Habit Vigorous annual. **Flowers** Tiny,
insignificant, in whorled spikes, borne in summer.
White. **Leaves** Pointed, broadly oval, and glossy.
Purple, green, or bronze, with frilly margins.
• NATIVE HABITAT Himalayas to eastern Asia.
• CULTIVATION Grow in fertile, moist but well-
drained soil, in sun or part-shade. Good as
contrast in a bedding scheme.
• PROPAGATION Sow seed at 55–64°F (13–18°C)
in spring.
• OTHER NAME *P. frutescens* var. *nankinensis.*

☼ ◊

HEIGHT
3ft (1m)

SPREAD
12in (30cm)

Malvaceae	BLACK HOLLYHOCK

ALCEA ROSEA 'Nigra'

Habit Upright perennial, grown as a biennial.
Flowers Funnel-shaped, glossy, 2–4in (5–10cm)
across, in tall clusters, from summer. Deep
chocolate-maroon, with a yellow center. **Leaves**
Rounded, shallowly lobed, hairy. Mid-green.
• NATIVE HABITAT Garden origin.
• CULTIVATION Grow in any moderately fertile,
well-drained soil, in sun. Suitable for a mixed
border and cottage gardens.
• PROPAGATION Sow seed *in situ* in mid-summer.
• OTHER NAME *Althaea rosea* 'Nigra'.

☼ ◊

Z 3–9

HEIGHT
6ft (2m)

SPREAD
12in (30cm)

TAGETES

The genus *Tagetes*, commonly known as marigolds, consists of about 50 species of strongly aromatic, bushy annuals and perennials, of which there are four main hybrid groups in cultivation, all blooming in long succession between late spring and autumn. Afro-French, French, and Signet marigolds are generally more compact and better suited to border edging or mixed and annual borders. All of these groups are ideal for cutting and suit window boxes, hanging baskets, and patio tubs.
African Derived from *T. erecta*, African marigolds are compact, with large, very double, pompon-like flowers up to 5in (12cm) across. They are ideal for use as formal bedding.
Afro-French Derived from crosses between *T. erecta* and *T. patula*, the Afro-French marigolds bear many small, single or double, yellow or orange flowerheads, 1–2⅜in (2.5–6cm) across.

French Derived from *T. patula*, French marigolds generally produce double flowerheads, about 2in (5cm) across, with red-brown, yellow, or orange part-colored ray florets and disk florets in a range of bright colors.
Signet Derived from *T. tenuifolia*, Signet marigolds produce a mass of small, single flowerheads to 1in (2.5cm) across, with yellow or orange florets.

Grow in any moderately fertile, well-drained soil, in full sun. Deadhead regularly to prolong flowering and keep well watered in dry periods. Use a soil-based potting mix for container-grown plants outdoors. Water well and apply a balanced liquid fertilizer weekly during the growing season.

Sow seed *in situ* in late spring or under glass at 70°F (21°C) in early spring. Flowers begin to appear within a few weeks, and are generally trouble-free.

T. **'Vanilla'**
Habit Bushy, upright annual.
Flowers Daisy-like, very double, borne freely from late spring through to early autumn. Creamy-white.
Leaves Lance-shaped, finely divided into leaflets, sharply toothed, and glossy. Dark green.
• HEIGHT 14in (35cm).
• SPREAD 18in (45cm).

T. **'Vanilla'**
(African)

☼ ◊

T. **'Gold Coins'**
Habit Vigorous, bushy, upright annual.
Flowers Large, daisy-like, fully double, borne from summer through to autumn. Yellow or orange.
Leaves Lance-shaped, divided into leaflets, sharply toothed, glossy. Dark green.
• HEIGHT 36in (90cm).
• SPREAD 12–18in (30–45cm).

T. **'Gold Coins'**
(African)

☼ ◊

T. Solar Series
Habit Bushy annuals.
Flowers Large, very
double, some with a
crested center, borne
freely from late spring
through to early autumn.
Orange, sulfur-yellow,
or golden-yellow.
Leaves Lance-shaped,
divided into leaflets.
Dark green.
• HEIGHT 14in (35cm).
• SPREAD 12–16in
(30–40cm).

T. Solar Series
(Afro-French)

T. 'Lemon Gem'
Habit Neat, bushy,
compact annual.
Flowers Single,
daisy-like, borne
freely from late
spring through
to early autumn.
Lemon-yellow.
Leaves Narrowly
lance-shaped,
divided into leaflets.
Dark green.
• HEIGHT 9in (23cm).
• SPREAD 16in (40cm).

T. 'Lemon Gem'
(Gem Series)
(Signet)

☼ ◊

T. 'Boy-O-Boy'
Habit Compact,
bushy annual.
Flowers Double, borne
in late spring and early
summer. Yellow, gold,
orange, and mahogany
red, with a deep orange
or yellow crest.
Leaves Narrowly lance-
shaped, divided into
leaflets, and toothed.
Dark green.
• HEIGHT 6in (15cm).
• SPREAD 12in (30cm).

T. 'Boy-O-Boy'
(Boy Series)
(French)

☼ ◊

T. 'Naughty Marietta'
Habit Fast-growing,
bushy, upright annual.
Flowers Single, borne
from late spring through
to early autumn. Yellow,
marked red-maroon at
the petal base.
Leaves Narrowly lance-
shaped, divided into
leaflets. Dark green.
• HEIGHT 12–16in
(30–40cm).
• SPREAD 12in (30cm).

T. 'Naughty Marietta'
(French)

☼ ◊

T. 'Crackerjack'
Habit Vigorous, bushy,
upright annual.
Flowers Large, double,
borne throughout
summer and early
autumn. In shades of
orange and yellow.
Leaves Lance-shaped,
divided into leaflets,
sharply toothed,
glossy. Dark green.
• HEIGHT 24in (60cm).
• SPREAD 12–18in
(30–45cm).

T. 'Crackerjack'
(African)

 ◊

T. 'Orange Winner'
Habit Bushy,
compact annual.
Flowers Double,
with a crested center,
from summer through
to early autumn.
Bright orange.
Leaves Narrowly
lance-shaped,
divided into
leaflets, toothed.
Dark green.
• HEIGHT 6in (15cm).
• SPREAD 12in (30cm).

T. 'Orange Winner'
(French)

T. 'Tangerine Gem'
Habit Compact,
bushy, upright annual.
Flowers Small, single,
borne freely from
late spring through
to early autumn.
Deep tangerine-
orange, with a
darker center.
Leaves Narrowly lance-
shaped, divided into
leaflets. Dark green.
• HEIGHT 8in (20cm).
• SPREAD 12in (30cm).

T. 'Tangerine Gem'
(Signet)

T. Inca Series
Habit Compact, upright,
bushy annual.
Flowers Double, daisy-
like, borne in late spring
through to early autumn.
In single or mixed
colors of yellow,
orange, and gold.
Leaves Divided, lance-
shaped, sharply toothed,
glossy. Dark green.
• HEIGHT 12in (30cm).
• SPREAD 12–18in
(30–45cm).

T. Inca Series
(African)

T. 'Safari Gem'
Habit Fast-growing, bushy annual.
Flowers Double, broad-petaled, from late spring through to early autumn. Rich tangerine-orange.
Leaves Narrowly lance-shaped, divided into leaflets, and toothed. Dark green.
• HEIGHT 8–10in (20–25cm).
• SPREAD to 12in (30cm).

T. 'Safari Gem'
(French)

T. 'Zenith Orange Brown'
Habit Dense, bushy, upright annual.
Flowers Large, double, borne from late spring through to autumn. Rich orange-brown.
Leaves Lance-shaped, divided into leaflets, Dark green.
• HEIGHT 12in (30cm).
• SPREAD 12–16in (30–40cm).

T. 'Zenith Orange Brown'
(Afro-French)

T. 'Cinnabar'
Habit Robust, fast-growing, bushy annual.
Flowers Single, daisy-like, rounded, borne from summer through to early autumn. Rust-red, with a yellow-red underside.
Leaves Narrowly lance-shaped, finely divided into leaflets, and toothed. Dark green.
• HEIGHT 12in (30cm).
• SPREAD 12in (30cm).

T. 'Paprika'
Habit Bushy, upright, compact annual.
Flowers Single, daisy-like, borne from summer through to early autumn. Dark red, with gold-edged petals and a golden-yellow center.
Leaves Narrowly lance-shaped, divided into leaflets. Dark green.
• HEIGHT 6in (15cm).
• SPREAD 12in (30cm).

T. 'Paprika'
(Signet)

T. 'Hero Spry'
Habit Robust annual.
Flowers Large, double, borne in late spring through to early autumn. Yellow, red, orange, or mahogany, with a crested yellow center.
Leaves Lance-shaped, divided into leaflets, toothed. Dark green.
• HEIGHT 8–10in (20–25cm).
• SPREAD 12in (30cm).

T. 'Hero Spry'
(French)

T. 'Cinnabar'
(French)

ZINNIA

The *Zinnia* genus consists of 20 species of annuals, perennials, and sub-shrubs, of which the most important in cultivation are the cultivars of *Z. elegans* and *Z. haageana*. These cultivars are valued for their long-stemmed, solitary, single or double, daisy-like flowerheads. The flowers are borne throughout summer until early autumn, in a range of bright colors. Zinnias flower best in long, hot summers, and are ideal for summer bedding, annual or mixed borders, or as cut flowers. The more compact cultivars are suitable for edging, or for window boxes and other containers.

Zinnias tolerate a range of well-drained soils, including dry ones, but for best results, grow in fertile, well-drained soil in full sun, in a warm, sheltered site. They dislike humid conditions, and the flowers, especially of the large-flowered cultivars, may be damaged by heavy rain. Pinch out the growing tips of young plants to promote a bushy habit. Regular dead-heading will help prolong flowering. Tall cultivars may need to be staked.

Sow seed in early spring at 61–64°F (16–18°C) and grow on young plants in well-ventilated conditions at a minimum of 61°F (16°C). Harden off and plant out when the danger of frost has passed. Zinnias dislike root disturbance and are best sown in, or pricked out into, individual, biodegradable pots or modular trays. Alternatively, carefully sow seed *in situ* in late spring, and thin out seedlings as soon as they are large enough to handle. Avoid disturbing the roots of the remaining seedlings. Sow in succession for a longer flowering display.

Zinnias are generally trouble-free, but may be infected by mildew if grown in crowded or humid conditions. The risk is reduced if they are planted in an open site with good air circulation.

Z. ELEGANS
Peppermint Stick Series
Habit Sturdy, upright annuals.
Flowers Pompon-like, borne from summer to autumn. In varied colors, with streaked, blotched petals.
Leaves Oval to lance-shaped. Bright green.
• HEIGHT 24in (60cm).
• SPREAD 12in (30cm).

Z. elegans **Peppermint Stick Series**
☼ ◊ Min. 50°F (10°C)

Z. ELEGANS
'Ruffles Mixed'
Habit Sturdy, upright annual. Weather-resistant.
Flowers Pompon-like, 2⅜in (6cm) across, ruffled petals, borne from summer to autumn. Varied color range.
Leaves Oval to lance-shaped. Bright green.
• HEIGHT 24in (60cm).
• SPREAD 12in (30cm).

Z. elegans **'Ruffles Mixed'** (Ruffles Series)
☼ ◊ Min. 50°F (10°C)

Z. ELEGANS
Thumbelina Series
Habit Compact, dwarf annuals. Weather-resistant.
Flowers Single or semi-double, 4in (10cm) across, borne from summer to early autumn. In shades of pink, red, and yellow.
Leaves Oval to lance-shaped. Bright green.
• HEIGHT 6in (15cm).
• SPREAD 12in (30cm).

Z. elegans **Thumbelina Series**
☼ ◊ Min. 50°F (10°C)

Z. ELEGANS
Whirlygig Series
Habit Sturdy, upright annuals.
Flowers Double, 2⅜in (6cm) across, from summer to autumn. Varied colors, with petal tips in contrasting and toning shades.
Leaves Oval to lance-shaped. Bright green.
• HEIGHT 24in (60cm).
• SPREAD 12in (30cm).

Z. elegans **Whirlygig Series**
☼ ◊ Min. 50°F (10°C)

Z. ELEGANS 'Envy'
Habit Sturdy, upright
annual. Shade-tolerant.
Flowers Large, semi-
double to double,
neatly formed,
with slightly quilled
petals, borne from
summer to autumn.
Chartreuse-green.
Leaves Oval to lance-
shaped. Pale to
mid-green.
• HEIGHT 30in (75cm).
• SPREAD 12in (30cm).

Z. elegans 'Envy'

☼ ◊
Min. 50°F (10°C)

**Z. ELEGANS
'Belvedere'**
Habit Compact,
dwarf annual.
Weather-resistant.
Flowers Large,
double, with broad
petals, from summer
to autumn. Varied
bright colors.
Leaves Oval to
lance-shaped.
Bright green.
• HEIGHT 12in (30cm).
• SPREAD 12in (30cm).

Z. elegans
'Belvedere'

☼ ◊
Min. 50°F (10°C)

**Z. ELEGANS
'Peter Pan Gold'**
Habit Compact,
dwarf, early-
flowering annual.
Flowers Double,
4in (10cm) across,
borne in summer.
Golden-yellow.
Leaves Oval to
lance-shaped, and
sparsely hairy.
Bright green.
• HEIGHT 8in (20cm).
• SPREAD 12in (30cm).

Z. elegans
'Peter Pan Gold'
(Peter Pan Series)
☼ ◊
Min. 50°F (10°C)

**Z. HAAGEANA
'Persian Carpet'**
Habit Dwarf,
compact, upright,
bushy annual.
Flowers Double and
semi-double, 1⅝in
(4cm) across, from
summer. Red, orange,
and yellow, in bi- and
tricolored shades.
Leaves Lance-shaped.
Mid-green.
• HEIGHT 16in (40cm).
• SPREAD 12in (30cm).

Z. haageana
'Persian Carpet'

☼ ◊

Z. Burpee Hybrids
Habit Sturdy, upright
annuals.
Flowers Large, cactus
dahlia-like, double,
with wavy, quilled
petals, borne from
summer to early
autumn. Varied
bright colors.
Leaves Oval to lance-
shaped, and sparsely
hairy. Bright green.
• HEIGHT 24in (60cm).
• SPREAD 12in (30cm).

Z. Burpee Hybrids
(Elegans Group)

☼ ◊
Min. 50°F (10°C)

Polemoniaceae	QUEEN ANNE'S THIMBLES

GILIA CAPITATA

Habit Upright annual. **Flowers** Tiny, to ⅜in (9mm) long, in rounded, pincushion-like heads, borne from summer. Lavender-blue. **Leaves** Feathery, divided into narrow leaflets. Mid-green.
• NATIVE HABITAT Dry, sunny sites, eastern N. America.
• CULTIVATION Grow in light, well-drained soil, in full sun. Ideal for a wildflower, annual, or mixed border.
• PROPAGATION Sow seed *in situ* in autumn or mid-spring.

HEIGHT
18–24in
(45–60cm)

SPREAD
8–9in
(20–23cm)

Asclepiadaceae	

TWEEDIA CAERULEA

Habit Twining, scrambling sub-shrub, grown as an annual. **Flowers** Saucer-shaped, 5-petaled, from summer to early autumn. Sky-blue. **Leaves** Narrow to lance-shaped, downy. Light green.
• NATIVE HABITAT Scrub, Brazil to Uruguay.
• CULTIVATION Grow in moist but well-drained, fertile soil, in sun. In cooler climates, grow as a house- or conservatory plant. Allow it to twine through other shrubs.
• PROPAGATION Sow seed at 59°F (15°C) in spring.
• OTHER NAME *Amblyopetalum caeruleum*.

Z 9–11

HEIGHT
2–3ft
(0.6–1m)

Linaceae	COMMON FLAX, LINSEED

LINUM USITATISSIMUM

Habit Upright annual. **Flowers** Saucer-shaped, 5-petaled, ⅜–¾in (1–2cm) across, in leafy clusters, borne in summer. Clear sky-blue. **Leaves** Narrow to lance-shaped. Mid-green. **Fruits** Rounded capsules. Straw-colored.
• NATIVE HABITAT Uncertain, probably Asia.
• CULTIVATION Seed heads are good for drying. Grow in light, moderately fertile, well-drained soil, in full sun. Ideal in an annual border.
• PROPAGATION Sow seed *in situ* in spring or autumn.

HEIGHT
24–36in
(60–90cm)

SPREAD
8in (20cm)

Malvaceae	

ANODA CRISTATA 'Silver Cup'

Habit Vigorous, erect, spreading annual, or short-lived perennial. *Flowers* Saucer-shaped, single, mallow-like, 2in (5cm) across, borne singly or in pairs in the upper leaf axils, from summer to autumn. In shades of white, some with a blue tinge. *Leaves* Oval, lobed or unlobed, toothed. Mid-green.
• NATIVE HABITAT Garden origin. The species occurs in damp soils, in moist meadows, and in open areas by streambanks, in southwestern US to Mexico, S. America, and W. Indies.

• CULTIVATION Grow in moist but well-drained, moderately fertile soil, in full sun. Provide support. Deadhead regularly to prolong flowering. *A. cristata* 'Silver Cup' is valued for its long flowering season and is ideally suited for use in a mixed border, an annual border, or for in-filling in a herbaceous border. Plants will overwinter in frost-free areas if given a deep, dry winter mulch.
• PROPAGATION Sow seed under glass at 55–59°F (13–15°C) in early spring, or *in situ* in mid-spring.

Z 10–11

HEIGHT
5ft (1.5m)

SPREAD
24in (60cm)

Commelinaceae	DAY FLOWER, WIDOW'S TEARS

COMMELINA COELESTIS

Habit Upright, tuberous perennial, grown as an annual. *Flowers* Saucer-shaped, 3-petaled, in clusters, from late summer to autumn. Mid-blue. *Leaves* Lance-shaped. Bright green.
• NATIVE HABITAT Forests, C. and S. America.
• CULTIVATION Grow in fertile, well-drained soil, in a warm, sheltered site. Mulch deeply in winter, or lift tubers in autumn and store in a frost-free place.
• PROPAGATION Sow seed in spring, at 55–64°F (13–18°C). Divide mature tubers in spring.

☀ ◌

Z 9–10

HEIGHT
to 36in
(90cm)

SPREAD
18in (45cm)

Compositae/Asteraceae	BACHELOR'S BUTTONS

CENTAUREA CYANUS

Habit Upright annual. *Flowers* Hemispherical, borne from late spring to mid-summer, with lobed florets. Dark blue, with violet-blue inner florets. *Leaves* Lance-shaped, with a hairy underside. Gray-green.
• NATIVE HABITAT Dry slopes, northern temperate regions.
• CULTIVATION Grow in well-drained, moderately fertile soil, in full sun. Good for cut flowers.
• PROPAGATION Sow seed *in situ* in spring or autumn.

☀ ◌

HEIGHT
8–31in
(20–80cm)

SPREAD
6in (15cm)

Labiatae/Lamiaceae	

PLECTRANTHUS THYRSOIDEUS

Habit Perennial, grown as an annual. *Flowers* In terminal spikes, borne intermittently, year-round. Violet-blue. *Leaves* Heart-shaped. Mid-green.
• NATIVE HABITAT C. Africa.
• CULTIVATION Grow in well-drained soil and part-shade. In cooler climates, grow as a house- or conservatory plant. Ideal in summer bedding. Under glass, use a soil-based potting mix.
• PROPAGATION Sow seed at 66–75°F (19–24°C) in autumn or early spring.
• OTHER NAME *Coleus thyrsoideus.*

☀ ◌

Min. 39°F
(4°C)

HEIGHT
to 36in
(90cm)

SPREAD
to 24in
(60cm)

Boraginaceae	BORAGE

BORAGO OFFICINALIS

Habit Bushy, branching annual. *Flowers* Star-shaped, to 1in (2.5cm) across, in branched clusters, borne throughout summer. Bright blue. *Leaves* Lance-shaped to oval, bristly. Dull green.
• NATIVE HABITAT Dry, rocky places, Europe.
• CULTIVATION Grow in any well-drained soil, in full sun. Ideal for a herb garden, and well suited for a cottage- or wildflower garden. Tolerates dry soils. Young leaves and flowers are edible.
• PROPAGATION Sow seed *in situ* in autumn or spring. Self-sows freely.

☀ ◌

HEIGHT
24in (60cm)

SPREAD
18in (45cm)

Gramineae	BROME GRASS, CHESS

BROMUS MACROSTACHYS

Habit Annual grass. **Flowers** Dense, narrow clusters of spikelets, to 8in (20cm) long, with long, conspicuous awns, borne in summer. Purple-tinged. **Leaves** Narrow, flat, and soft. Mid-green.
• NATIVE HABITAT Dry wasteland around the Mediterranean.
• CULTIVATION Grows best in light, well-drained soil, in sun. Flowerheads are well suited for dried arrangements, and should be cut and air-dried before fully ripe.
• PROPAGATION Sow seed *in situ* in spring.

☀ ◊

HEIGHT
20in (50cm)

SPREAD
4in (10cm)

Gramineae/Poaceae	HARE'S-TAIL

LAGURUS OVATUS

Habit Tufted, annual grass. **Flowers** Soft, hairy, in dense, oval clusters of spikelets, 2⅜in (6cm) long, borne in summer. Pale green, sometimes purple-flushed. **Leaves** Flat, narrow. Pale green.
• NATIVE HABITAT Coastal sands, Mediterranean and southern Europe.
• CULTIVATION Grow in light, sandy, well-drained soil, in full sun. Good for dried arrangements and as a filler in a mixed or herbaceous border.
• PROPAGATION Sow seed *in situ* in spring or in containers in a cold frame in autumn.

☀ ◊

HEIGHT
20in (50cm)

SPREAD
12in (30cm)

Gramineae/Poaceae	SQUIRREL TAIL GRASS

HORDEUM JUBATUM

Habit Erect or arching, annual or perennial grass. **Flowers** Dense clusters of spikelets, to 5in (13cm) long, with long, silky bristles, from early to mid-summer. Pale green.
Leaves Upright or arching, narrow. Pale green.
• NATIVE HABITAT Disturbed land, northeast Asia, N. America.
• CULTIVATION Grow in light, well-drained, moderately fertile soil, in sun. Good for drying, and for an annual or mixed border.
• PROPAGATION Sow *in situ* in spring or autumn.

☀ ◊

Z 4–8

HEIGHT
20in (50cm)

SPREAD
12in (30cm)

Gramineae	BEARD GRASS, RABBIT'S FOOT GRASS

POLYPOGON MONSPELIENSIS

Habit Slender, clump-forming, annual grass.
Flowers Narrowly oval to cylindrical heads, to 6in (15cm) long, in silky, bristled spikelets, from summer to autumn. Green, aging to brown.
Leaves Flat, narrow, and rough. Mid-green.
• NATIVE HABITAT Sparse grassland, Europe.
• CULTIVATION Grow in a mixed or annual border, in light, well-drained, moderately fertile soil, in sun. Flowerheads are good for cutting and drying.
• PROPAGATION Sow seed *in situ* in spring or autumn.

☀ ◌

HEIGHT
to 24in
(60cm)

SPREAD
8in (20cm)

Leguminosae/ Mimosaceae	HUMBLE PLANT, SENSITIVE PLANT

MIMOSA PUDICA

Habit Bushy annual or short-lived perennial.
Flowers Spherical, borne from summer. Light pink to lilac. **Leaves** Divided into narrow leaflets that fold when touched. Bright green.
• NATIVE HABITAT Forest, N. and S. America.
• CULTIVATION Grow under glass in soilless or soil-based potting mix in good light, with shade from hot sun. In cool climates, grow as a house- or conservatory plant. Water moderately.
• PROPAGATION Sow seed at 64–75°F (18–24°C) in spring.

☀ ◌

Min. 55°F
(13°C)

HEIGHT
12–30in
(30–75cm)

SPREAD
16–36in
(40–90cm)

Gramineae/Poaceae	GREATER QUAKING GRASS, PUFFED WHEAT

BRIZA MAXIMA

Habit Slender, upright, tufted, annual grass.
Flowers Open heads, to 4in (10cm) long, of drooping, oval to heart-shaped spikelets, from late spring and summer. Green, turning buff when ripe.
Leaves Long, narrow, and bristly. Pale green.
• NATIVE HABITAT Bare ground, Mediterranean.
• CULTIVATION Grow in a mixed or annual border in light, moderately fertile, well-drained soil, in sun. Flowerheads are good for cutting and drying.
• PROPAGATION Sow seed *in situ* in spring or autumn.

☀ ◌

HEIGHT
18–24in
(45–60cm)

SPREAD
10in (25cm)

Gramineae	FOXTAIL MILLET, ITALIAN MILLET

SETARIA ITALICA

Habit Robust annual grass. **Flowers** Dense, lobed, spike-like heads, often drooping, in clusters, from late summer. Creamy-brown. **Leaves** Narrow to lance-shaped. Mid-green. **Fruits** Cylindrical, lobed seedheads. Golden-yellow.
• NATIVE HABITAT Warm temperate Asia.
• CULTIVATION Grow in light, well-drained, fertile soil, in sun. Seedheads are good for attracting birds into the garden and for dried arrangements.
• PROPAGATION Sow seed *in situ* in spring.

☀ ◌

HEIGHT
to 5ft
(1.5m)

SPREAD
to 3ft (1m)

Euphorbiaceae	

RICINUS COMMUNIS 'Zanzibarensis'

Habit Evergreen shrub, grown as an annual.
Flowers In oval spikes, male flowers below female flowers, from summer. Male flower, greenish-yellow. Female flower, purple, with a red stigma. **Leaves** Hand-shaped. Bright green.
• NATIVE HABITAT Garden origin.
• CULTIVATION Grow in fertile, moist but well-drained soil in a warm, sheltered site. Good as fillers in formal bedding. All parts are toxic.
• PROPAGATION Sow pre-soaked seed at 70°F (21°C), in individual pots, in spring.

Z 8–10

HEIGHT
6–10ft
(2–3m)

SPREAD
to 3ft (1m)

Gramineae/Poaceae	WITCH GRASS

PANICUM CAPILLARE

Habit Loosely tufted annual grass. **Flowers** Dense clusters of tiny spikelets on slender stems, from late summer. Brownish-green.
Leaves Narrowly lance-shaped, flat. Mid-green.
• NATIVE HABITAT Grasslands, N. America.
• CULTIVATION Grow in moderately fertile, well-drained soil, in sun. Suitable for a mixed or annual border. Flowerheads are also good for drying.
• PROPAGATION Sow seed at 55–64°F (13–18°C) in spring.

HEIGHT
2–3ft
(0.6–1m)

SPREAD
24in (60cm)

Chenopodiaceae	BURNING BUSH, SUMMER CYPRESS

BASSIA SCOPARIA f. TRICHOPHYLLA

Habit Dense, bushy, conical annual. **Flowers** Insignificant. **Leaves** Narrowly lance-shaped. Emerald green, turning red or purple in autumn.
• NATIVE HABITAT Disturbed ground, Asia, N. America, and southern Europe.
• CULTIVATION Grow in fertile, well-drained soil in a warm, sunny and sheltered site. Grow for foliage effect in bedding or as temporary screening.
• PROPAGATION Surface-sow seed at 61°F (16°C) in early spring, or *in situ* in late spring.
• OTHER NAME *Kochia trichophylla*.

HEIGHT
1–5ft
(0.3–1.5m)

SPREAD
12–18in
(30–45cm)

Labiatae/Lamiaceae	BELLS OF IRELAND, SHELL FLOWER

MOLUCCELLA LAEVIS

Habit Upright, branching annual.
Flowers Tiny, 2-lipped, fragrant, enclosed in papery bracts, borne in whorled spikes, from late summer. White, with green bracts.
Leaves Broadly oval, scalloped. Pale green.
• NATIVE HABITAT Stony slopes, Caucasus, Turkey, Syria, and Iraq.
• CULTIVATION Grow in moist but well-drained soil, in sun. Good for cutting and drying.
• PROPAGATION Chill seed for two weeks then sow at 55–64°F (13–18°C) in spring.

☼ ◊

HEIGHT
24–36in
(60–90cm)

SPREAD
9in (23cm)

Gramineae/Poaceae	JOB'S TEARS

COIX LACRYMA-JOBI

Habit Tufted, annual grass. *Flowers* Arching clusters, with separate male and female spikelets, from late summer to early autumn. Greenish-yellow. *Leaves* Narrowly lance-shaped, flat. Bright green. *Fruits* Hard, shiny, teardrop-shaped, pearly seeds. Gray-purple.
• NATIVE HABITAT Grasslands, southeast Asia.
• CULTIVATION Grow in light, well-drained soil, in a warm site. Good for dried arrangements.
• PROPAGATION Sow seed at 55–61°F (13–16°C) in late winter or early spring.

☼ ◊

HEIGHT
18–36in
(45–90cm)

SPREAD
12in (30cm)

Gramineae/Poaceae	SORGHUM, GREAT MILLET

SORGHUM BICOLOR

Habit Robust, clump-forming annual. *Flowers* Dense, branching clusters, to 24in (60cm) long, from summer. Pink, purple, or pale green. *Leaves* Narrow, flat, waxy. Mid-green, with a white midrib. *Fruits* Large seed grains, varied colors.
• NATIVE HABITAT China, S. Africa.
• CULTIVATION Grow in well-drained, fertile soil. Seedheads are good for drying and attracting birds.
• PROPAGATION Sow seed at 55–64°F (13–18°C) in early spring.
• OTHER NAME *S. vulgare.*

☼ ◊

HEIGHT
6–10ft
(2–3m)

SPREAD
24in (60cm)

Gramineae/Poaceae	VARIEGATED CORN

ZEA MAYS 'Gracillima Variegata'

Habit Upright, rapid-growing annual. *Flowers* Male flowers, spike-like tassels in terminal heads, from summer. Female flowers, enclosed in a bract, with silky styles, from summer. *Leaves* Lance-shaped, striped. Green and white. *Fruits* Female flowers give rise to a cob of flat seeds. Yellow.
• NATIVE HABITAT Garden origin.
• CULTIVATION Grow in fertile, moist but well-drained soil, in a warm, sunny, sheltered site.
• PROPAGATION Sow seed at 64°F (18°C) in late winter or early spring.

☀ ◊

HEIGHT
36in (90cm)

SPREAD
12–18in
(30–45cm)

Cucurbitaceae	CALABASH GOURD, BOTTLE GOURD

LAGENARIA SICERARIA

Habit Scrambling or climbing annual. *Flowers* Solitary, bell-shaped, from summer. Creamy-yellow. *Leaves* Oval to heart-shaped. Mid-green. *Fruits* Bottle-shaped, smooth, can be dried. Green-yellow.
• NATIVE HABITAT Throughout the tropics.
• CULTIVATION Grow in moist, well-drained, fertile soil rich in organic matter, in a sheltered site, in sun. Ripen fruits in a dry place indoors.
• PROPAGATION Sow pre-soaked seed at 70–75°F (21–24°C) in early spring.

☀ ◊

HEIGHT
to 30ft
(10m)

Scrophulariaceae	MULLEIN

VERBASCUM BOMBYCIFERUM

Habit Rosette-forming biennial or short-lived perennial. *Flowers* Saucer-shaped, to 1⅝in (4cm) across, in dense, sparsely branched, silky spikes, borne freely from summer. Pale yellow. *Leaves* Oval, woolly. White.
• NATIVE HABITAT Dry stony hills, Turkey.
• CULTIVATION Grow in low-fertility, well-drained, alkaline soil, in sun. Good for mixed borders.
• PROPAGATION Sow seed in containers in a cold frame in late spring or early summer.
• OTHER NAME *V. broussa.*

☀ ◊

Z 5–8

HEIGHT
to 6ft (2m)

SPREAD
24in (60cm)

Apiaceae/Umbelliferae	PERFOLIATE ALEXANDERS

SMYRNIUM PERFOLIATUM

Habit Upright biennial. **Flowers** Tiny, in domed clusters, from late spring. Greenish-yellow. **Leaves** Stem leaves, rounded, perfoliate. Yellow-green. Basal leaves, divided. Pale green.
• NATIVE HABITAT Scrub, rocky places, and woodland margins. Europe, southwest Asia, N. Africa.
• CULTIVATION Grow in moist but well-drained, moderately fertile soil, in sun or part-shade. Good for cutting, and for wild and woodland gardens.
• PROPAGATION Sow seed *in situ* in spring or autumn, or in containers in a cold frame in spring.

Z 8–10

HEIGHT
2–5ft
(0.6–1.5m)

SPREAD
24in (60cm)

Compositae/Asteraceae	SWEET SULTAN

AMBERBOA MOSCHATA

Habit Upright annual. **Flowers** Cornflower-like, scented, with fringed ray florets, 2in (5cm) across, from spring to summer. White, pink, purple, or yellow. **Leaves** Lance-shaped, entire at base, lobed or divided on the stem. Gray-green.
• NATIVE HABITAT Turkey, Caucasus.
• CULTIVATION Grow in light, well-drained soil, in sun. Good for cut flowers and cottage gardens.
• PROPAGATION Sow *in situ* in spring or autumn, with cloche protection for autumn sowings.
• OTHER NAME *Centaurea moschata.*

HEIGHT
24in (60cm)

SPREAD
9in (23cm)

Scrophulariaceae	YELLOW FOXGLOVE

DIGITALIS GRANDIFLORA

Habit Clump-forming biennial, or short-lived perennial. **Flowers** Tubular, in open clusters, from early to mid-summer. Pale yellow, with brown veins. **Leaves** Narrow to oval, toothed. Mid-green.
• NATIVE HABITAT Europe, Siberia, Turkey.
• CULTIVATION Grow in moist, well-drained soil rich in leaf mold, in partial shade. Good for a woodland garden, mixed or herbaceous border.
• PROPAGATION Sow seed in containers in a cold frame in late spring. May self-seed.
• OTHER NAMES *D. ambigua, D. orientalis.*

Z 3–8

HEIGHT
to 3ft (1m)

SPREAD
18in (45cm)

Scrophulariaceae	WHITE MULLEIN

VERBASCUM LYCHNITIS

Habit Rosette-forming biennial. *Flowers* Saucer-shaped, on branching, pyramidal stems, borne from mid- to late summer. Creamy-yellow. *Leaves* Narrowly oval. Mid-green, with a white underside.
• NATIVE HABITAT Hedgerows and rocky places, western Europe to western Asia.
• CULTIVATION Grow in low-fertility, well-drained, alkaline soil, in sun. Good for mixed borders.
• PROPAGATION Sow seed in containers in a frame in late spring or early summer.

Z 5–8

HEIGHT
to 5ft
(1.5m)

SPREAD
24in (60cm)

Scrophulariaceae	

VERBASCUM OLYMPICUM

Habit Rosette-forming, woolly perennial, dies after flowering (in year 2 or 3). *Flowers* Saucer-shaped, 1¼in (3cm) across, on candelabra-like, branching plumes, from summer. Golden-yellow. *Leaves* Lance-shaped, woolly. White.
• NATIVE HABITAT Dry stony hills, Greece.
• CULTIVATION Grow in low-fertility, well-drained, alkaline soil, in sun. Good for mixed borders.
• PROPAGATION Sow seed in containers in a cold frame in late spring. Also by root cuttings in winter.
• OTHER NAME *V. longifolium* var. *pannosum.*

Z 5–8

HEIGHT
6ft (2m)

SPREAD
24in (60cm)

Papaveraceae	DEVIL'S FIG, PRICKLY POPPY

ARGEMONE MEXICANA

Habit Clump-forming annual. *Flowers* Solitary, poppy-like, to 3in (8cm) across, from late summer to early autumn. Pale to deep yellow. *Leaves* Prickly, lobed. Blue-green, veined silver-white.
• NATIVE HABITAT Dry scrub, southern US to C. America.
• CULTIVATION Grow in sharply drained, low-fertility, gritty or stony soil, in full sun. Suitable for a dry border or gravel garden. Will self-seed.
• PROPAGATION Sow seed at 64°F (18°C) in modular or individual containers in early spring.

HEIGHT
to 3ft (1m)

SPREAD
to 16in
(40cm)

Onagraceae	EVENING PRIMROSE

OENOTHERA BIENNIS

Habit Upright annual or biennial. **Flowers** Bowl-shaped, fragrant, to 2in (5cm) across, in spike-like heads, from summer. Pale or golden-yellow. **Leaves** Narrow to lance-shaped, in basal rosettes. Mid-green, with red-veins.
• NATIVE HABITAT Dry places, eastern N. America.
• CULTIVATION Grow in poor to moderately fertile, well-drained soil, in full sun. Suitable for a mixed or herbaceous border, or dry sunny bank.
• PROPAGATION Sow seed in containers in a cold frame in early spring.

☀ ◊

Z 3–7

HEIGHT
3–5ft
(1–1.5m)

SPREAD
24in
(60cm)

Compositae/Asteraceae	STAR DAISY

LINDHEIMERA TEXANA

Habit Upright, red-stemmed annual. **Flowers** Star-shaped, 1in (2.5cm) across, in loose clusters, from late spring to summer. Pale to golden-yellow. **Leaves** Oval to lance-shaped, basal leaves divided. Mid-green.
• NATIVE HABITAT Prairies, Texas.
• CULTIVATION Grow in light, well-drained, moderately fertile soil, in sun. Good in a wildflower border, cottage garden, mixed or annual border.
• PROPAGATION Sow seed in containers in a cold frame in early spring, or *in situ* in mid-spring.

☀ ◊

HEIGHT
24in (60cm)

SPREAD
12in (30cm)

Compositae/Asteraceae	

TOLPIS BARBATA

Habit Upright, branching annual. **Flowers** Daisy-like, ⅜–1¼in (1–3cm) across, with fringed ray florets, borne from late spring to summer. Bright yellow, with a dark maroon disk. **Leaves** Lance-shaped, mostly basal, hairy. Bright green.
• NATIVE HABITAT Sandy places. Mediterranean.
• CULTIVATION Grow in light, well-drained, moderately fertile soil, in sun. Good for a mixed, wildflower, or annual border.
• PROPAGATION Sow seed *in situ* in mid-spring.

☀ ◊

HEIGHT
12–24in
(30–60cm)

SPREAD
12in (30cm)

Compositae/Asteraceae	POT MARIGOLD

CALENDULA OFFICINALIS
Kablouna Series

Habit Sturdy, upright annuals. **Flowers** Daisy-like, to 4in (10cm) across, with crested disk florets and quilled petals, from summer to autumn. Yellow, gold, or orange. **Leaves** Lance- to spoon-shaped, finely hairy. Bright green.
• NATIVE HABITAT Garden origin.
• CULTIVATION Grow in any well-drained soil, in sun. Good for mixed borders and cottage gardens.
• PROPAGATION Sow *in situ* in spring or autumn, with cloche protection for autumn sowings.

☀ ◊

HEIGHT
to 24in
(60cm)

SPREAD
12in (30cm)

Plumbaginaceae	STATICE

LIMONIUM SINUATUM
Sunburst Series (mixed)

Habit Upright perennials grown as annuals.
Flowers Tiny, funnel-shaped, in clustered sprays
of spikelets, from late summer. Rose, apricot,
blue, or peach. *Leaves* Lance-shaped, wavy-
margined, in basal rosettes. Dark green.
• NATIVE HABITAT Garden origin.
• CULTIVATION Grow in well-drained, moderately
fertile soil, in full sun. Good for cutting and drying.
• PROPAGATION Sow seed at 55–64°F (13–18°C)
in early spring.

☼ ◊

Z 8–10

HEIGHT
30in (75cm)

SPREAD
12in (30cm)

Cruciferae/Brassicaceae	WOAD

ISATIS TINCTORIA

Habit Tap-rooted biennial or short-lived
perennial. *Flowers* Cross-shaped, 4-petaled,
in plumes, from early summer. Yellow. *Leaves*
Lance-shaped, in basal rosettes. Gray-green.
• NATIVE HABITAT Waste ground, Europe.
• CULTIVATION Grow in moist, well-drained soil,
in sun. Good for a wildflower or herb garden.
Fermenting the leaves with ammonia yields
a blue pigment.
• PROPAGATION Sow seed in autumn or spring
in containers in a cold frame.

 ☼ ◊

Z 4–8

HEIGHT
to 4ft
(1.2m)

SPREAD
18in (45cm)

Solanaceae	PAINTED TONGUE

SALPIGLOSSIS SINUATA Casino Series

Habit Compact, free-flowering, weather-resistant
annuals. *Flowers* Funnel-shaped, from summer
to autumn, or from spring under glass. Purple, red,
blue, yellow, or orange, heavily veined. *Leaves*
Lance-shaped, wavy-margined. Mid-green.
• NATIVE HABITAT Garden origin.
• CULTIVATION Grow in moist, well-drained,
fertile soil, in sun, or a soil-based potting mix
under glass. Ideal for summer bedding.
• PROPAGATION Sow seed at 64–75°F (18–24°C)
in spring, or in autumn or late winter for pot plants.

☼ ◊

HEIGHT
18–24in
(45–60cm)

SPREAD
12in (30cm)

Papaveraceae	TULIP POPPY

HUNNEMANNIA FUMARIIFOLIA 'Sunlite'

Habit Fast-growing perennial, grown as an annual. **Flowers** Saucer-shaped, poppy-like, to 3in (8cm) across, with glossy petals, from mid-summer to autumn. Clear yellow.
Leaves Narrow, finely divided into 3 lobes. Blue-green.
• NATIVE HABITAT Garden origin.
• CULTIVATION Grow in well-drained, moderately fertile soil, in a warm, sheltered site, in full sun. Good as a filler in a mixed or herbaceous border.
• PROPAGATION Sow seed *in situ* in mid-spring.

☼ ◊

Z 10–11

HEIGHT
to 24in
(60cm)

SPREAD
8in (20cm)

Compositae/Asteraceae	CORN MARIGOLD

CHRYSANTHEMUM SEGETUM

Habit Upright, slightly fleshy annual. **Flowers** Solitary, daisy-like, with broad ray florets, from summer to autumn. Golden-yellow, with a yellow central disk. **Leaves** Lance-shaped. Gray-green.
• NATIVE HABITAT Cultivated and disturbed land, Mediterranean.
• CULTIVATION Grow in light, preferably sandy, well-drained soil, in sun. Good for an annual meadow, or a wildflower or annual border.
• PROPAGATION Sow seed *in situ* in spring, or in autumn, with cloche protection over winter.

☼ ◊

HEIGHT
to 31in
(80cm)

SPREAD
12in (30cm)

Compositae/Asteraceae	PALM SPRINGS DAISY

CLADANTHUS ARABICUS

Habit Branching annual. **Flowers** Daisy-like, to 2in (5cm) across, from summer. Golden-yellow ray florets, with a yellow central disk. **Leaves** Finely divided into narrow lobes. Bright green.
• NATIVE HABITAT Dry pasture, southern Europe, northwest Africa.
• CULTIVATION Grow in light, well-drained soil, in sun. Good for cut flowers and suitable for a sunny border, window box, or other container.
• PROPAGATION Sow seed at 55–61°F (13–16°C) in early spring, or *in situ* later in spring.

☼ ◊

HEIGHT
16–24in
(40–60cm)

SPREAD
to 16in
(40cm)

Compositae/Asteraceae	

COREOPSIS GRANDIFLORA 'Sunray'

Habit Clump-forming perennial, usually grown as an annual. **Flowers** Double, daisy-like, with unevenly cut ray florets, borne throughout summer. Deep golden-yellow. **Leaves** Lance-shaped, lobed. Mid-green.
• NATIVE HABITAT Garden origin.
• CULTIVATION Grow in light, well-drained soil, in sun. Good for cut flowers, and as a filler in a mixed border. Deadhead to prolong flowering.
• PROPAGATION Sow seed at 55–61°F (13–16°C) in late winter or early spring.

☼ ◊

Z 4–9

HEIGHT
20–30in
(50–75cm)

SPREAD
18in (45cm)

Compositae/Asteraceae	

COREOPSIS TINCTORIA

Habit Upright, stiff-stemmed annual. **Flowers** Solitary, daisy-like, 2in (5cm) across, from summer. Bright yellow, red at the base of the ray florets, with a dark red disk. **Leaves** Lance-shaped, or finely divided into narrow leaflets. Mid-green.
• NATIVE HABITAT Prairies, N. America.
• CULTIVATION Grow in light, well-drained soil, in sun. Good for cutting and for an annual border.
• PROPAGATION Sow seed *in situ*, in succession from spring to early summer.
• OTHER NAME *Calliopsis tinctoria*.

☀ ◊

HEIGHT
to 4ft
(1.2m)

SPREAD
12–18in
(30–45cm)

Compositae/Asteraceae	CROWN DAISY

CHRYSANTHEMUM CORONARIUM

Habit Vigorous, branching annual. **Flowers** Single, daisy-like, 2in (5cm) across, from spring to summer. Bright yellow. **Leaves** Fern-like, finely cut. Bright green.
• NATIVE HABITAT Mediterranean.
• CULTIVATION Grow in light, fertile, well-drained soil, in sun. Good in an annual or wildflower border and in cottage gardens. Provide support.
• PROPAGATION Sow seed at 55°F (13°C) in early spring, or *in situ* in spring or in autumn, with cloche protection over winter.

☀ ◊

HEIGHT
to 31in
(80cm)

SPREAD
to 16in
(40cm)

Scrophulariaceae	

CALCEOLARIA INTEGRIFOLIA

Habit Evergreen perennial, usually grown as an annual. **Flowers** Slipper-like, pouched, 1in (2.5cm) long, borne in clusters during summer. Yellow. **Leaves** Lance-shaped. Gray-green.
• NATIVE HABITAT Mexico.
• CULTIVATION Grow as bedding, in well-drained soil in a warm, sheltered site, in sun or part-shade.
• PROPAGATION Surface sow seed at 64°F (18°C) in spring or in autumn and overwinter in frost-free conditions. Also by heeled cuttings in summer.
• OTHER NAME *C. rugosa*.

☀ ◊

Z 8–10

HEIGHT
to 4ft
(1.2m)

SPREAD
9–12in
(23–30cm)

Compositae/Asteraceae	

BRACTEANTHA BRACTEATA
'Dargan Hill Monarch'

Habit Vigorous annual or short-lived perennial. **Flowers** Daisy-like, with papery ray florets, from summer to autumn. Golden-yellow. **Leaves** Lance-shaped. Gray-green.
• NATIVE HABITAT Garden origin.
• CULTIVATION Grow in moderately fertile, well-drained soil, in sun. Good for cutting and drying.
• PROPAGATION Sow seed in spring at 64°F (18°C).
• OTHER NAME *Helichrysum bracteatum* 'Dargan Hill Monarch'.

☀ ◊

Z 10–11

HEIGHT
24–36in
(60–90cm)

SPREAD
12in (30cm)

Papaveraceae	YELLOW HORNED POPPY

GLAUCIUM FLAVUM

Habit Rosette-forming perennial, usually grown as a biennial, on branching stems. *Flowers* Poppy-like, fine-textured, 2in (5cm) across, from summer. Bright golden-yellow. *Leaves* Oval, lobed, and toothed. Blue-green.
• NATIVE HABITAT Disturbed ground, Europe, Canary Islands, N. Africa, western Asia.
• CULTIVATION Grow in poor to moderately fertile, sharply drained soil. Good for an annual border.
• PROPAGATION Sow seed *in situ* in spring or autumn.

Z 6–9

HEIGHT
12–36in
(30–90cm)

SPREAD
18in (45cm)

Compositae/Asteraceae	

COREOPSIS TINCTORIA 'Golden Crown'

Habit Upright, stiff-stemmed annual. *Flowers* Solitary, daisy-like, 2in (5cm) across, from summer to autumn. Deep yellow, with a red-brown central disk. *Leaves* Lance-shaped, or divided into narrow leaflets. Dark green.
• NATIVE HABITAT Garden origin.
• CULTIVATION Grow in light, well-drained soil, in sun. Good for cutting and for an annual border.
• PROPAGATION Sow seed *in situ*, in succession from spring to early summer.
• OTHER NAME *Calliopsis tinctoria* 'Golden Crown'.

HEIGHT
24in (60cm)

SPREAD
8in (20cm)

Plumbaginaceae	STATICE

LIMONIUM SINUATUM 'Forever Gold'

Habit Upright perennials, grown as annuals. *Flowers* Tiny, funnel-shaped, to ⅜in (1cm) long, in clustered sprays, borne freely from late summer. Yellow. *Leaves* Deeply lobed, wavy-margined, slightly fleshy, in basal rosettes. Dark green.
• NATIVE HABITAT Garden origin.
• CULTIVATION Grow in well-drained, moderately fertile soil in full sun. Good for cutting and drying.
• PROPAGATION Sow seed at 55–64°F (13–18°C) in early spring.

Z 8-10

HEIGHT
24in (60cm)

SPREAD
12in (30cm)

Gramineae/Poaceae	VARIEGATED CORN

ZEA MAYS 'Strawberry Corn'

Habit Upright, rapid-growing annual. *Flowers* Male flowers, spike-like tassels in terminal sprays, from summer. Green. Female flowers, silky styles, borne in leaf axils, from summer. Green. *Leaves* Lance-shaped, arching. Green and white. *Fruits* Cob of flattened seeds. Burgundy-red, or yellow.
• NATIVE HABITAT Garden origin.
• CULTIVATION Grow in fertile, moist but well-drained soil, in a warm, sunny, sheltered site.
• PROPAGATION Sow seed at 64°F (18°C) in late winter or early spring.

HEIGHT
4ft (1.2m)

SPREAD
24in (60cm)

Compositae/Asteraceae	POT MARIGOLD

CALENDULA OFFICINALIS 'Art Shades'

Habit Sturdy, upright annual. **Flowers** Double, daisy-like, to 4in (10cm) across, from summer to autumn. Pastel shades of cream, apricot, or orange. **Leaves** Lance- to spoon-shaped, finely hairy. Bright green.
• NATIVE HABITAT Garden origin.
• CULTIVATION Grow in any well-drained soil, in sun. Good for mixed borders and cottage or herb gardens. Flowers are edible and good for cutting.
• PROPAGATION Sow *in situ* in spring or autumn, with cloche protection for autumn sowings.

☼ ◊

HEIGHT
to 24in
(60cm)

SPREAD
24in (60cm)

Compositae/Asteraceae	GLORIOSA DAISY

RUDBECKIA HIRTA 'Goldilocks'

Habit Upright biennial or perennial, grown as an annual. **Flowers** Double or semi-double, daisy-like, 2¾in (7cm) across, from summer to autumn. Golden-orange, with a brown-purple central disk. **Leaves** Oval. Dark green.
• NATIVE HABITAT Garden origin.
• CULTIVATION Grow in moist but well-drained, moderately fertile soil. Good for cutting.
• PROPAGATION Sow seed at 61–64°F (16–18°C) in spring.
• OTHER NAME *R. gloriosa* 'Goldilocks'.

☼ ◊

Z 3–7

HEIGHT
to 24in
(60cm)

SPREAD
12in (30cm)

Compositae/Asteraceae	

COSMOS SULPHUREUS 'Sunset'

Habit Bushy, upright annual. **Flowers** Bowl-shaped, to 2¼in (6cm) across, borne throughout summer. Rich orange-bronze. **Leaves** Narrow, finely divided into lobes. Mid-green.
• NATIVE HABITAT Garden origin.
• CULTIVATION Grow in moist but well-drained, moderately fertile soil, in full sun. Ideal for cut flowers and suitable for a mixed or annual border.
• PROPAGATION Sow seed at 61°F (16°C) in mid-spring, or *in situ* in late spring.

☼ ◊

HEIGHT
36in (90cm)

SPREAD
18in (45cm)

Bignoniaceae	CHILEAN GLORY FLOWER

ECCREMOCARPUS SCABER

Habit Slender evergreen climber, often grown as an annual. **Flowers** Tubular, 1in (2.5cm) long, borne in clusters, from early summer to autumn. Orange-red. **Leaves** Divided into oval leaflets. Light green.
• NATIVE HABITAT Scrub and forest margins, Chile.
• CULTIVATION Grow in fertile, well-drained soil, in a warm, sunny site. Good for trellis or scrambling through other shrubs.
• PROPAGATION Sow seed at 55–61°F (13–16°C) in late winter or early spring.

☼ ◊

Z 10–11

HEIGHT
10–15ft
(3–5m)

| Acanthaceae | BLACK-EYED SUSAN VINE |

THUNBERGIA ALATA

Habit Evergreen perennial climber, often grown as an annual. **Flowers** Saucer-shaped, with 5 spreading lobes, 1¼–1⅝in (3–4cm) across, borne singly in the leaf axils, from summer to autumn. Creamy-white, yellow, or bright orange, sometimes with a brown-purple center.
Leaves Oval to triangular, toothed, lobed at the base, with winged stalks. Mid-green.
• NATIVE HABITAT Forests of tropical Africa.
• CULTIVATION Grow in fertile, moist but well-drained soil, in sun or partial shade, in a warm, sheltered site. In cool climates, grow as a house- or conservatory plant. Under glass, use a soilless or soil-based potting mix. Admit full light but provide shade from hot sun. Water freely when in growth, sparingly in winter. Ideal for trellis, arch or other supports, or for twining through shrubs in a mixed border.
• PROPAGATION Sow seed at 61–64°F (16–18°C) in spring. May also be increased by softwood cuttings in early summer, or semi-ripe cuttings in mid- to late summer.

Z 9–10

HEIGHT
5–6ft
(1.5–2m)

Scrophulariaceae	MASK FLOWER

ALONSOA LINEARIS

Habit Upright sub-shrub, grown as an annual.
Flowers Spurred, 2-lipped, 1in (2.5cm) across,
in loose plumes, borne throughout summer.
Brick red, with black spots at the throat. *Leaves*
Narrow to lance-shaped, pointed. Dark green.
• NATIVE HABITAT Scrub, in Peru and Chile.
• CULTIVATION Grow in fertile, well-drained
soil, in sun. Good for summer bedding.
• PROPAGATION Sow seed at 64°F (18°C) in
early spring.
• OTHER NAME *A. linifolia.*

☼ ◊

Z 11

HEIGHT
to 3ft (1m)

SPREAD
12in (30cm)

Acanthaceae	

THUNBERGIA GREGORII

Habit Evergreen perennial climber, often
grown as an annual. *Flowers* Saucer-shaped,
1¼in (4.5cm) across, from summer. Clear orange.
Leaves Oval to triangular. Mid-green.
• NATIVE HABITAT Tropical Africa.
• CULTIVATION Grow in fertile, moist but well-
drained soil, in sun or part-shade, in a warm,
sheltered site. Ideal for trellis, or other supports.
• PROPAGATION Sow seed at 64–70°F (18–21°C) in
spring. May also be increased by softwood or semi-
ripe cuttings in early or mid-summer respectively.

☼ ◊

Z 9–10

HEIGHT
7ft (2.2m)

Compositae/Asteraceae	MEXICAN SUNFLOWER

TITHONIA ROTUNDIFOLIA 'Torch'

Habit Vigorous, branching annual. *Flowers*
Single, dahlia-like, on branched stems, from late
summer to autumn. Bright orange-red. *Leaves*
Oval to triangular, entire or 3-lobed. Dark green.
• NATIVE HABITAT Garden origin.
• CULTIVATION Grow in moderately fertile,
well-drained soil. Good for cut flowers and
mixed borders.
• PROPAGATION Sow seed at 55–64°F (13–18°C)
in mid- to late spring, or *in situ* in late spring.
• OTHER NAME *T. speciosa* 'Torch'.

☼ ◊

HEIGHT
to 6ft (2m)

SPREAD
12in (30cm)

Compositae/Asteraceae	GLORIOSA DAISY

RUDBECKIA HIRTA 'Rustic Dwarfs'

Habit Upright biennial or perennial, grown as
an annual. *Flowers* Daisy-like, 2¼in (7cm) across,
from summer to autumn. Red-brown, yellow, or
orange-bronze, including bicolors, with a brown-
purple central disk. *Leaves* Oval. Dark green.
• NATIVE HABITAT Garden origin.
• CULTIVATION Grow in moist, well-drained,
moderately fertile soil. Good for cutting.
• PROPAGATION Sow seed at 61–64°F
(16–18°C) in spring.
• OTHER NAME *R. gloriosa* 'Rustic Dwarfs'.

☼ ◊

Z 3–7

HEIGHT
to 24in
(60cm)

SPREAD
to 12in
(30cm)

Compositae/Asteraceae	

BRACTEANTHA BRACTEATA
Monstrosum Series

Habit Vigorous annuals or short-lived perennials.
Flowers Daisy-like, double, with papery florets,
from summer to autumn. White, pink, red, yellow,
or orange. *Leaves* Lance-shaped. Gray-green.
• NATIVE HABITAT Garden origin.
• CULTIVATION Grow in moderately fertile, well-
drained soil, in sun. Good for cutting and drying.
• PROPAGATION Sow seed in spring at 64°F (18°C).
• OTHER NAME *Helichrysum bracteatum*
Monstrosum Series.

☼ ◊

Z 10–11

HEIGHT
to 36in
(90cm)

SPREAD
12in (30cm)

Compositae/Asteraceae	FLORA'S PAINTBRUSH

EMILIA COCCINEA

Habit Rosette-forming annual. *Flowers*
Double, hemispherical, from ⅗in (1.5cm)
across, borne singly or in clusters, from summer.
Scarlet or orange-red. *Leaves* Lance-shaped.
Grayish-green.
• NATIVE HABITAT Stony slopes, tropical Africa.
• CULTIVATION Grow in well-drained soil, in
full sun. Good for cutting and drying.
• PROPAGATION Sow seed at 64°F (18°C) in spring.
• OTHER NAMES *E. flammea, E. javanica, Cacalia
coccinea, C. sagittata.*

☼ ◊

HEIGHT
18–24in
(45–60cm)

SPREAD
12–24in
(30–60cm)

Compositae/Asteraceae	POT MARIGOLD

CALENDULA OFFICINALIS 'Geisha Girl'

Habit Sturdy, upright annual. *Flowers* Daisy-
like, double, to 4in (10cm) across, with incurved
ray florets, from summer to autumn. Deep orange.
Leaves Lance- to spoon-shaped, finely hairy.
Bright green.
• NATIVE HABITAT Garden origin.
• CULTIVATION Grow in any well-drained soil, in
sun. Good for mixed borders and cottage or herb
gardens. Flowers are edible and good for cutting.
• PROPAGATION Sow *in situ* in spring or autumn,
with cloche protection for autumn sowings.

☼ ◊

HEIGHT
24in (60cm)

SPREAD
12–24in
(30–60cm)

Compositae/Asteraceae	

DAHLIA 'Dandy'

Habit Bushy perennial, grown as an annual.
Flowers Daisy-like, to 2¾in (7cm) across, with
quilled petals, from summer. White, red, yellow,
or orange, with paler petals around disk.
Leaves Oval, divided into leaflets. Mid-green.
• NATIVE HABITAT Garden origin.
• CULTIVATION Grow in fertile, moist but well-
drained soil, in full sun. Good for cutting,
bedding and containers.
• PROPAGATION Sow at 61°F (16°C) in early spring.
Pinch out growing tip to encourage bushiness.

☼ ◊

Z 8–10

HEIGHT
24in (60cm)

SPREAD
24in (60cm)

Compositae/Asteraceae

ARCTOTIS Harlequin Hybrids 'Torch'

Habit Upright, well-branched, slow-growing perennial, grown as an annual. *Flowers* Daisy-like, 3in (8cm) across, from mid-summer to early autumn. Rich bronze. *Leaves* Oval, lobed, felted. Silver-green.
• NATIVE HABITAT Garden origin.
• CULTIVATION Grow in light, moderately fertile, sharply drained but fairly moist soil, in full sun. In cool climates, grow as a house- or conservatory plant. Under glass, use a soil-based potting mix and provide full light.

Water moderately when in growth, and apply a balanced liquid fertilizer every two weeks. Ideal as cut flowers and suitable for a warm, sunny bank or annual border.
• PROPAGATION Sow seed at 64°F (18°C) in spring, or in autumn for growing under glass. Seedlings are best pricked out individually into 3½in (9cm) pots to reduce root disturbance on planting out. Also by stem cuttings at any time of the year; overwinter young plants in frost-free conditions under glass.
• OTHER NAME x *Venidioarctotis* 'Torch'.

☼ ◌

Min. 41°F
(5°C)

HEIGHT
18in (45cm)

SPREAD
18in (45cm)

Solanaceae	

BROWALLIA SPECIOSA 'White Troll'

Habit Compact, bushy perennial, grown as an annual. *Flowers* Saucer-shaped, 5-lobed, borne in the leaf axils, starting in summer. Pure white. *Leaves* Narrow to oval. Mid-green.
• NATIVE HABITAT Garden origin.
• CULTIVATION Grow in soil-based potting mix, in full light, shaded from hot sun. In cool climates, grow as a house- or conservatory plant. Water moderately and apply balanced fertilizer monthly.
• PROPAGATION Sow seed at 64°F (18°C) in early spring, or in late summer for winter flowers.

☀ ◊

Min 55°F (13°C)

HEIGHT to 10in (25cm)

SPREAD 10in (25cm)

Cruciferae/Brassicaceae	CANDYTUFT

IBERIS AMARA

Habit Upright, branching annual. *Flowers* Scented, 4-petaled, in domed clusters, starting in summer. White or purplish-white. *Leaves* Lance- to spoon-shaped. Mid-green.
• NATIVE HABITAT Open sites on freely draining, lime-rich soils, western Europe.
• CULTIVATION Grow in poor to moderately fertile, well-drained, neutral to alkaline soil, in sun. Good for bedding and borders.
• PROPAGATION Sow seed *in situ* in succession in spring or autumn, or in late winter at 61°F (16°C).

☀ ◊

HEIGHT 6–18in (15–45cm)

SPREAD 6in (15cm)

Plumbaginaceae	STATICE

LIMONIUM SINUATUM 'Iceberg'

Habit Upright, rosette-forming perennial. *Flowers* Tiny, funnel-shaped, in plumes of clustered spikelets, from summer to autumn. Pure white. *Leaves* Narrowly lance-shaped, lobed. Mid-green.
• NATIVE HABITAT Garden origin.
• CULTIVATION Grow in light, well-drained soil in full sun. Good for cutting and drying; cut when flowers are almost fully open. One of the California Series.
• PROPAGATION Sow seed in early spring at 55–64°F (13–18°C).

☀ ◊

Z 8–10

HEIGHT 16in (40cm)

SPREAD 12in (30cm)

Cruciferae/Brassicaceae	SWEET ALYSSUM

LOBULARIA MARITIMA 'Snow Crystals'

Habit Compact, mound-forming annual. *Flowers* Cross-shaped, fragrant, in dense, rounded clusters, from summer. Pure white. *Leaves* Narrow to lance-shaped. Grayish-green.
• NATIVE HABITAT Garden origin.
• CULTIVATION Grow in well-drained soil, in full sun. Good for bedding, edging, and containers.
• PROPAGATION Sow seed in early spring at 55–64°F (13–18°C), or *in situ* in late spring.
• OTHER NAME *Alyssum maritimum* 'Snow Crystals'.

☀ ◊

HEIGHT 10in (25cm)

SPREAD 8–10in (20–25cm)

Boraginaceae	VENUS'S NAVELWORT

OMPHALODES LINIFOLIA

Habit Upright, fairly fast-growing, slender, low-branching annual.
Flowers Short-tubed, slightly scented, to ⅗in (1.5cm) across, on slender stems, in loose, airy clusters, borne freely from spring to summer. Available in white, sometimes with a blue tint, or pale blue.
Leaves Narrowly lance- to spoon-shaped, to 4in (10cm) long, with smaller, very narrow, stalkless stem leaves. Gray-green, sparsely clothed in white hair, mostly in basal tufts.

• NATIVE HABITAT Dry, open sites, frequently on alkaline soils, southwest Europe.
• CULTIVATION Grow in light, well-drained, moderately fertile, preferably neutral to alkaline soil, in an open site in full sun. Ideal for an annual border, a wildflower border, as a filler in a mixed or herbaceous border, or in gravel plantings. Well suited for cutting and arranging, giving a similar airy effect to that of *Gypsophila elegans*.
• PROPAGATION Sow seed *in situ* in spring. Often self-seeds freely.

HEIGHT
12–16in
(30–40cm)

SPREAD
6in (15cm)

Hydrophyllaceae	FIVE-SPOT

NEMOPHILA MACULATA

Habit Spreading, fleshy-stemmed annual.
Flowers Saucer-shaped, long-stalked, from summer. White, with violet-blue markings.
Leaves Divided into oval leaflets. Bright green.
• NATIVE HABITAT Western slopes of the Sierra Nevada, California.
• CULTIVATION Grow in moist but well-drained soil, in sun. Good for border edges and containers. Water freely during prolonged dry spells.
• PROPAGATION Sow seed *in situ* in autumn or early spring. Self-sows freely.

HEIGHT
6–12in
(15–30cm)

SPREAD
6–12in
(15–30cm)

Compositae/Asteraceae	RAIN DAISY, WEATHER PROPHET

DIMORPHOTHECA PLUVIALIS

Habit Upright, hairy annual. **Flowers** Single, daisy-like, 2⅜in (6cm) across, from summer. White, with a brownish-violet disk. **Leaves** Lance-shaped, coarsely toothed. Dark green.
• NATIVE HABITAT Semi-arid areas, Namibia, S. Africa.
• CULTIVATION Grow in light, well-drained soil in shelter. Ideal for cutting, bedding, and borders.
• PROPAGATION Sow seed at 64°F (18°C) in early spring, or *in situ* in mid-spring.
• OTHER NAME *D. annua.*

HEIGHT
to 16in
(40cm)

SPREAD
6–12in
(15–30cm)

Polemoniaceae	MOUNTAIN PHLOX

LINANTHUS GRANDIFLORUS

Habit Slender, upright, branching annual.
Flowers Funnel-shaped, with spreading lobes, to 1⅛in (3cm) across, borne in dense heads, from spring to summer. White, lavender-pink, or lilac, with white flecks. **Leaves** Divided into narrow lobes. Mid-green.
• NATIVE HABITAT Dry sites, southern California.
• CULTIVATION Grow in light, well-drained soil, in sun. Ideal in a mixed, annual, or wildflower border. Good for cutting.
• PROPAGATION Sow seed *in situ* in spring.

HEIGHT
12–20in
(30–50cm)

SPREAD
9in (23cm)

Compositae/Asteraceae	

OSTEOSPERMUM 'Whirligig'

Habit Sub-shrub, grown as an annual. **Flowers** Daisy-like, 3in (8cm) across, with spoon-shaped ray florets, from late spring to autumn. White, with a slate-blue underside, around a blue central disk. **Leaves** Lance-shaped, toothed. Gray-green.
• NATIVE HABITAT Garden origin.
• CULTIVATION Grow in well-drained soil in a warm, sunny, sheltered site. Good for cutting.
• PROPAGATION Sow seed at 64°F (18°C) in spring. Take stem tip cuttings in spring or summer.
• OTHER NAME O. 'Tauranga'.

☀ ◊

Z 8–10

HEIGHT
to 24in
(60cm)

SPREAD
24in (60cm)

Resedaceae	COMMON MIGNONETTE

RESEDA ODORATA

Habit Upright, hairless, low-branching annual. **Flowers** Star-shaped, ¼in (7mm) across, very fragrant, in conical heads, from summer to early autumn. White, yellow-green, or reddish-green. **Leaves** Oval to spoon-shaped, lobed. Mid-green.
• NATIVE HABITAT Scrub and stony hills, N. Africa.
• CULTIVATION Grow in well-drained, alkaline, moderately fertile soil, in sun or part-shade. Ideal for cutting and drying.
• PROPAGATION Sow seed at 55°F (13°C) in late winter, or in situ in spring or autumn.

☀ ◊

HEIGHT
12–24in
(30–60cm)

SPREAD
9in (23cm)

Euphorbiaceae	GHOST WEED, SNOW ON THE MOUNTAIN

EUPHORBIA MARGINATA

Habit Single-stemmed, branching annual. **Flowers** In terminal clusters, to 2in (5cm) across, enclosed in a ring of bracts, from late summer to autumn. Greenish-white, margined, spotted, and variegated. **Leaves** Oval. Mid-green, with white veins and margins.
• NATIVE HABITAT N. America.
• CULTIVATION Grow in light, well-drained soil in sun. Ideal for cut flowers.
• PROPAGATION Sow seed in situ in spring.
• OTHER NAME E. variegata.

☀ ◊

HEIGHT
12–36in
(30–90cm)

SPREAD
12in (30cm)

Dipsacaceae	

SCABIOSA STELLATA

Habit Wiry-stemmed, branching annual. **Flowers** Spherical heads, from summer. Pale blue. **Leaves** Lance-shaped. Mid-green. **Fruits** Rounded seedheads in bracts. Silver-cream.
• NATIVE HABITAT Sunny, rocky slopes, southern Europe.
• CULTIVATION Grow in light, moderately fertile, neutral to slightly alkaline, well-drained soil, in full sun. Seedheads are good for drying.
• PROPAGATION Sow seed at 43–54°F (6–12°C) in early spring, or in situ in mid-spring.

☀ ◊

HEIGHT
to 18in
(45cm)

SPREAD
9in (23cm)

Compositae/Asteraceae	SWAN RIVER DAISY

BRACHYSCOME IBERIDIFOLIA
'White Splendour'

Habit Spreading annual. *Flowers* Daisy-like, 1⅝in (4cm) across, from summer. White, with a yellow central disk. *Leaves* Divided into narrow leaflets, with soft down. Gray-green.
• NATIVE HABITAT Garden origin.
• CULTIVATION Grow in fertile, well-drained soil in a warm, sunny, sheltered site. Good for bedding, edging, containers, and dry, sunny banks. Moderately drought-tolerant.
• PROPAGATION Sow seed at 18°F (64°C) in spring.

☼ ◊

Z 8–10

HEIGHT
12in (30cm)

SPREAD
14in (35cm)

Solanaceae	CUPFLOWER

NIEREMBERGIA CAERULEA 'Mont Blanc'

Habit Upright, branching perennial, grown as an annual. *Flowers* Cup-shaped, 2in (⅘cm) across, from summer. White, with a yellow throat. *Leaves* Narrowly spoon-shaped, pointed. Bright green.
• NATIVE HABITAT Garden origin.
• CULTIVATION Grow in light, moist but well-drained soil, in a sheltered site in full sun. Good for bedding and border edging.
• PROPAGATION Sow seed at 59°F (15°C) in spring. Also by stem-tip cuttings in late summer.
• OTHER NAME *N. hippomannica* 'Mont Blanc'.

☼ ◊

Z 8–10

HEIGHT
to 8in
(20cm)

SPREAD
8in (20cm)

Compositae/Asteraceae	

COSMOS BIPINNATUS 'Sonata White'

Habit Compact, well-branched annual. *Flowers* Solitary, single, saucer-shaped, to 3in (8cm) across, from summer. Pure white, with a yellow center. *Leaves* Feathery, finely divided. Bright green.
• NATIVE HABITAT Garden origin.
• CULTIVATION Grow in fertile, moist, but well-drained soil, in sun. Good for cutting, for an annual border, or as fillers in a mixed or herbaceous border.
• PROPAGATION Sow seed at 61°F (16°C) in spring, or *in situ* in late spring.

☼ ◊

HEIGHT
18in (45cm)

SPREAD
12in (30cm)

Compositae/Asteraceae	

ARCTOTIS FASTUOSA 'Zulu Prince'

Habit Spreading perennial, grown as an annual.
Flowers Daisy-like, from mid-summer to autumn.
Creamy-yellow, with black and orange zones at
the base. *Leaves* Oval, deeply lobed. Silver-white.
• NATIVE HABITAT Garden origin.
• CULTIVATION Grow in light, sharply drained but
fairly moist soil, in a warm, sunny site. In cooler
climates, grow as a house- or conservatory plant.
Ideal for cutting, or for an annual or mixed border.
• PROPAGATION Sow seed at 61–64°F (16–18°C)
in early spring, or take stem cuttings in summer.

Z 8–10

Min. 41°F
(5°C)

HEIGHT
12–24in
(30–60cm)

SPREAD
12in (30cm)

Compositae/Asteraceae	

ERIGERON KARVINSKIANUS 'Profusion'

Habit Rhizomatous perennial, grown as an
annual. *Flowers* Daisy-like, ⅘in (2cm) across.
White or pink, with a yellow disk. *Leaves*
Oval to lance-shaped, hairy. Gray-green.
• NATIVE HABITAT Garden origin.
• CULTIVATION Grow in fertile, moist but
well-drained soil, preferably in mid-day shade.
Ideal for hanging baskets and other containers.
• PROPAGATION Sow seed in containers in a
cold frame in early to mid-spring.
• OTHER NAME *E. mucronatus* 'Profusion'.

Z 6–9

HEIGHT
8–12in
(20–30cm)

SPREAD
20in (50cm)

Compositae/Asteraceae	

CREPIS RUBRA

Habit Rosette-forming annual or short-lived
perennial. *Flowers* Dandelion-like, to 1in
(2.5cm) across, borne in pairs or singly on stiff
stems, from spring to summer. Pinkish-red.
Leaves Lance-shaped, toothed, hairy. Pale green.
• NATIVE HABITAT Stony slopes, Balkans,
southern Italy, Greece.
• CULTIVATION Grow in any well-drained soil,
in sun. Good for an annual or mixed border.
• PROPAGATION Sow seed in spring, or when
ripe, in a cold frame.

Z 5–7

HEIGHT
12–16in
(30–40cm)

SPREAD
6in (15cm)

Gentianaceae	PRAIRIE GENTIAN

EUSTOMA GRANDIFLORUM
Heidi Series

Habit Annuals or biennials. *Flowers* Bell-shaped, satiny, from summer. White, pink, or blue, with bicolors. *Leaves* Narrow to oval. Gray-green.
• NATIVE HABITAT Garden origin.
• CULTIVATION Grow in sheltered, well-drained, neutral to alkaline soil, in sun. In cooler climates, grow as a house- or conservatory plant.
• PROPAGATION Sow seed at 55–61°F (13–16°C) in autumn or late winter.
• OTHER NAME *Lisianthus russellianus* Heidi Series.

☼ ◊

Z 8–10

HEIGHT
24–36in
(60–90cm)

SPREAD
12in (30cm)

Caryophyllaceae	ROSE OF HEAVEN

SILENE COELI-ROSA

Habit Upright, slender annual. *Flowers* Deeply notched petals, borne in loose clusters, from summer. Rose-pink, with a white center. *Leaves* Narrow to lance-shaped. Gray-green.
• NATIVE HABITAT Mediterranean.
• CULTIVATION Grow in well-drained, neutral to slightly alkaline soil, in sun or dappled shade.
• PROPAGATION Sow seed *in situ* in autumn or spring.
• OTHER NAMES *Agrostemma coeli-rosa*, *Lychnis coeli-rosa*, *Viscaria elegans*.

☼ ◊

HEIGHT
to 20in
(50cm)

SPREAD
6in (15cm)

Compositae/Asteraceae	FLOSS FLOWER

AGERATUM HOUSTONIANUM
'Swing Pink'

Habit Compact, mound-forming annual. *Flowers* Tiny, fluffy, in rounded heads, from mid-summer to autumn. Pink. *Leaves* Oval, downy. Mid-green.
• NATIVE HABITAT Garden origin.
• CULTIVATION Grow in moist but well-drained fertile soil, in a sunny, sheltered site. Good for bedding, edging, and containers. Deadhead to promote a second flush of flowers.
• PROPAGATION Sow seed at 61–64°F (16–18°C) in early spring.

☼ ◊

HEIGHT
6–8in
(15–20cm)

SPREAD
6–8in
(15–20cm)

Ranunculaceae	LARKSPUR

CONSOLIDA AJACIS Dwarf Rocket Series

Habit Compact annuals. *Flowers* Spurred, in dense spikes, from summer. White, pink, purple, or blue. *Leaves* Finely cut leaflets. Bright green.
• NATIVE HABITAT Garden origin.
• CULTIVATION Grow in light, fertile, well-drained soil, in sun. Suitable for an annual or mixed border or as a filler in herbaceous borders. Water freely in dry periods. Deadhead to prolong flowering. The flower-spikes are ideal as cut flowers and are also very attractive when dried. Cut flowers for drying when half of the buds in the spike are open, strip the leaves from the stem, and air-dry by hanging upside down in a dry, airy place. Flowers can also be preserved in silica or borax.
• PROPAGATION Sow seed *in situ* from early spring to early summer. Autumn-sowings should be given cloche protection over winter. The cultivar may self-seed, but the offspring will be variable, and many will revert to the single flowered form.
• OTHER NAMES *C. ambigua, Delphinium consolida, D ajacis.*

HEIGHT
12–20in
(30–50cm)

SPREAD
6–10in
(15–25cm)

ANTIRRHINUM

The genus *Antirrhinum*, commonly known as snapdragons, consists of 30–40 species of annuals, perennials, and sub-shrubs. The most common in cultivation are the cultivars of *A. majus* described here. The species is a half-hardy, low-branching, woody-based perennial bearing upright clusters of fragrant, 2-lipped flowers. In cultivated selections, the flowers are available in a range of colors, including many bicolors. *A. majus* and its cultivars are short-lived if grown as perennials, but flower freely in their first year from seed and give the best flowering performance when treated as annuals. The cultivars fall into the following three size categories:

Tall These grow to 3ft (1m) high, with a spread of 18in (45cm). They are ideal as cut flowers or fillers in mixed borders.

Intermediate These grow 12–24in (30–60cm) high, with a spread of 18in (45cm), and are well suited for bedding.

Dwarf Cultivars in this group grow to 12in (30cm) tall, with a spread of 12in (30cm). They are ideal for edging, small bedding schemes, and containers.

Grow in well-drained, fertile soil in a warm site in full sun. Pinch out young plants at 2¼–4in (7–10cm) high to encourage a bushy habit. Deadhead frequently to maintain the flowering display. Tall cultivars may need staking in exposed positions.

Sow seed at 61–64°F (16–18°C), in early spring, for setting out in late spring or early summer. Alternatively, sow in late summer or early autumn, and overwinter the young plants in a frost-free greenhouse, at about 39–45°F (4–7°C). Harden off all plants before setting out.

Antirrhinums are susceptible to antirrhinum rust, powdery mildew, and aphids. The flowers are also sometimes pierced by bees in their search for nectar.

A. Tahiti Series
Habit Compact, vigorous, rust-resistant annuals.
Flowers Borne from summer to autumn. White, rose-pink, red, yellow, bronze, or orange, with some bicolors.
Leaves Lance-shaped, glossy. Dark green.
• HEIGHT to 8in (20cm).
• SPREAD to 12in (30cm).

A. Tahiti Series
(Dwarf)

A. Sonnet Series
Habit Bushy, early-flowering, many flowered, wet weather-resistant annuals.
Flowers Borne from early summer to autumn. White, pink, carmine-red, crimson, burgundy, yellow, or mauve.
Leaves Lance-shaped, glossy. Dark green.
• HEIGHT 12–24in (30–60cm).
• SPREAD 12in (30cm).

A. Sonnet Series
(Intermediate)

A. Coronette Series
Habit Vigorous, bushy, many-flowered. Weather- and rust-resistant.
Flowers Neat, dense spikes, borne from summer to autumn. Shades of white, pink, scarlet, purple, lemon-yellow, or salmon-orange.
Leaves Lance-shaped, glossy. Dark green.
• HEIGHT 26in (65cm).
• SPREAD 18in (45cm).

A. Coronette Series
(Tall)

A. 'Magic Carpet Mixed'
Habit Bushy, vigorous, well-branched annual.
Flowers Broadly tubular, borne freely from early summer to autumn. White, pink, carmine-red, crimson, burgundy, yellow, or bronze.
Leaves Lance-shaped, glossy. Dark green.
• HEIGHT 6in (15cm).
• SPREAD 12in (30cm).

A. 'Magic Carpet Mixed'
(Dwarf)

A. Princess Series

Habit Upright, well-branched perennials, grown as annuals.
Flowers Tubular flowers, 2-lipped, borne freely from summer to autumn. Available in crimson, streaked white, with a yellow eye.
Leaves Lance-shaped, glossy. Dark green.
• HEIGHT 18in (45cm).
• SPREAD 18in (45cm).

A. Princess Series
(Intermediate)

☀ ◊

A. 'Bells'

Habit Early-flowering perennial, grown as an annual.
Flowers Rounded, hyacinth-like, 2-lipped, in upright clusters, borne freely from summer to autumn. Crimson.
Leaves Lance-shaped, glossy. Deep green.
• HEIGHT 8–12in (20–30cm).
• SPREAD 12in (30cm).

A. 'Bells'
(Dwarf)

☀ ◊   Z 6–9

A. Madame Butterfly Series

Habit Vigorous, upright, many-flowered annuals.
Flowers Double, azalea-like, in broad, dense spikes, borne from summer to autumn. Pink, red, yellow, apricot, peach, or orange.
Leaves Lance-shaped, glossy. Dark green.
• HEIGHT 24–30in (60–75cm).
• SPREAD 18in (45cm).

A. Madame Butterfly Series
(Tall)

☀ ◊

A. Royal Carpet Series

Habit Compact, bushy, vigorous, rust-resistant annuals.
Flowers Borne from early summer to autumn. White, pale to deep pink, red to bronze-red, or shades of yellow.
Leaves Lance-shaped, glossy. Dark green.
• HEIGHT 8in (20cm).
• SPREAD 12in (30cm).

A. Royal Carpet Series
(Dwarf)

☀ ◊

A. 'Trumpet Serenade'

Habit Compact, vigorous, upright annual.
Flowers Open, trumpet-shaped, borne from summer to autumn. Bicolored, in varied range of colors, including pastel shades.
Leaves Lance-shaped, glossy. Dark green.
• HEIGHT 12in (30cm).
• SPREAD 12in (30cm).

A. 'Trumpet Serenade'
(Dwarf)

☀ ◊

A. Hyacinth-flowered Series

Habit Vigorous, strongly upright, free-flowering annuals.
Flowers Large, wide, open-faced, hyacinth-like, in dense spikes, borne from summer to autumn. Varied warm colors.
Leaves Lance-shaped, glossy. Dark green.
• HEIGHT 18in (45cm).
• SPREAD 18in (45cm).

A. Hyacinth-flowered Series
(Intermediate)

☀ ◊

A. Floral Carpet Series

Habit Compact, vigorous annuals.
Flowers Neat, uniform, long-lasting spikes, borne from early summer to autumn. Bright pink, purplish-pink, red, or bronze-yellow.
Leaves Lance-shaped, glossy. Dark green.
• HEIGHT 8in (20cm).
• SPREAD to 12in (30cm).

A. Floral Carpet Series
(Dwarf)

☀ ◊

BEGONIA

The enormously diverse genus *Begonia* consists of some 900 species of annuals, perennials, shrubs, and climbers, including many that are grown as house- or conservatory plants. The Semperflorens begonias described here are evergreen hybrid perennials derived from crosses involving *B. cucullata* var. *hookeri*, *B. schmidtiana*, and other species. In frost-prone areas, they are most commonly grown as annuals and can be used as summer bedding, edging, or in a wide range of container plantings, including window boxes and hanging baskets. They can also be grown indoors as perennial houseplants.

   The Semperflorens begonias all have well-branched, succulent stems, rounded, green or bronzed leaves, and bear small, single or double flowers, measuring up to 1in (2.5cm) across, throughout the summer months.

Grow in well-drained, fertile, neutral to acid soil that is rich in organic matter. The plants flower well in partial shade and will tolerate sun, but need protection from direct mid-day sun. To grow under glass or as houseplants, grow in a soilless or soil-based potting mix in bright light, but with shade from direct sun. Ventilate well. Water moderately and apply a balanced liquid fertilizer weekly when in full growth. In winter, keep the potting medium just moist and maintain a temperature of 50–59°F (10–15°C).

   Surface-sow seed in early spring at 70°F (21°C). The dust-fine seed may be mixed with fine silver sand to ensure even sowing. Alternatively, take basal cuttings in spring. Harden off before setting out when all danger of frost has passed.

   The plants are susceptible to caterpillars, thrips, vine weevils, grey mold (*Botrytis*), powdery mildew, and stem rot.

B. 'Olympia White'
Habit Bushy, compact, fibrous-rooted, well-branched perennial. Weather-resistant.
Flowers Single, neatly formed, borne freely throughout summer. Pure white.
Leaves Rounded. Mid-green.
• HEIGHT 8in (20cm).
• SPREAD 8in (20cm).

B. 'Olympia White'
(Olympia Series)
(Semperflorens)
☼ ◊
Min. 55°F (13°C)

B. Cocktail Series
Habit Compact, fibrous-rooted, evergreen perennials.
Flowers Single, borne throughout summer. Shades of white, pink, or red. Some bicolors.
Leaves Rounded, glossy. Dark bronze-green.
• HEIGHT 8–12in (20–30cm).
• SPREAD 12in (30cm).

B. Cocktail Series
(Semperflorens)
☼ ◊
Min. 55°F (13°C)

B. Coco Series
Habit Bushy, very compact, fibrous-rooted, evergreen perennials.
Flowers Neat, single, borne throughout summer. Bicolored. Shades of white, rose-pink, red, or scarlet.
Leaves Rounded, glossy. Bronze.
• HEIGHT 6–8in (15–20cm).
• SPREAD 6–8in (15–20cm).

B. Coco Series
(Semperflorens)

☼ ◊
Min. 55°F (13°C)

B. 'Organdy'
Habit Compact, fibrous-rooted, evergreen perennial. Weather-resistant.
Flowers Single, borne throughout summer. Mixed shades of white, rose-pink, pink, and scarlet.
Leaves Rounded, waxy, glossy. Green or bronze.
• HEIGHT 6in (15cm).
• SPREAD 6in (15cm).

B. 'Organdy'
(Semperflorens)

☼ ◊
Min. 55°F (13°C)

B. Devon Gems
Habit Compact, evergreen perennial. Weather-resistant.
Flowers Large, single, borne from summer. Shades of white, pink, or red.
Leaves Rounded, waxy, and glossy. Bronze and chocolate-brown.
• HEIGHT 6–7½in (15–18cm).
• SPREAD 6–7½in (15–18cm).

B. Devon Gems
(Semperflorens)

☼ ◊
Min. 55°F (13°C)

B. 'Olympia Red'
Habit Bushy, compact, fibrous-rooted, evergreen perennial, grown as an annual. Weather-resistant.
Flowers Single, neatly formed, borne freely from summer to autumn. Red.
Leaves Rounded. Mid-green.
• HEIGHT 8in (20cm).
• SPREAD 8in (20cm).

B. 'Olympia Red'
(Olympia Series)
(Semperflorens)

☼ ◊
Min. 55°F (13°C)

B. 'Red Ascot'
Habit Compact, many-flowered, fibrous-rooted, evergreen perennial.
Flowers Small, single, borne freely throughout summer. Self-colored, crimson-red.
Leaves Rounded, glossy. Bright emerald green.
• HEIGHT 6in (15cm).
• SPREAD 6in (15cm).

B. 'Red Ascot'
(Semperflorens)

☼ ◊
Min. 55°F (13°C)

DIANTHUS

A genus of over 300 species, *Dianthus* includes annuals, biennials, evergreen perennials, and sub-shrubs. Those grown as annuals are derived from *D. caryophyllus*, the wild carnation, or *D. chinensis*, the Chinese or Indian pink. These are true perennials or biennials, but are short-lived. They do, however, flower freely in their first year from seed, and generally produce more flowers when grown as annuals. *D. barbatus* (Sweet William) is a short-lived perennial or, more usually, a biennial, although many cultivars flower in their first year if sown in late winter or early spring.

The cultivars described here are grown mainly for their beautifully scented flowers, borne in early summer and early autumn. They are available as both biennials and annuals, and are ideal for the cutting border. They may be used as fillers in a mixed border, in bedding, or grown in massed plantings in an annual border.

Grow in open, well-drained, neutral to alkaline soil, in a warm position in full sun. Prior to planting, apply a dressing of a balanced, granular fertilizer at the manufacturer's recommended rate. Deadhead frequently to maintain the flowering display. If biennials are dead-headed immediately after flowering, they may bloom a second time. Cultivars of *D. barbatus* may need staking if grown in exposed sites on very fertile soils.

Sow seed of annuals at 55–59°F (13–15°C) in early spring. Sow seed of biennials outdoors in late spring, or under glass in early spring, as for annuals. Harden off and plant out in their flowering site in early summer.

The plants may be damaged by slugs, and infestation by aphids can transmit fusarium wilt and virus diseases. The leaves of *D. barbatus* cultivars can also be badly affected by rust.

D. CARYOPHYLLUS
Knight Series (white)
Habit Dwarf, bushy perennial, grown as an annual.
Flowers Double, in loose heads on stiff stems, borne freely from summer. White.
Leaves Flattened, soft. Mid-green.
• HEIGHT 12in (30cm).
• SPREAD 9in (23cm).

D. caryophyllus
Knight Series (white)

 Z 6–9

D. CHINENSIS
Heddewigii Group
Habit Bushy, short-lived perennials or biennials, grown as annuals.
Flowers Small, single, fragrant, fringed or cut, borne freely in summer. White, pink, or red, some with a purple eye.
Leaves Lance-shaped. Pale to mid-green.
• HEIGHT 10–12in (25–30cm).
• SPREAD 12in (30cm).

D. chinensis
Heddewigii Group

 Z 7–10

D. BARBATUS
Monarch Series
Habit Bushy, short-lived perennials, grown as biennials.
Flowers Single, fragrant, from late spring or early summer. White, pink, crimson, or purple, some patterned or with an eye.
Leaves Lance-shaped. Dark green.
• HEIGHT 24in (60cm).
• SPREAD 12in (30cm).

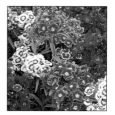

D. barbatus
Monarch Series

Z 3–9

D. *CHINENSIS*
'Fire Carpet'
Habit Bushy, neat,
compact perennial,
grown as an annual.
Flowers Single,
in terminal clusters,
borne from early
to late summer.
Rich scarlet,
self-colored.
Leaves Lance-shaped.
Mid-green.
• HEIGHT 8in (20cm).
• SPREAD 12in (30cm).

D. *chinensis*
'Fire Carpet'
(Carpet Series)

☀ ◌   Z 7–10

D. 'Telstar Crimson'
Habit Bushy,
short-lived perennial,
grown as an annual
or biennial.
Flowers Single,
weather-resistant,
in terminal clusters,
borne freely
in summer.
Crimson.
Leaves Lance-shaped.
Dark gray-green.
• HEIGHT 8in (20cm).
• SPREAD 9in (23cm).

D. 'Telstar Crimson'
(Telstar Series)

☀ ◌   Z 4–10

D. *BARBATUS*
Roundabout Series
Habit Compact,
bushy perennials,
grown as annuals
or biennials.
Flowers Single, fragrant,
borne in early to late
summer. Shades of
white or pink, some
bicolored or with an eye.
Leaves Lance-shaped.
Dark green.
• HEIGHT 8in (20cm).
• SPREAD 12in (30cm).

D. *barbatus*
Roundabout Series

☀ ◌   Z 3–9

D. *CHINENSIS*
Baby Doll Series
Habit Compact, bushy
perennials or biennials,
grown as annuals.
Flowers Large, single,
intricately patterned,
borne freely in summer.
Shades of white,
pink, or crimson.
Leaves Lance-shaped.
Pale to mid-green.
• HEIGHT 6–8in
(15–20cm).
• SPREAD 8in (20cm).

D. *chinensis*
Baby Doll Series

☀ ◌   Z 7–10

Compositae/Asteraceae	

RHODANTHE CHLOROCEPHALA subsp. *ROSEA*

Habit Slender, erect annual. **Flowers** Daisy-like, 1¼–3in (2.5–8cm) across, surrounded by papery bracts, from summer. Yellow disk, with white or pink bracts. **Leaves** Narrow. Gray-green.
• NATIVE HABITAT Arid areas, southwest Australia.
• CULTIVATION Grow in light, well-drained, low-fertility soil, in full sun. Good for drying.
• PROPAGATION Sow seed at 61°F (16°C) in spring.
• OTHER NAMES *Acroclinium roseum*, *Helipterum roseum*.

HEIGHT 12–24in (30–60cm)

SPREAD 6in (15cm)

Papaveraceae	CALIFORNIA POPPY

ESCHSCHOLZIA CALIFORNICA Ballerina Series

Habit Mat-forming annuals. **Flowers** Double or semi-double, fluted, shallowly cupped, from summer. Pink, red, yellow, or orange. **Leaves** Lance-shaped, finely cut. Mid-green.
• NATIVE HABITAT Garden origin.
• CULTIVATION Grow in poor, well-drained soil, in full sun. Good for cut flowers and suitable for an annual or mixed border.
• PROPAGATION Sow seed *in situ* in spring, and in succession for continuous display.

HEIGHT 12in (30cm)

SPREAD 6in (15cm)

Cruciferae/Brassicaceae	

IBERIS UMBELLATA Fairy Series

Habit Mound-forming annuals. **Flowers** Tiny, scented, cross-shaped, in flattened plumes, from spring to summer. White, pink, lilac-purple, or red-pink. **Leaves** Narrow to lance-shaped. Mid-green.
• NATIVE HABITAT Garden origin.
• CULTIVATION Grow in poor to moderately fertile, moist but well-drained soil, in full sun. Suitable for bedding, edging, borders, and containers.
• PROPAGATION Sow seed *in situ* in autumn or spring.

HEIGHT 6–12in (15–30cm)

SPREAD 9in (23cm)

Solanaceae	BUTTERFLY FLOWER

SCHIZANTHUS PINNATUS 'Hit Parade'

Habit Upright annual. **Flowers** Tubular, 2-lipped, from spring to autumn. White, pink, red, purple, or yellow, with contrasting markings. **Leaves** Lance-shaped, finely cut. Bright green.
• NATIVE HABITAT Garden origin.
• CULTIVATION Grow in fertile, moist, but well-drained soil in a sheltered site, in full sun. In cooler climates, grow as a house- or conservatory plant. Ideal for cut flowers, bedding, or containers.
• PROPAGATION Sow seed at 61°F (16°C) in mid-spring.

Min. 41°F (5°C)

HEIGHT 9–12in (23–30cm)

SPREAD 9–12in (23–30cm)

Compositae/Asteraceae	CHINA ASTER

CALLISTEPHUS CHINENSIS
Milady Series

Habit Bushy annuals. *Flowers* Double, chrysanthemum-like, from late summer to autumn. White, rose-pink, red, scarlet, or blue. *Leaves* Oval to triangular, toothed. Mid-green.
• NATIVE HABITAT Garden origin.
• CULTIVATION Grow in fertile, neutral to alkaline, moist but well-drained soil, in a sheltered site. Bred for use in bedding.
• PROPAGATION Sow seed at 61°F (16°C) in early spring.

☼ ◊

HEIGHT
12in (30cm)

SPREAD
10in (25cm)

Plumbaginaceae	STATICE

LIMONIUM SINUATUM

Habit Upright perennial, grown as an annual. *Flowers* Tiny, funnel-shaped, to ⅝in (1.5cm) long, in plumes of clustered spikelets, from late summer to autumn. White, pink, or blue. *Leaves* Narrow to lance-shaped, wavy-margined, in basal rosettes. Deep green.
• NATIVE HABITAT Coastal areas, Mediterranean.
• CULTIVATION Good for drying; cut when almost fully open. Prefers sandy, well-drained soil in sun.
• PROPAGATION Sow seed at 55–64°F (13–18°C) in early spring.

☼ ◊

Z 8–10

HEIGHT
16in (40cm)

SPREAD
12in (30cm)

Compositae/Asteraceae	CHINA ASTER

CALLISTEPHUS CHINENSIS
Thousand Wonders Series

Habit Bushy, compact annuals. *Flowers* Double, chrysanthemum-like, from summer to autumn. White, pink, red, purple, or blue. *Leaves* Oval to triangular. Mid-green.
• NATIVE HABITAT Garden origin.
• CULTIVATION Grow in fertile, neutral to alkaline, moist but well-drained soil, in a sheltered site. Ideal for bedding and containers.
• PROPAGATION Sow seed at 61°F (16°C) in early spring.

☼ ◊

HEIGHT
8in (20cm)

SPREAD
12in (30cm)

Apocynaceae	

CATHARANTHUS ROSEUS
'Pink Periwinkle'

Habit Evergreen perennial. *Flowers* Saucer-shaped, from spring to summer. Rose-pink. *Leaves* Narrowly oval, glossy. Mid- to dark green.
• NATIVE HABITAT Garden origin.
• CULTIVATION Grow in fertile, well-drained soil, in sun. In cooler climates, grow as a house- or conservatory plant. Ideal for bedding.
• PROPAGATION Sow seed at 64°F (18°C) in early spring. Also by softwood cuttings in summer.
OTHER NAME *Vinca rosea* 'Pink Periwinkle'.

☼ ◊

Z 9–10

HEIGHT
12–24in
(30–60cm)

SPREAD
12–24in
(30–60cm)

Cruciferae/Brassicaceae	VIRGINIAN STOCK

MALCOLMIA MARITIMA

Habit Low-branching annual. **Flowers**
Cross-shaped, very fragrant, to ⅜in (1cm) across,
borne in open spikes, from spring to autumn.
In shades of red or purple. **Leaves** Oval,
toothed or entire. Mid-green.
• NATIVE HABITAT Waste ground, Mediterranean.
• CULTIVATION Grow in moderately fertile,
well-drained soil, in sun with mid-day shade.
Good as a filler in a mixed or herbaceous border.
• PROPAGATION Sow seed *in situ*, in succession,
starting in late spring. Will self-sow.

☼ ◊

HEIGHT
8–16in
(20–40cm)

SPREAD
4–6in
(10–15cm)

Cruciferae/Brassicaceae	ORNAMENTAL CABBAGE

BRASSICA OLERACEA

Habit Upright, tap-rooted annuals, grown as
winter foliage plants. **Flowers** Insignificant.
Leaves Rounded to oval, entire or fringed,
in loose or tight rosettes, to 18in (45cm) across.
Gray- or blue-green, splashed white, pink, or red.
• NATIVE HABITAT Garden origin.
• CULTIVATION Grow in well-drained, alkaline
soil in sun. Good for borders, bedding and
containers. Best foliage color develops at
temperatures below 50°F (10°C).
• PROPAGATION Sow seed *in situ* in spring.

☼ ◊

HEIGHT
18in (45cm)

SPREAD
18in (45cm)

Caryophyllaceae	

SILENE ARMERIA 'Electra'

Habit Sticky-haired annual or biennial.
Flowers In dense clusters, to ⅜in (1.5cm)
across, with shallowly notched petals, starting
in late summer. Deep carmine-pink. **Leaves**
Spoon- or lance-shaped. Gray-green.
• NATIVE HABITAT Garden origin.
• CULTIVATION Grow in moderately fertile,
neutral to alkaline, well-drained soil in sun, or
dappled shade. Good for a mixed or annual border.
• PROPAGATION Sow seed *in situ* in autumn
or spring.

☼ ◊

Z 8–10

HEIGHT
12in (30cm)

SPREAD
6in (15cm)

Labiatae/Lamiaceae	COLEUS

SOLENOSTEMON SCUTELLARIOIDES

Habit Evergreen perennial, grown as an annual
foliage plant. **Flowers** Insignificant. **Leaves**
Oval, toothed. Light to dark green, with patterns
in shades of white, pink, red, purple, or yellow.
• NATIVE HABITAT Garden origin.
• CULTIVATION Grow in fertile soil that is rich
in organic matter, in sun or part-shade. In cooler
climates, grow as a house- or conservatory plant.
• PROPAGATION By seed at 75°F (24°C) in
early spring.
• OTHER NAME *Coleus blumei* var. *verschaffeltii*.

☼ ◊

Min. 39°F
(4°C)

HEIGHT
to 24in
(60cm)

SPREAD
24in (60cm)

Caryophyllaceae	

SILENE COELI-ROSA 'Rose Angel'

Habit Upright, slender annual. **Flowers** In loose clusters, to 1in (2.5cm) across, with deeply notched petals, from summer. Deep magenta-pink. **Leaves** Narrow to lance-shaped. Gray-green.
• NATIVE HABITAT Garden origin.
• CULTIVATION Grow in well-drained, neutral to slightly alkaline soil, in sun or dappled shade.
• PROPAGATION By seed *in situ* in autumn or spring.
• OTHER NAMES *Agrostemma coeli-rosa* 'Rose Angel', *Lychnis coeli-rosa* 'Rose Angel'.

HEIGHT
12in (30cm)

SPREAD
6in (15cm)

Onagraceae	

CLARKIA 'Arianna'

Habit Slender, upright annual. **Flowers** Semi-double, rosette-like, with frilled, waved petals, in spikes, from summer and early autumn. Deep rose-pink. **Leaves** Lance-shaped. Mid-green.
• NATIVE HABITAT Garden origin.
• CULTIVATION Grow in moderately fertile, moist but well-drained, slightly acid soil, in sun or partial shade. Good for cutting, and for an annual border.
• PROPAGATION Sow seed *in situ* in early spring or in autumn. Provide cloche protection for young plants during winter.

HEIGHT
18in (45cm)

SPREAD
12in (30cm)

Portulacaceae	

CALANDRINIA UMBELLATA 'Amaranth'

Habit Compact, mound-forming perennial, grown as an annual. **Flowers** Upturned, cup-shaped, in clusters, from summer. Rich crimson-magenta. **Leaves** Narrow to lance-shaped. Gray-green.
• NATIVE HABITAT Garden origin.
• CULTIVATION Grow in sharply drained, slightly acid soil that is rich in organic matter, in full sun. Good for edging, for an annual border, and containers. Ideal as a pot plant.
• PROPAGATION Sow seed at 61–64°F (16–18°C) in early spring.

Z 7–9

HEIGHT
8in (20cm)

SPREAD
6–8in
(15–20cm)

Scrophulariaceae	

CALCEOLARIA
Monarch Series (Grandiflora)

Habit Bushy annuals. *Flowers* Slipper-like, pouched, in dense clusters, from spring or summer. Red or yellow, often speckled. *Leaves* Oval, soft-haired. Light green.
• NATIVE HABITAT Garden origin.
• CULTIVATION Grow in light, moderately fertile, acid soil, in sun or part-shade. Grow as bedding or as a short-term house- or greenhouse plant.
• PROPAGATION Surface-sow seed at 64°F (18°C) in late summer or spring.

☀ ◊

HEIGHT
12in (30cm)

SPREAD
10in (25cm)

Scrophulariaceae	

NEMESIA STRUMOSA Carnival Series

Habit Bushy, low-branching annuals. *Flowers* 2-lipped, in terminal clusters, from mid- to late summer. In white, pink, red, purple, yellow, bronze, or orange, all with purple veins. *Leaves* Lance-shaped, slightly hairy. Mid-green.
• NATIVE HABITAT Garden origin.
• CULTIVATION Grow in moderately fertile, moist but well-drained, slightly acid soil, in sun. Good for bedding and containers. Water well in dry periods.
• PROPAGATION Sow seed at 59°F (15°C) from early to late spring.

☀ ◊

HEIGHT
7–9in
(17–23cm)

SPREAD
4–6in
(10–15cm)

Malvaceae	MUSK MALLOW

ABELMOSCHUS MOSCHATUS
Pacific Series

Habit Neat, bushy perennial. *Flowers* Hibiscus-like, borne in summer. Pink or scarlet, with a white center. *Leaves* Broadly oval, lobed. Mid-green.
• NATIVE HABITAT Garden origin.
• CULTIVATION Grow in fertile, well-drained soil, in sun. In cooler climates, grow as a house- or conservatory plant. Good for bedding, or in an annual border.
• PROPAGATION Sow seed *in situ* in mid- to late spring, or in early spring at 50–55°F (10–13°C).

☀ ◊

Min 41°F
(5°C)

HEIGHT
12–16in
(30–40cm)

SPREAD
16in (40cm)

Compositae/Asteraceae	

DAHLIA 'Rigoletto'

Habit Bushy, tuberous perennial, grown as an annual. *Flowers* Double, up to 2¾in (7cm) across, from summer to autumn. In a range of colors, including white, pink, red, yellow, or orange. *Leaves* Divided into oval leaflets. Mid-green.
• NATIVE HABITAT Garden origin.
• CULTIVATION Grow in fertile, moist but well-drained soil, in full sun. Ideal for cutting, bedding, and containers.
• PROPAGATION Sow seed at 61°F (16°C) in late winter or early spring.

☀ ◊

Z 8–10

HEIGHT
15in (38cm)

SPREAD
15in (38cm)

Compositae/Asteraceae	

DAHLIA Coltness Hybrids

Habit Compact, bushy, tuberous perennials, grown as annuals. *Flowers* Daisy-like, single, 2–2¼in (5–7cm) across, from summer to autumn. In a range of bright colors, including white, pink, purple, red, or yellow. *Leaves* Divided into oval leaflets. Mid- to dark green.

• NATIVE HABITAT Garden origin.

• CULTIVATION Grow in fertile, moist but well-drained soil that is rich in organic matter, in an open, sunny site. Bred for bedding, but also suitable for other massed plantings, for border edging, as fillers in a mixed or herbaceous border, and in containers. Provides long-lasting cut flowers. To improve flowering performance, apply a high-nitrogen fertilizer weekly in early summer, then a high-potash fertilizer every week from mid-summer to early autumn. Pinch out growing tips when young to encourage a bushy habit. Bedding dahlias do not need stopping or disbudding, but regular deadheading prolongs flowering period.

• PROPAGATION Sow seed at 61°F (16°C) in late winter or early spring.

Z 8–10

HEIGHT
18in (45cm)

SPREAD
18in (45cm)

Tropaeolaceae	NASTURTIUM

TROPAEOLUM 'Empress of India'

Habit Dwarf, bushy annual. **Flowers** Spurred, semi-double, to 2⅜in (6cm) across, from summer to autumn. Rich velvety-red. **Leaves** Rounded to kidney-shaped, wavy-margined. Deep green.
• NATIVE HABITAT Garden origin.
• CULTIVATION Grow in moist but well-drained, poor to moderately fertile soil, in full sun. Suitable for an annual border and containers. Too rich a soil promotes leaf growth at the expense of flowers.
• PROPAGATION Sow seed at 55–61°F (13–16°C) in early spring, or *in situ* in mid-spring.

☼ ◊

HEIGHT
12in (30cm)

SPREAD
18in (45cm)

Lythraceae	

CUPHEA × PURPUREA 'Firefly'

Habit Bushy sub-shrub, grown as an annual. **Flowers** 2-petaled, to 1⅛in (3cm) long, in terminal clusters, from spring to autumn. Cherry-red. **Leaves** Oval to lance-shaped. Dark green.
• NATIVE HABITAT Garden origin.
• CULTIVATION Grow in moderately fertile, well-drained soil, in sun or part-shade. Use as bedding.
• PROPAGATION Sow seed at 55–61°F (13–16°C) in early spring, or *in situ* in late spring.
• OTHER NAMES *C. llavea* 'Firefly', *C. llavea* var. *miniata* 'Firefly', *C. miniata* 'Firefly'.

☼ ◊

Z 10–11

HEIGHT
12–24in
(30–60cm)

SPREAD
9–18in
(23–45cm)

Cruciferae/Brassicaceae	WALLFLOWER

ERYSIMUM CHEIRI 'Blood Red'

Habit Sub-shrubby, evergreen perennial, grown as a biennial. **Flowers** Cross-shaped, fragrant, to 1in (2.5cm) across, in clusters, from spring. Dark red. **Leaves** Lance-shaped. Dark green.
• NATIVE HABITAT Garden origin.
• CULTIVATION Grow in poor to moderately fertile, well-drained, neutral to alkaline soil, in sun. Good for borders and bedding.
• PROPAGATION Sow seed in a seed bed from late spring to early summer.
• OTHER NAME *Cheiranthus cheiri* 'Blood Red'.

☼ ◊

Z 3–7

HEIGHT
18in (45cm)

SPREAD
18in (45cm)

Linaceae	

LINUM GRANDIFLORUM 'Rubrum'

Habit Slender, low-branching annual. **Flowers** Saucer-shaped, to 1½in (4cm) across, in loose heads, from summer. Brilliant crimson. **Leaves** Oval to lance-shaped. Gray-green.
• NATIVE HABITAT Garden origin.
• CULTIVATION Grow in light, well-drained, moderately fertile soil that is rich in organic matter, in full sun. Good for an annual border and as a filler in a mixed or herbaceous border.
• PROPAGATION Sow seed *in situ* in autumn or spring.

☼ ◊

HEIGHT
to 18in
(45cm)

SPREAD
6in (15cm)

Amaranthaceae

AMARANTHUS TRICOLOR 'Illumination'

Habit Upright, bushy annual, grown as a foliage plant. *Flowers* Tiny, ornamentally insignificant, in flattened, terminal or axillary clusters, from summer to early autumn. Green or red. *Leaves* Narrow to oval, to 8in (20cm) or more in length. Bright rose-red, with gold markings on emergence, contrasting or toning with bronze or coppery-brown older leaves.
• NATIVE HABITAT Garden origin.
• CULTIVATION Grow in moist but well-drained, moderately fertile soil, in a warm, sunny, and sheltered site. Keep well watered during prolonged dry periods. Under glass and in containers, use a soilless or soil-based potting mix and site in full light. Water containerized plants freely when in full growth. Plants are suitable for bedding or other massed plantings, and may also be used as fillers. Also good for containers, either outdoors on a sheltered patio, or in the home or conservatory.
• PROPAGATION Sow seed at 68°F (20°C) in mid-spring.

HEIGHT
18in (45cm)

SPREAD
12in (30cm)

Amaranthaceae	CRESTED COCKSCOMB

CELOSIA ARGENTEA 'Jewel Box' (mixed)

Habit Well-branched annual. *Flowers* Coral-like, from summer. Pink, red, yellow, or gold.
Leaves Oval to lance-shaped. Pale green.
• NATIVE HABITAT Garden origin.
• CULTIVATION Grow as pot plants in soil-based potting mix, in full light. Shade lightly when in bloom. Water moderately and apply a balanced liquid fertilizer every two weeks. One of the Cristata Group.
• PROPAGATION Sow seed at 64°F (18°C) in early to late spring.

☼ ◊

HEIGHT
9in (23cm)

SPREAD
9in (23cm)

Labiatae/Lamiaceae	COLEUS

SOLENOSTEMON SCUTELLARIOIDES 'Brightness'

Habit Evergreen perennial, grown as an annual.
Flowers Insignificant. *Leaves* Oval. Rust-red.
• NATIVE HABITAT Garden origin.
• CULTIVATION Grow in fertile, moist, but well-drained soil that is rich in organic matter, in sun or part-shade. In cooler climates, grow as a house- or conservatory plant. Remove flowers as they appear.
• PROPAGATION By seed at 75°F (24°C) in early spring.
• OTHER NAME *Coleus blumei* 'Brightness'.

☼ ◊

Min. 39°F
(4°C)

HEIGHT
18in (45cm)

SPREAD
12in (30cm)

Labiatae/Lamiaceae	COLEUS

SOLENOSTEMON SCUTELLARIOIDES Wizard Series

Habit Evergreen perennials, grown as annuals.
Flowers Insignificant. *Leaves* Oval. Light green, patterned in white, pink, red, purple, or yellow.
• NATIVE HABITAT Garden origin.
• CULTIVATION Grow in fertile, moist, drained soil rich in organic matter, in sun or shade. In cooler climates, grow as a house- or conservatory plant.
• PROPAGATION By seed at 75°F (24°C) in early spring.
• OTHER NAME *Coleus blumei* Wizard Series.

☼ ◊

Min. 39°F
(4°C)

HEIGHT
to 8in
(20cm)

SPREAD
12in (30cm)

Compositae/Asteraceae	FLOSS FLOWER

AGERATUM HOUSTONIANUM 'Bavaria'

Habit Compact, mound-forming annual. **Flowers** Tiny, fluffy, in rounded clusters, 2–4in (5–10cm) across, from mid-summer to autumn. White and lavender. **Leaves** Oval, soft-haired. Mid-green.
• NATIVE HABITAT Garden origin.
• CULTIVATION Grow in moist but well-drained fertile soil, in a sunny, sheltered site. Good for bedding, edging, and containers. Deadhead to promote a second flush of flowers.
• PROPAGATION Sow seed at 61–64°F (16–18°C) in early spring.

☼ ◊

HEIGHT
10in (25cm)

SPREAD
10in (25cm)

Scrophulariaceae	

LINARIA MAROCCANA 'Fairy Lights'

Habit Slender, upright annual. **Flowers** Tiny, 2-lipped, to ⅝in (1.5cm) long, in slender spikes, from summer. Pink, red, purple, or yellow, with a white throat. **Leaves** Narrow. Light green.
• NATIVE HABITAT Garden origin.
• CULTIVATION Grow in light, moderately fertile, well-drained, preferably sandy soil, in full sun. Good for an annual border, sunny bank, or gravel garden.
• PROPAGATION Sow seed *in situ* in early spring. Will self-seed.

☼ ◊

HEIGHT
8in (20cm)

SPREAD
6in (15cm)

Plumbaginaceae	

PSYLLIOSTACHYS SUWOROWII

Habit Rosette-forming annual. **Flowers** Tiny, in cylindrical, branched spikes, to 8in (20cm) or more long, from summer to early autumn. Pale mauve. **Leaves** Lance-shaped. Light green.
• NATIVE HABITAT Sandy plains, C. Asia.
• CULTIVATION Grow in light, moist but well-drained soil, in a warm, sunny, sheltered site. Good for cutting and drying.
• PROPAGATION Sow seed at 70°F (21°C) in spring.
• OTHER NAMES *Limonium suworowii, Statice suworowii.*

☼ ◊

HEIGHT
12–18in
(30–45cm)

SPREAD
12in (30cm)

Compositae/Asteraceae	FLOSS FLOWER

AGERATUM HOUSTONIANUM 'Adriatic'

Habit Compact, bushy annual. **Flowers** Tiny, fluffy, in rounded clusters, 2–4in (5–10cm) across, from mid-summer to autumn. Clear blue. **Leaves** Oval, softly downy. Mid-green.
• NATIVE HABITAT Garden origin.
• CULTIVATION Grow in moist but well-drained, fertile soil, in a sunny, sheltered site. Good for bedding, edging, and containers. One of the Adriatic Series.
• PROPAGATION Sow seed at 61–64°F (16–18°C) in early spring.

☼ ◊

HEIGHT
6–8in
(15–20cm)

SPREAD
6–8in
(15–20cm)

IMPATIENS

The *Impatiens* genus, commonly known as busy lizzies, consists of some 850 species of fully hardy to frost-tender annuals, evergreen perennials, and sub-shrubs. The most significant *Impatiens* in cultivation are derived from the frost-tender annual *I. balsamina* and the tender evergreen perennial *I. walleriana*. The latter are treated as annuals, as they will not overwinter in frost-prone areas, and are most productive of flowers in their first year. They tend to become leggy when treated as perennials.

Impatiens are valued for the profusion of small, spurred, 5-petaled flowers borne throughout summer. The flowers are available in a range of bright colors, including white, shades of pink, red, purple, violet, and orange. Many also have attractively colored foliage. *Impatiens* cultivars are well suited for bedding and for outdoor containers,

including hanging baskets and window boxes. Most cultivars also tend to make good house- or conservatory plants.

Grow in moist, well-drained, fertile soil that is rich in organic matter, in partial shade, with shelter from strong winds. The cultivars tolerate part-day sun, but need protection from the hot mid-day sun. Under glass, use a soilless or soil-based potting mix. Admit bright, filtered light. Water moderately and apply a balanced liquid fertilizer every 2–4 weeks during spring and summer. In winter, water sparingly and do not feed.

Sow seed in early spring, at 61–64°F (16–18°C). Harden off before planting out. Cultivars of *I. walleriana* and the New Guinea Group may be propagated by softwood cuttings in spring or early summer.

Seedlings are very prone to damping off, and flowerbuds may be affected by gray mold (*Botrytis*) in damp conditions.

I. BALSAMINA
Habit Sparsely branched, hairy annual.
Flowers Hooded, cup-shaped, borne singly, or in clusters of 2–3, from summer to early autumn. White, pink, red, or purple.
Leaves Narrowly oval to narrowly lance-shaped, deeply toothed. Pale green.
• **HEIGHT** 30in (75cm).
• **SPREAD** 18in (45cm).

I. balsamina

☀ ◗ Min. 41°F (5°C)

I. 'Deco Pink'
Habit Sub-shrubby perennial, grown as an annual.
Flowers Spurred, 5-petaled, borne singly or in clusters, from summer. Mid-pink, with a deep pink eye.
Leaves Oval to lance-shaped, slightly toothed. Bronze-green.
• **HEIGHT** to 8in (20cm).
• **SPREAD** to 8in (20cm).

I. 'Deco Pink'
(Deco Series)

☀ ◗ Min. 50°F (10°C)

I. Super Elfin Series
Habit Neat, dwarf, sub-shrubby perennials, grown as annuals.
Flowers Large, flattened, borne throughout summer. White, pink, red, violet, or orange, including pastel colors and picotees.
Leaves Oval to lance-shaped, and toothed. Mid-green.
• **HEIGHT** 10in (25cm).
• **SPREAD** 10in (25cm).

I. Super Elfin Series

☀ ◗ Min. 50°F (10°C)

I. New Guinea Group
Habit Sub-shrubby perennials, grown as annuals.
Flowers Produced from summer to early autumn. White, pink, scarlet, lavender, salmon, orange, with some bicolors.
Leaves Lance-shaped, variegated. Mid-green.
• **HEIGHT** 14in (35cm).
• **SPREAD** 12in (30cm).

I. New Guinea Group

☀ ◗ Min. 50°F (10°C)

I. Rosette Series

Habit Sub-shrubby
perennials, grown
as annuals.
Flowers Flat, double
or semi-double,
borne freely from
early summer to
autumn. White,
pink, red, or orange.
Leaves Oval to
lance-shaped, toothed.
Mid-green.
• HEIGHT 12in (30cm).
• SPREAD 12in (30cm).

I. Rosette Series

☼ ◑
Min. 50°F (10°C)

I. 'Lipstick'

Habit Neat, dwarf,
sub-shrubby perennial,
grown as an annual.
Flowers Flattened,
borne singly or in
clusters, from
summer through
to early autumn.
Rose-red.
Leaves Oval to lance-
shaped, toothed.
Fresh green.
• HEIGHT 8in (20cm).
• SPREAD 8in (20cm).

I. 'Lipstick'
(Super Elfin Series)

☼ ◑
Min. 50°F (10°C)

I. Confection Series

Habit Sub-shrubby
perennials, grown
as annuals.
Flowers Flat, double
or semi-double, from
summer to autumn.
Pink, red, or orange.
Leaves Oval to lance-
shaped, toothed.
Deep green.
• HEIGHT 9–12in
(23–30cm).
• SPREAD 9–12in
(23–30cm).

I. Confection Series

☼ ◑
Min. 50°F (10°C)

I. 'Red Star'

Habit Sub-shrubby
perennial, grown
as an annual.
Flowers Small,
flattened, borne singly
or in clusters, from
spring to autumn.
Bright red, with a
white central star.
Leaves Oval to lance-
shaped, toothed.
Fresh green.
• HEIGHT 6in (15cm).
• SPREAD 6in (15cm).

I. 'Red Star'
(Novette Series)

☼ ◑
Min. 50°F (10°C)

I. Novette Series

Habit Sub-shrubby
perennials, grown
as annuals.
Flowers Flattened,
borne from spring to
autumn. Salmon-pink,
red, or orange, with
some bicolors or star-
shaped central marks.
Leaves Oval to lance-
shaped, toothed.
Fresh green.
• HEIGHT 6in (15cm).
• SPREAD 6in (15cm).

I. Novette Series

☼ ◑
Min. 50°F (10°C)

I. 'Tempo Lavender'

Habit Neat, dwarf,
sub-shrubby perennial,
grown as an annual.
Flowers Flat, borne
singly or in clusters,
from summer. Pink, red,
lavender-blue, violet,
or orange, with some
bicolors and picotees.
Leaves Oval to lance-
shaped, toothed.
Mid-green.
• HEIGHT 9in (23cm).
• SPREAD 9in (23cm).

I. 'Tempo Lavender'
(Tempo Series)

☼ ◑
Min. 50°F (10°C)

I. BALSAMINA 'Blackberry Ice'

Habit Sparsely
branched annual.
Flowers Hooded,
cup-shaped, double,
borne in abundance from
summer to early autumn.
Purple, splashed white.
Leaves Oval to
narrowly lance-shaped,
deeply toothed.
Pale green.
• HEIGHT 28in (70cm).
• SPREAD 18in (45cm).

I. balsamina
'Blackberry Ice'

☼ ◑
Min. 41°F (5°C)

I. BALSAMINA Tom Thumb Series

Habit Dwarf,
slightly hairy annual.
Flowers Large,
double, camellia-like,
borne freely from
summer to early
autumn. White, pink,
scarlet, or violet.
Leaves Oval to narrowly
lance-shaped, deeply
toothed. Pale green.
• HEIGHT 12in (30cm).
• SPREAD 12in (30cm).

I. balsamina
Tom Thumb Series

☼ ◑
Min. 41°F (5°C)

NICOTIANA

The *Nicotiana* genus consists of some 67 species of annuals, biennials, and perennials. The plants have narrow, lance-shaped, or broadly oval leaves that are often hairy and sticky. The leaves are borne mostly in basal rosettes. Tubular, trumpet-shaped, or saucer-shaped flowers are borne in clusters from summer to autumn. The flowers are often fragrant and, in many cases, night-scented; they frequently open only in early evening and at night. A few will remain open during the day if grown in partial shade. Cultivars of *N.* x *sanderae* have flat, upward-facing flowers that remain open in bright sunlight. Nicotianas flower freely during their first year from seed and are best grown as annuals. However, with mulch protection, these short-lived perennials can occasionally overwinter in areas where temperatures seldom fall much below 41°F (5°C).

All of the nicotianas described here are notably free-flowering and resistant to both hot and wet weather. Contact with the foliage may irritate the skin.

Nicotianas are suitable for annual borders and as fillers in a mixed or herbaceous border. The compact cultivars are ideal for planting in containers. Many, especially those with green flowers, are valued by flower arrangers.

Grow in moist but well-drained, fertile soil, in full sun, or in partial or dappled shade. Tall cultivars may need unobtrusive support in exposed positions.

Surface-sow seed at 64°F (18°C) in early to mid-spring. Nicotiana seeds need light for germination. Harden off young plants before setting out when the danger of frost has passed.

Use biological control or insecticide to prevent plants being affected by aphids, mildew, or gray mold (*Botrytis*).

N. x *SANDERAE*
Domino Series
Habit Compact, upright, sticky annuals.
Flowers Saucer-shaped, from summer to autumn. In white, red, crimson, purple, or lime-green, some with a white eye.
Leaves Spoon-shaped to narrowly oval. Mid-green.
• HEIGHT 12–18in (30–45cm).
• SPREAD 12–16in (30–40cm).

N. x *sanderae*
Domino Series

N. x *SANDERAE*
'Salmon Pink'
Habit Compact, upright, sticky annual.
Flowers Saucer-shaped, upward-facing, to 3in (8cm) long, borne from summer to autumn. Salmon-pink.
Leaves Oval to paddle-shaped. Mid-green.
• HEIGHT 12–18in (30–45cm).
• SPREAD 12–16in (30–40cm).

N. x *sanderae*
'Salmon Pink'
(Domino Series)

N. x *SANDERAE*
'Havana Apple Blossom'
Habit Compact, upright, sticky annual.
Flowers Saucer-shaped, in open clusters, borne from summer to autumn. White, tinted rose-pink, with pink petal reverse.
Leaves Spoon-shaped to narrowly oval. Mid-green.
• HEIGHT 14in (35cm).
• SPREAD 12–16in (30–40cm).

N. x *sanderae* **'Havana Apple Blossom'**
(Havana Series)

N. × SANDERAE
Nikki Series
Habit Sticky, upright, many-flowered annuals.
Flowers Saucer-shaped, scented, from summer to autumn. In white, and shades of pink, red, or purple. Available in mixed or single colors.
Leaves Spoon-shaped to narrowly oval. Mid-green.
• HEIGHT 15in (38cm).
• SPREAD 12–16in (30–40cm).

N. × sanderae
Nikki Series

N. × SANDERAE
Sensation Series
Habit Sticky, upright, many-flowered annuals.
Flowers Saucer-shaped, fragrant, from summer to autumn. In white, greenish-white, and shades of pink, red, crimson, or purple.
Leaves Spoon-shaped to narrowly oval. Mid-green.
• HEIGHT 24–36in (60–90cm).
• SPREAD 12in (30cm).

N. × sanderae
Sensation Series

N. LANGSDORFFII
Habit Low-branching, free-flowering, sticky annual.
Flowers Tubular, in nodding clusters, 2in (5cm) long, with flared, 5-lobed mouths, borne from summer to autumn. Apple-green.
Leaves Large, oval, in basal rosettes. Mid-green.
• HEIGHT to 5ft (1.5m).
• SPREAD to 14in (35cm).

N. langsdorffii

N. 'Lime Green'
Habit Upright, free-flowering, sticky annual.
Flowers Large, saucer-shaped, in open clusters. Night-scented, long-tubed, to 4½in (12cm) in length, borne freely from mid- to late summer to autumn. Bright lime-green.
Leaves Spoon-shaped. Mid-green.
• HEIGHT 24in (60cm).
• SPREAD 10in (25cm).

N. 'Lime Green'

PAPAVER

Of the 70 species of annual, biennial, and perennial poppies that make up the genus *Papaver*, the annuals described here are among the least demanding and most rewarding to grow. They produce often brilliantly colored, bowl- or saucer-shaped flowers throughout summer. In many cases, especially in cultivars of *P. somniferum*, these flowers are followed by ornamental, "pepper-pot" seedheads that are perfect for dried arrangements. Under suitable conditions, many cultivars will self-seed freely if the seedheads are left in place. The flowers produced by *P. croceum* and its cultivars, the Icelandic poppies, are ideal as cut flowers. Most poppies are suitable for informal, cottage-style gardens, for the annual border, and for a mixed border.

The vigorous, large-flowered cultivars of *P. somniferum* associate particularly well with perennials, and are ideal for use as fillers in a mixed or herbaceous border. All parts of *P. somniferum* cultivars are potentially harmful, and are capable of causing stomach upsets if ingested.

Grow in any poor to moderately fertile, well-drained soil, in full sun. Staking or other support is seldom necessary, even with tall cultivars. Deadhead to prevent self-seeding. Flowers of Icelandic poppies should be cut just as the buds begin to color, and the ends of the cut stems should be scalded before arranging.

Sow seed of annuals *in situ*, in spring or early summer, or in autumn. Provide cloche protection for autumn-sown seedlings in areas prone to severe frost. Sow seed of biennials *in situ* in late spring or early summer.

The various plants of the genus *Papaver* described here are highly susceptible to attack from aphids, fungal wilts, and, in wet weather, to downy mildew.

P. RHOEAS
Shirley Series
(double)
Habit Upright, sparsely hairy annual.
Flowers Bowl-shaped, double, from summer. White and shades of pink, red, crimson, yellow, or salmon, with some bicolors.
Leaves Finely divided, and downy. Light green.
• HEIGHT 24in (60cm).
• SPREAD 12in (30cm).

P. rhoeas
Shirley Series
(double)

☀ ◊

P. RHOEAS
'Mother of Pearl'
Habit Branching, sparsely hairy annual.
Flowers Bowl-shaped, from summer. Soft pink, peach-pink, dove-gray, or lilac-blue, some speckled or with zoning.
Leaves Finely divided, and downy. Light green.
• OTHER NAME
P. rhoeas 'Fairy Wings'.
• HEIGHT 14in (35cm).
• SPREAD 10in (25cm).

P. rhoeas
'Mother of Pearl'

☀ ◊

P. RHOEAS
Shirley Series (single)
Habit Upright, sparsely hairy annual.
Flowers Solitary, bowl-shaped, single, borne in summer. White and shades of pink, red, crimson, or salmon, with some bicolors.
Leaves Finely divided, and downy. Light green.
• HEIGHT 24in (60cm).
• SPREAD 12in (30cm).

P. rhoeas
Shirley Series (single)

P. SOMNIFERUM
'Hen and Chickens'
Habit Erect annual.
Flowers Bowl-shaped, from summer. White, pink, red, or mauve-purple, with dark spots.
Leaves Narrow, deeply lobed. Blue-green.
• TIP Grown mainly for seedheads.
• HEIGHT 2–3ft (0.6–1m).
• SPREAD 12–18in (30–45cm).

P. somniferum
'Hen and Chickens'

P. COMMUTATUM
'Ladybird'
Habit Upright, branching annual.
Flowers Single, solitary, bowl-shaped, 3in (8cm) across, borne in summer. Glossy crimson-red, with neat, black, satiny basal marks.
Leaves Finely cut into lance-shaped segments, and downy. Mid-green.
• HEIGHT 18in (45cm).
• SPREAD 6in (15cm).

P. commutatum
'Ladybird'

P. CROCEUM
'Champagne Bubbles'
Habit Tufted perennial grown as a biennial.
Flowers Bowl-shaped, from summer. In pink, red, apricot, or yellow.
Leaves Finely divided, and hairy. Blue-green.
• OTHER NAME
P. nudicaule 'Champagne Bubbles'.
• HEIGHT 18in (45cm).
• SPREAD 6in (15cm).

P. croceum
'Champagne Bubbles'

  Z 3–8

P. CROCEUM
'Summer Breeze'
Habit Erect, tuft-forming, hairy perennial, grown as a biennial.
Flowers Tubular, from summer. White, yellow, golden-yellow, or orange.
Leaves Lance-shaped to oval, hairy. Blue-green.
• OTHER NAME
P. nudicaule 'Summer Breeze'.
• HEIGHT 12–14in (30–35cm).
• SPREAD to 6in (15cm).

P. croceum
'Summer Breeze'

  Z 3–8

Solanaceae	BUTTERFLY FLOWER, POOR MAN'S ORCHID

SCHIZANTHUS PINNATUS

Habit Upright, bushy, moderately fast-growing annual. *Flowers* Tubular, 2-lipped, flared at the mouth, to 3in (8cm) across, in terminal open plumes, borne freely from spring to autumn. Available in a range of shades, including white, pink, red, purple, or yellow, splashed violet or contrasting colors, with a yellow throat. *Leaves* Lance-shaped, finely dissected, fern-like. Bright green.
• NATIVE HABITAT Dry rocky slopes and canyons, Chile.

• CULTIVATION Grow in fertile, moist but well-drained soil, in a sheltered site in full sun. In cooler climates grow as a house- or conservatory plant. Ideal for cut flowers, bedding, an annual border, or containers in a courtyard or patio garden. Provide light support using twigs. Under glass, use a soil-based potting mix. Grow in full light with shade from the hottest sun. Water moderately and apply a high-potash fertilizer every two weeks.
• PROPAGATION Sow seed at 61°F (16°C) in mid-spring.

Min. 41°F
(5°C)

HEIGHT
8–20in
(20–50cm)

SPREAD
9–12in
(23–30cm)

Compositae/Asteraceae	

BRACHYSCOME IBERIDIFOLIA
'Purple Splendour'

Habit Spreading annual. *Flowers* Daisy-like, 1⅝in (4cm) across, from summer. Purple, with a dark central disk. *Leaves* Finely divided, softly downy. Gray-green.
• NATIVE HABITAT Garden origin.
• CULTIVATION Grow in fertile, well-drained soil, in a warm, sunny, sheltered site. Well suited for bedding, edging, and containers, and can also be grown on sunny banks.
• PROPAGATION Sow seed at 64°F (18°C) in spring.

HEIGHT
12in (30cm)

SPREAD
12in (30cm)

Scrophulariaceae	CHINESE HOUSES

COLLINSIA GRANDIFLORA

Habit Bushy, slender-stemmed annual. *Flowers* Asymmetrically 2-lipped, in whorled clusters, from spring to summer. Pale pink-purple upper lips, with deep blue-purple lower lips. *Leaves* Oval to narrowly lance-shaped. Mid-green.
• NATIVE HABITAT Western N. America.
• CULTIVATION Good for an annual or mixed border, or in a wildflower garden. Grow in moist well-drained soil rich in organic matter, in full sun.
• PROPAGATION Sow seed *in situ* in autumn or early spring.

HEIGHT
6–12in
(15–30cm)

SPREAD
8–12in
(20–30cm)

Gentianaceae	PERSIAN VIOLET

EXACUM AFFINE

Habit Bushy annual or short-lived evergreen perennial. *Flowers* Saucer-shaped, scented, from summer. White, pink, or lavender-blue, with yellow stamens. *Leaves* Oval, shiny. Mid-green.
• NATIVE HABITAT Streambanks, Yemen.
• CULTIVATION Grow as a short-term house- or conservatory plant, in soil-based potting mix. Admit full light and water freely when in growth.
• PROPAGATION Sow seed at 64°F (18°C) in early spring.

Min.
45–50°F
(7–10°C)

HEIGHT
9–12in
(23–30cm)

SPREAD
9–12in
(23–30cm)

Campanulaceae	CUP-AND-SAUCER

CAMPANULA MEDIUM 'Bells of Holland'

Habit Clump-forming biennial. *Flowers* Bell-shaped, single, to 1⅝in (4cm) long, in clusters, borne freely from spring to summer. Shades of white, pink, or blue. *Leaves* Oval to lance-shaped. Mid-green.
• NATIVE HABITAT Garden origin.
• CULTIVATION Grow in fertile, neutral to alkaline, moist but well-drained soil, in sun or part-shade. Good for cutting, and for a mixed or annual border.
• PROPAGATION Sow seed in containers in a cold frame in spring.

Z 5–8

HEIGHT
16–18in
(40–45cm)

SPREAD
12in (30cm)

Plumbaginaceae	STATICE

LIMONIUM SINUATUM
Petite Bouquet Series

Habit Compact perennials, grown as annuals.
Flowers Tiny, funnel-shaped, in clustered
spikelets, borne in plumes, produced freely
from summer to autumn. Pinkish-purple.
Leaves Narrow to lance-shaped. Mid-green.
• NATIVE HABITAT Garden origin.
• CULTIVATION Grow in light, well-drained
soil, in full sun. Good for cutting and drying.
• PROPAGATION Sow seed in early spring at
55–64°F (13–18°C).

Z 8–10

HEIGHT
12in (30cm)

SPREAD
9in (23cm)

Labiatae/Lamiaceae	DRAGON'S HEAD

DRACOCEPHALUM MOLDAVICA

Habit Bushy, upright, aromatic annual. **Flowers**
Tubular, 2-lipped, sage-like, to 1in (2.5cm) long,
in whorled, spike-like heads, starting in summer.
Violet-blue. **Leaves** Narrowly lance-shaped,
oval, or triangular. Gray-green.
• NATIVE HABITAT Europe, C. Asia, Siberia, China.
• CULTIVATION Grow in moderately fertile,
well-drained soil, in sun or partial shade. Good
as a filler in a mixed or herbaceous border.
• PROPAGATION Sow seed *in situ* in mid-spring.
• OTHER NAME *D. moldavicum*.

HEIGHT
12–24in
(30–60cm)

SPREAD
12in (30cm)

Boraginaceae	

ECHIUM VULGARE Dwarf Hybrids

Habit Upright, bushy biennials. **Flowers** Broadly
bell-shaped, in short, dense spikes, from early
summer. White, pink, purple, or lilac-blue. **Leaves**
Narrowly lance-shaped, bristly-haired. Mid-green.
• NATIVE HABITAT Garden origin.
• CULTIVATION Good for a mixed or wildflower
border, or for bedding. Grow in well-drained,
moderately fertile soil that is rich in organic
matter, in sun.
• PROPAGATION Sow seed at 55–61°F (13–16°C)
in summer.

Z 3–8

HEIGHT
12–18in
(30–45cm)

SPREAD
12in (30cm)

Solanaceae	CUPFLOWER

NIEREMBERGIA CAERULEA
'Purple Robe'

Habit Upright perennial, grown as an annual.
Flowers Cup-shaped, ⅔in (2cm) across, from summer. Rich violet-blue. **Leaves** Pointed, narrowly spoon-shaped. Bright green.
• NATIVE HABITAT Garden origin.
• CULTIVATION Use as bedding or edging. Grow in moist but well-drained soil, in a sheltered site.
• PROPAGATION Sow seed at 59°F (15°C) in spring. Also by stem-tip cuttings in late summer.
• OTHER NAME *N. hippomannica* 'Purple Robe'.

☼ ◊

Z 7–9

HEIGHT
8in (20cm)

SPREAD
8in (20cm)

Compositae/Asteraceae	

PERICALLIS × HYBRIDA 'Spring Glory'

Habit Bushy perennial, grown as an annual.
Flowers Daisy-like, in heads, to 3in (8cm) across, from winter to spring. Pink, carmine, blue, or copper. **Leaves** Heart-shaped. Mid-green.
• NATIVE HABITAT Garden origin.
• CULTIVATION Grow in soil-based potting mix in good light. In cooler climates, grow as a house- or conservatory plant. Water moderately.
• PROPAGATION By seed at 55–64°F (13–18°C) from spring to mid-summer.
• OTHER NAMES *Cineraria cruentus*, *C.* × *hybrida*.

☼ ◊

Min. 45°F
(7°C)

HEIGHT
8in (20cm)

SPREAD
10in (25cm)

Cruciferae/Brassicaceae	

ORYCHOPHRAGMUS VIOLACEUS

Habit Upright annual or biennial. **Flowers** Cross-shaped, to 1in (2.5cm) across, in terminal clusters, from late spring and early summer. Violet. **Leaves** Finely divided basal leaves, with entire leaves clasping the stem. Pale green.
• NATIVE HABITAT Fallow or waste ground, China.
• CULTIVATION Grow in fertile, well-drained soil in a warm, sunny, sheltered site. Suitable for bedding and containers.
• PROPAGATION Sow seed *in situ* in spring or early summer. Also in autumn in frost-free areas.

☼ ◊

Z 6–9

HEIGHT
12–24in
(30–60cm)

SPREAD
12in (30cm)

Convolvulaceae	MORNING GLORY

CONVOLVULUS TRICOLOR 'Blue Flash'

Habit Spreading annual or short-lived perennial.
Flowers Open funnel-shaped, to 1⅔in (4cm) wide, borne throughout summer. Brilliant blue, with a white and yellow center. **Leaves** Oval to lance-shaped. Dark green.
• NATIVE HABITAT Garden origin.
• CULTIVATION Grows best in poor, well-drained soil in a warm, sunny, sheltered site. Good for a dry sunny bank, or the front of a border.
• PROPAGATION Sow seed *in situ* in mid-spring.
• OTHER NAME *C. minor* 'Blue Flash'.

☼ ◊

Z 9–10

HEIGHT
8–12in
(20–30cm)

SPREAD
8in (20cm)

Scrophulariaceae	WISHBONE FLOWER

TORENIA FOURNIERI Clown Series

Habit Compact annuals. *Flowers* Tubular,
2-lipped, flared at the mouth, in summer. White,
pink, deep purple, or lavender-blue, with a yellow-
marked throat. *Leaves* Oval, pointed. Pale green.
• NATIVE HABITAT Garden origin.
• CULTIVATION Grow in fertile, moist but well-
drained soil, in partial shade. In cooler climates,
grow as house- or conservatory plants. Suitable
for bedding.
• PROPAGATION Sow seed at 64°F (18°C) in
mid-spring.

☀: ◊

Min. 41°F
(5°C)

HEIGHT
8–10in
(20–25cm)

SPREAD
6–9in
(15–23cm)

Scrophulariaceae	WISHBONE FLOWER

TORENIA FOURNIERI

Habit Upright annual. *Flowers* Tubular,
2-lipped, in summer. Lilac-blue, with dark
purple lower lips and a yellow-marked throat.
Leaves Oval. Pale green.
• NATIVE HABITAT Woodlands of tropical
Asia and Africa.
• CULTIVATION Grow in fertile, moist but well-
drained soil, in partial shade. In cooler climates,
grow as a house- or conservatory plant.
• PROPAGATION Sow seed at 64°F (18°C) in
mid-spring.

☀: ◊

Min. 41°F
(5°C)

HEIGHT
12in (30cm)

SPREAD
6–9in
(15–23cm)

Boraginaceae	HELIOTROPE

HELIOTROPIUM ARBORESCENS 'Marine'

Habit Compact, short-lived shrub, grown as an
annual. *Flowers* Fragrant, tubular, in dense heads
to 6in (15cm) across, from summer. Deep violet-
blue. *Leaves* Oval to lance-shaped, wrinkled.
Contact may irritate skin and eyes. Dark green.
• NATIVE HABITAT Garden origin.
• CULTIVATION Grow in any fertile, moist but
well-drained soil, in full sun. Ideal for bedding
and containers.
• PROPAGATION Sow seed at 61–64°F (16–18°C)
in spring.

☼ ◊

Z 11

HEIGHT
to 18in
(45cm)

SPREAD
12–18in
(30–45cm)

Plumbaginaceae	STATICE

LIMONIUM SINUATUM Fortress Series

Habit Upright, rosette-forming perennial, usually
grown as an annual. *Flowers* Tiny, funnel-shaped,
in clustered spikelets, borne in broad clusters,
from summer to autumn. White, magenta, purple,
bright blue, yellow, and apricot. *Leaves* Narrow
to lance-shaped, lobed. Mid-green.
• NATIVE HABITAT Garden origin.
• CULTIVATION Grow in light, well-drained
soil, in full sun. Good for cutting and drying.
• PROPAGATION Sow seed in early spring at
55–64°F (13–18°C).

☼ ◊

Z 8–10

HEIGHT
to 24in
(60cm)

SPREAD
12in (30cm)

Scrophulariaceae	

NEMESIA STRUMOSA 'KLM'

Habit Bushy, low-branching annual. **Flowers** 2-lipped, to 1in (2.5cm) across, in terminal clusters, from mid- to late summer. Bicolored blue and white, with a yellow and pink throat. **Leaves** Lance-shaped, slightly hairy. Mid-green.
• NATIVE HABITAT Garden origin.
• CULTIVATION Grow in moderately fertile, moist but well-drained, slightly acid soil, in sun. Good for bedding and containers. Water well in dry periods.
• PROPAGATION Sow seed at 59°F (15°C) from early to late spring.

HEIGHT
7½–12in
(18–30cm)

SPREAD
4–6in
(10–15cm)

Boraginaceae	

ECHIUM VULGARE 'Blue Bedder'

Habit Upright, bushy biennial. **Flowers** Broadly bell-shaped, in short, dense spikes, from early summer. Light blue, aging to bluish-pink. **Leaves** Narrowly lance-shaped, bristly-haired. Mid-green.
• NATIVE HABITAT Garden origin.
• CULTIVATION Grow in well-drained, moderately fertile soil that is rich in organic matter, in sun. Good for a mixed or wildflower border, or for bedding.
• PROPAGATION Sow seed at 55–61°F (13–16°C) in summer.

Z 3–8

HEIGHT
to 18in
(45cm)

SPREAD
12in (30cm)

Polemoniaceae	BIRD'S EYES

GILIA TRICOLOR

Habit Mound-forming annual. **Flowers** Saucer-shaped, to ⅗in (1.5cm) across, borne singly or in clusters, from late spring to late summer. Pale violet. **Leaves** Finely divided. Bright green.
• NATIVE HABITAT Grasslands, western N. America.
• CULTIVATION Grow in moderately fertile, well-drained soil, in full sun. Ideal for a mixed, annual, or wildflower border, and for dry, sunny banks.
• PROPAGATION Sow seed *in situ* in autumn or spring.

HEIGHT
12–18in
(30–45cm)

SPREAD
9in (23cm)

Campanulaceae	

CAMPANULA ISOPHYLLA 'Stella Blue'

Habit Trailing perennial, often grown as an annual. **Flowers** Star-shaped, 1⅜in (3.5cm) across, in loose heads, from summer. Soft violet-blue. **Leaves** Heart-shaped, toothed. Light green.
• NATIVE HABITAT Garden origin.
• CULTIVATION Grow in fertile, well-drained soil, in sun or dappled shade. Good for hanging baskets and other containers. One of the Krystal Hybrids.
• PROPAGATION Sow seed at 59°F (15°C) in late winter. Also by stem-tip cuttings in early spring.

Z 6–9

HEIGHT
6–8in
(15–20cm)

SPREAD
12in (30cm)

Ranunculaceae	LOVE-IN-A-MIST

NIGELLA DAMASCENA **Persian Jewel Series**

Habit Slender, stiffly upright, fast-growing annuals. *Flowers* Solitary, saucer-shaped, to 1¾in (4.5cm) across, with petal-like sepals and 2-lipped true petals, finely divided at the tips, borne freely from summer. White, rose-pink, deep pink, sky-blue, or deep violet-blue, each with a wispy, bright green ruff beneath. Sometimes offered as separate colors. *Leaves* Oval, finely cut. Bright green. *Fruits* Inflated, round seed capsule, in 10 segments, with persistent styles.

• NATIVE HABITAT Garden origin. The species occurs in rocky places and fallow fields in Europe and N. Africa.
• CULTIVATION Grow in any well-drained soil, in sun. Good for a cottage garden, or as fillers in an annual or mixed border. The flowers are good for cutting and last well in water, and the seed capsules dry well for winter arrangements. Self-sows freely.
• PROPAGATION Sow seed *in situ* in mid-spring or autumn.

☼ ◊

HEIGHT
16in (40cm)

SPREAD
9in (23cm)

Solanaceae	

BROWALLIA SPECIOSA 'Blue Troll'

Habit Compact, bushy perennial, grown as an annual. *Flowers* Saucer-shaped, 5-lobed, to 2in (5cm) across, borne in the leaf axils, starting in summer. Clear blue. *Leaves* Oval. Mid-green.
• NATIVE HABITAT Garden origin.
• CULTIVATION Grow in soil-based potting mix, in full light; shade from hot sun. Used in bedding, or as a short-term house- or conservatory plant. Water moderately and apply balanced fertilizer monthly.
• PROPAGATION Sow seed at 64°F (18°C) in early spring, or in late summer for winter flowers.

☼ ◊

Min 55°F
(13°C)

HEIGHT
to 10in
(25cm)

SPREAD
10in (25cm)

Compositae/Asteraceae	FLOSS FLOWER

AGERATUM HOUSTONIANUM 'Blue Mink'

Habit Vigorous, open annual. *Flowers* Tiny, fluffy, 2–4in (5–10cm) across, in rounded heads, from mid-summer to autumn. Powder-blue. *Leaves* Oval, soft-haired. Mid-green.
• NATIVE HABITAT Garden origin.
• CULTIVATION Grow in moist but well-drained, fertile soil, in a sunny, sheltered site. Good for bedding, edging, and containers.
• PROPAGATION Sow seed at 61–64°F (16–18°C) in early spring.

☼ ◊

HEIGHT
8–12in
(20–30cm)

SPREAD
8–12in
(20–30cm)

Ranunculaceae	LOVE-IN-A-MIST

NIGELLA DAMASCENA 'Miss Jekyll'

Habit Slender annual. *Flowers* Semi-double, saucer-shaped, to 1¾in (4.5cm) across, with a ruff of finely divided foliage beneath, from summer. Sky-blue. *Leaves* Finely cut. Bright green. *Fruits* Inflated seed capsule, with persistent styles.
• NATIVE HABITAT Garden origin.
• CULTIVATION Grow in any well-drained soil, in sun. Good for a cottage garden, or an annual or mixed border, and for cut flowers. Self-sows freely.
• PROPAGATION Sow seed *in situ* in mid-spring or autumn.

☼ ◊

HEIGHT
18in (45cm)

SPREAD
9in (23cm)

Scrophulariaceae	

NEMESIA STRUMOSA 'Blue Gem'

Habit Bushy, low-branching annual. *Flowers* Single, 2-lipped, to 1in (2.5cm) across, in terminal clusters, from mid- to late summer. Bright blue, with a white throat. *Leaves* Lance-shaped, slightly hairy. Mid-green.
• NATIVE HABITAT Garden origin.
• CULTIVATION Grow in moderately fertile, moist but well-drained, slightly acid soil, in sun. Good for bedding and containers. Water well in dry periods.
• PROPAGATION Sow seed at 59°F (15°C) from early to late spring.

☼ ◊

HEIGHT
8–10in
(20–25cm)

SPREAD
4–6in
(10–15cm)

Solanaceae	

NOLANA PARADOXA

Habit Spreading, creeping, fleshy-stemmed annual or perennial. *Flowers* Broadly trumpet-shaped, 5-petaled, to 2in (5cm) across, borne singly or in clusters in the leaf axils, from summer. Flowers open fully only in sun. Sky-blue, with a white eye and a creamy-yellow throat. *Leaves* Inversely lance-shaped, stalkless, in a basal rosette, with oval stem leaves. Mid-green.
• NATIVE HABITAT Garden origin. Species occurs in arid and coastal areas of Chile and Peru.

• CULTIVATION Grow in any moderately fertile, well-drained soil, in a warm site in full sun. Suitable for a hanging basket, window box, or other container, and for a mixed or annual border. May also be grown as a short-term houseplant. Under glass, use a soil-based potting mix. Admit full light, maintain good ventilation, and water moderately.
• PROPAGATION Sow seed at 55–59°F (13–15°C) in early spring, or *in situ* in late spring. May also be sown in autumn for spring-flowering pot plants.

Z 9–10

HEIGHT
6–8in
(15–20cm)

SPREAD
6–8in
(15–20cm)

Hydrophyllaceae	BABY BLUE-EYES

NEMOPHILA MENZIESII

Habit Fleshy-stemmed annual. **Flowers** Solitary, saucer-shaped, to 1⅝in (4cm) across, from summer. Bright blue, with dark blue markings and a pale center. **Leaves** Finely divided. Gray-green.
• NATIVE HABITAT California.
• CULTIVATION Grow in fertile, moist but well-drained soil, in sun or partial shade. Good for edging and containers.
• PROPAGATION Sow seed *in situ* in early spring or autumn. Self-sows freely.
• OTHER NAME *N. insignis*.

 ☼ ◊

HEIGHT
8in (20cm)

SPREAD
12in (30cm)

Compositae/Asteraceae	SWAN RIVER DAISY

BRACHYSCOME IBERIDIFOLIA

Habit Spreading annual. **Flowers** Daisy-like, 1⅝in (4cm) across, from summer. White, violet-pink, or blue-purple, with a yellow central disk. **Leaves** Finely divided, soft-haired. Gray-green.
• NATIVE HABITAT Damp grassland, western and southern Australia.
• CULTIVATION Grow in fertile, well-drained soil, in a warm, sunny, sheltered site. Good for bedding, edging, containers, and dry, sunny banks.
• PROPAGATION Sow seed at 64°F (18°C) in spring.

 ☼ ◊

HEIGHT
to 18in
(45cm)

SPREAD
14in (35cm)

Compositae/Asteraceae	KINGFISHER DAISY

FELICIA BERGERIANA

Habit Mat-forming annual. **Flowers** Solitary, daisy-like, 1¼in (3cm) across, with slender ray florets, borne freely in summer. Brilliant blue, with a yellow central disk. **Leaves** Lance-shaped, soft-haired. Gray-green.
• NATIVE HABITAT Open sunny places, S. Africa.
• CULTIVATION Grow in poor to moderately fertile, well-drained soil, in sun. Suitable for bedding, borders, window boxes, and other containers. Good wind-resistance.
• PROPAGATION Sow seed at 64°F (18°C) in spring.

 ☼ ◊

HEIGHT
10in (25cm)

SPREAD
10in (25cm)

Boraginaceae	CHINESE FORGET-ME-NOT

CYNOGLOSSUM AMABILE 'Firmament'

Habit Upright, bushy annual or biennial. **Flowers** Drooping, forget-me-not-like, to ⅜in (1cm) across, in terminal heads, from late summer. Sky-blue. **Leaves** Oval to lance-shaped, hairy. Gray-green.
• NATIVE HABITAT Garden origin.
• CULTIVATION Grow in moderately fertile, moist but well-drained soil, in sun or partial shade. Suitable for an annual border or as a filler in a mixed or herbaceous border.
• PROPAGATION Sow seed *in situ* in mid-spring.

 ☼ ◊

Z 5–8

HEIGHT
16in (40cm)

SPREAD
to 12in
(30cm)

PELARGONIUM

The genus *Pelargonium* consists of some 230 species of mainly evergreen perennials, with some succulents, sub-shrubs, and shrubs. Few true species are grown; those most commonly seen are the many cultivars widely, but incorrectly, called geraniums. These are derived from complex crosses involving some 20 species. Angel pelargoniums, derived mainly from *P. crispum*, bear clusters of funnel-shaped flowers during summer. Ivy-leaved types have fleshy, lobed leaves and are either compact and short-jointed, or else trailing in habit. Newer, zonal pelargoniums include single-flowered, zonal cultivars of uniform habit bred for use in summer bedding or containers. These provide vibrant color throughout summer. Unlike older cultivars, which are raised annually from softwood cuttings, they bloom freely in their first year from seed and come true to color and type.

Pelargoniums may be overwintered in frost-free conditions, but grow vigorously from seed. Treating them as annuals saves greenhouse space in winter, reduces heating costs, and discourages disease.

Grow in fertile, well-drained, neutral to alkaline soil, in full sun. Deadhead regularly. In containers, use a soilless or soil-based potting mix. Water container-grown plants moderately when in growth. Apply a balanced liquid fertilizer every 10–14 days from spring and early summer, switching to a high-potash fertilizer as they begin to come into flower.

Sow seed in late winter or early spring, at 61–64°F (16–18°C). Maintain a constant temperature after sowing and when growing on. Temperature fluctuations lead to delayed germination and poor growth.

The plants are susceptible to vine weevils, leafhoppers, aphids, caterpillars, gray mold (*Botrytis*), and stem rot.

P. Horizon Series
Habit Bushy, compact perennials, grown as annuals. Wet weather-resistant.
Flowers Single, in clusters to 4½in (12cm) across, from early summer to autumn. White, pink, or red.
Leaves Rounded. Mid-green, with darker zones.
• HEIGHT 12in (30cm).
• SPREAD 10in (25cm).

P. Horizon Series
(Seed-raised, zonal)

☀ ◊
Min. 36°F (2°C)

P. Multibloom Series
Habit Bushy, early-flowering perennials, grown as annuals. Wet weather-resistant.
Flowers Single, in clusters, from summer to autumn. White, pink, or red, some with an eye.
Leaves Rounded. Mid-green, with darker zones.
• HEIGHT to 12in (30cm).
• SPREAD 12in (30cm).

P. Multibloom Series
(Seed-raised, zonal)

☀ ◊
Min. 36°F (2°C)

P. Breakaway Series
Habit Neat, compact perennials, grown as annuals.
Flowers Small, single, with upright, horizontal, and drooping stems, in open clusters, from summer to autumn. Red or salmon-pink.
Leaves Small, rounded. Mid-green.
• HEIGHT 10in (25cm).
• SPREAD 10in (25cm).

P. Breakaway Series
(Seed-raised, zonal)

☀ ◊
Min. 36°F (2°C)

P. 'Raspberry Ripple'
Habit Very bushy, evergreen perennial, grown as an annual.
Flowers Single, broadly trumpet-shaped, to 1⅛in (3cm) across, borne in flushes throughout summer. Pinkish-white, splashed with red.
Leaves Rounded, aromatic. Mid-green.
• HEIGHT 12in (30cm).
• SPREAD 12in (30cm).

P. 'Raspberry Ripple'
(Seed-raised, zonal)

☀ ◊
Min. 36°F (2°C)

P. 'Summer Showers'

Habit Low-branching, trailing perennial, grown as an annual.
Flowers Single, in clusters, borne from summer to autumn. White, pink, red, or lavender-blue.
Leaves Lobed, ivy-like, fleshy, firm, and glossy. Mid-green.
• HEIGHT 24in (60cm).
• SPREAD 36in (90cm).

P. 'Summer Showers'
(Seed-raised, ivy-leaved)

☼ ◊
Min. 36°F (2°C)

P. Sensation Series

Habit Bushy, compact, wet weather-resistant perennials, grown as annuals.
Flowers Single, in clusters, from early summer to autumn. Pink, red, or orange, some with a white eye. Single or mixed colors.
Leaves Rounded. Mid-green, with darker zones.
• HEIGHT 12in (30cm).
• SPREAD 10in (25cm).

P. Sensation Series
(Seed-raised, zonal)

☼ ◊
Min. 36°F (2°C)

P. 'Cherry Orbit'

Habit Well-branched, early-flowering perennial, grown as an annual.
Flowers Single, in clusters, to 5½in (14cm) across, borne freely from early summer to autumn. White, pink, violet-cerise, scarlet, or orange.
Leaves Rounded. Mid-green, finely zoned.
• HEIGHT 14in (35cm).
• SPREAD 10in (25cm).

P. 'Cherry Orbit'
(Orbit Series)
(Seed-raised, zonal)
☼ ◊
Min. 36°F (2°C)

P. Tornado Series

Habit Neat, compact perennials, grown as annuals.
Flowers Single, in clusters to 4½in (12cm) across, on short, trailing stems, from summer to autumn. Available in white or lilac.
Leaves Lobed, firm, fleshy, ivy-like, and glossy. Mid-green.
• HEIGHT 10in (25cm).
• SPREAD 8in (20cm).

P. Tornado Series
(Seed-raised, ivy-leaved)

☼ ◊
Min. 36°F (2°C)

P. Video Series

Habit Dwarf, bushy, compact perennials, grown as annuals.
Flowers Single, in clusters, to 4in (10cm) across, from summer to autumn. Pink, red, or salmon pink, in single colors or mixtures.
Leaves Rounded. Dark green, and strongly zoned.
• HEIGHT 8in (20cm).
• SPREAD 7½in (18cm).

P. Video Series
(Seed-raised, zonal)

☼ ◊
Min. 36°F (2°C)

P. 'Rose Diamond'

Habit Bushy, weather-resistant perennial, grown as an annual.
Flowers Single, in domed clusters, 4½in (12cm) across, from summer to autumn. Rose-pink or red.
Leaves Rounded. Mid-green, zoned bronze.
• HEIGHT 12–24in (30–60cm).
• SPREAD 12–24in (30–60cm).

P. 'Rose Diamond'
(Diamond Series)
(Seed-raised, zonal)
☼ ◊
Min. 36°F (2°C)

P. 'Orange Appeal'

Habit Bushy, free-flowering perennial, grown as an annual.
Flowers Single, in clusters up to 2¾in (7cm) across, borne from summer to autumn. Clear bright orange.
Leaves Rounded. Bright green.
• HEIGHT 12–16in (30–40cm).
• SPREAD 12in (30cm).

P. 'Orange Appeal'
(Seed-raised, zonal)

☼ ◊
Min. 36°F (2°C)

PETUNIA

The genus *Petunia* consists of some 40 species of annuals and perennials, of which the modern cultivars derived from *P. axillaris*, *P. integrifolia*, and *P. violacea* are the most horticulturally important. Petunias bloom freely from late spring to late autumn, bearing single or double, fluted, trumpet-shaped flowers. Colors range from white through to shades of pink, red, purple, violet-blue, and yellow, including many that are veined with darker shades. Also available are picotees and a few with "halos," or throats, of a contrasting color. Modern cultivars are divided into two main groups:

Grandiflora The flowers of Grandifloras grow to 4in (10cm) across, and many are susceptible to rain and wind damage. They are best used in hanging baskets in a sheltered site, or in a cool conservatory.
Multiflora These produce smaller flowers, measuring about 2in (5cm) across,

and are more weather-resistant than the Grandifloras. They are used in bedding schemes, in annual borders, and in a variety of containers.

Grow in light, well-drained, moderately fertile soil, in sun, with shelter from strong winds. Petunias tolerate coastal conditions and poor soils. Rich soils promote leaf growth at the expense of flowers. Deadhead regularly. In containers, use soilless or soil-based potting mix. Water freely when in growth and apply a high-potash fertilizer every two weeks as they begin to come into flower.

Sow seed at 55–64°F (13–18°C) in spring or autumn. Overwinter young plants under glass. Harden off before planting out when danger of frost has passed. Propagate Surfinia petunias from softwood cuttings in summer and overwinter under glass.

The plants are susceptible to aphids, slugs, and viruses, including potato virus.

P. Surfinia Series (white)
Habit Vigorous, branching, weather-resistant annual.
Flowers Trumpet-shaped, 4in (10cm) across, borne freely from summer to autumn. White.
Leaves Oval. Mid-green.
• HEIGHT 9–16in (23–40cm).
• SPREAD 12–36in (30–90cm).

P. Surfinia Series (white)
(Grandiflora)

☼ ◊

P. Recoverer Series
Habit Bushy, well-branched annuals.
Flowers Trumpet-shaped, single, 4in (10cm) across, from summer to autumn. White or varied colors, also available in mixtures.
Leaves Oval. Mid- to dark green.
• HEIGHT 6–12in (15–30cm).
• SPREAD 12in (30cm).

P. Recoverer Series
(Grandiflora)

☼ ◊

P. Victorious Series
Habit Bushy, well-branched annuals.
Flowers Double, trumpet-shaped, to 4in (10cm) across, with very ruffled petal margins, borne freely from summer to autumn. Available in a range of bright colors.
Leaves Oval. Mid-green.
• HEIGHT 6–12in (15–30cm).
• SPREAD 12in (30cm).

P. Victorious Series
(Grandiflora)

☼ ◊

P. Bonanza Series

Habit Dense, vigorous, free-flowering annuals.
Flowers Funnel-shaped, double, 2in (5cm) across, borne freely from summer to autumn. In white, pink, red, purple, violet, or blue, most with heavy veining.
Leaves Oval. Mid-green.
• HEIGHT 6–12in (15–30cm).
• SPREAD 12in (30cm).

P. Bonanza Series
(Multiflora)

P. 'Plum Pudding'

Habit Dense, spreading, weather-resistant annual.
Flowers Single, 2in (5cm) across, borne from summer to autumn. In deep-pink, purple, blue, or yellow, with a dark central disk and prominent lacy veining.
Leaves Oval. Mid-green.
• HEIGHT 8in (20cm).
• SPREAD 12–18in (30–45cm).

P. 'Plum Pudding'
(Multiflora)

P. Junior Series

Habit Dwarf, compact, clump-forming annuals.
Flowers Trumpet-shaped, 1in (2.5cm) across, from summer to autumn. White, pink, red, or blue.
Leaves Oval. Mid-green.
• TIPS Ideal for hanging baskets and containers.
• HEIGHT 4–6in (10–15cm).
• SPREAD 6in (15cm).

P. Junior Series
(Multiflora)

P. Resisto Series (rose-pink)

Habit Bushy, well-branched, rain-resistant perennial.
Flowers Single, trumpet-shaped, 2in (5cm) across, borne freely from summer to autumn. Rose-pink.
Leaves Oval. Mid-green.
• HEIGHT 6–12in (15–30cm).
• SPREAD 12in (30cm).

P. Resisto Series (rose-pink)
(Multiflora)

P. Falcon Series (mixed)

Habit Bushy, well-branched annuals.
Flowers Trumpet-shaped, single, 4in (10cm) across, borne freely from summer to autumn. Mixed colors, some veined or bicolored.
Leaves Oval. Mid-green.
• HEIGHT 9–12in (23–30cm).
• SPREAD 12in (30cm).

P. Falcon Series (mixed)
(Grandiflora)

P. 'Rose Star'

Habit Spreading, early-flowering, rain-resistant annual.
Flowers Trumpet-shaped, 4in (10cm) across, from summer to autumn. Rose-pink, with a white central star. Also available in a range of colors.
Leaves Oval. Mid-green.
• HEIGHT 12in (30cm).
• SPREAD 12–36in (30–90cm).

P. 'Rose Star'
(Ultra Series)
(Grandiflora)

P. Pirouette Series

Habit Dense, bushy annuals.
Flowers Double, trumpet-shaped, 2¼–4in (7–10cm) across, with ruffled petal margins, borne from summer to autumn. Bicolored, in varied strong, clear colors.
Leaves Oval-shaped. Mid-green.
• HEIGHT 15in (38cm).
• SPREAD 18in (45cm).

P. Pirouette Series
(Grandiflora)

P. Star Series

Habit Bushy, well-branched annuals.
Flowers Single, trumpet-shaped, 4in (10cm) across, from summer to autumn. In a range of rich colors, each petal with a broad, white, central stripe.
Leaves Oval-shaped. Mid-green.
• HEIGHT 6–12in (15–30cm).
• SPREAD 12in (30cm).

P. Star Series
(Grandiflora)

P. Resisto Series (red)

Habit Bushy, well-branched, rain-resistant annual.
Flowers Single, trumpet-shaped, 2in (5cm) across, borne freely from summer to autumn. Rich red.
Leaves Oval. Mid-green.
• HEIGHT 6–12in (15–30cm).
• SPREAD 12in (30cm).

P. Resisto Series (red)
(Multiflora)

P. 'Mirage Velvet'

Habit Dense, spreading, wet weather-resistant annual.
Flowers Single, 2½in (7cm) across, borne freely from summer to autumn. Deep red, with a dark center.
Leaves Oval-shaped. Mid- to dark green.
• HEIGHT 10in (25cm).
• SPREAD 12in (30cm).

P. 'Mirage Velvet'
(Mirage Series)
(Multiflora)

P. Falcon Series 'Salmon'

Habit Bushy, well-branched annual.
Flowers Trumpet-shaped, single, 4in (10cm) across, borne freely from summer to autumn. Salmon-pink.
Leaves Oval-shaped. Mid-green.
• HEIGHT 9–12in (23–30cm).
• SPREAD 12in (30cm).

P. Falcon Series 'Salmon'
(Grandiflora)

P. 'Horizon Red Halo'

Habit Dense, spreading annual.
Flowers Single, 2in (5cm) across, borne freely from summer to autumn. Red, with a white and yellow throat.
Leaves Oval-shaped. Mid-green.
• HEIGHT 14in (35cm).
• SPREAD 12–36in (30–90cm).

P. 'Horizon Red Halo'
(Horizon Series)
(Multiflora)

P. 'Purple Wave'

Habit Dense, trailing annual.
Flowers Single, widely trumpet-shaped, 2in (5cm) across, borne from summer to autumn. Brilliant magenta, with a dark center.
Leaves Oval-shaped. Mid-green.
• HEIGHT 18in (45cm).
• SPREAD 12–36in (30–90cm).

P. 'Purple Wave'
(Multiflora)

P. Resisto Series
Habit Bushy, well-branched, wet weather-resistant annuals.
Flowers Single, trumpet-shaped, 2in (5cm) across, borne freely from summer to autumn. Available in a range of colors.
Leaves Oval. Mid-green.
• HEIGHT 6–12in (15–30cm).
• SPREAD 12in (30cm).

P. Resisto Series
(Multiflora)

P. 'Lavender Storm'
Habit Dense, well-branched, compact, wet weather-resistant annual.
Flowers Large, saucer-shaped, 4in (10cm) across, borne freely throughout summer. Lavender, with lacy veining.
Leaves Oval-shaped. Mid-green.
• HEIGHT 10in (25cm).
• SPREAD 18in (45cm).

P. 'Lavender Storm'
(Grandiflora)

P. 'Sugar Daddy'
Habit Bushy, well-branched annual.
Flowers Trumpet-shaped, 4in (10cm) across, ruffled, borne freely from summer through to autumn. Purple, with dark veins.
Leaves Oval-shaped. Mid-green.
• HEIGHT 14in (35cm).
• SPREAD 12–36in (30–90cm).

P. 'Sugar Daddy'
(Daddy Series)
(Grandiflora)

P. 'Mirage Lavender'

Habit Dense, spreading annual.
Flowers Single, 2¾in (7cm) across, borne freely from summer to autumn. Pale lavender-blue, with lacy veining.
Leaves Oval-shaped. Mid-green.
• HEIGHT 12in (30cm).
• SPREAD 12–36in (30–90cm).

P. 'Mirage Lavender'
(Mirage Series)
(Multiflora)

P. 'Blue Frost'

Habit Bushy, well-branched annual.
Flowers Single, trumpet-shaped, 4in (10cm) across, with broad, slightly ruffled margins, from summer to autumn. Violet-blue, with white edges.
Leaves Oval-shaped. Mid-green.
• HEIGHT 6–12in (15–30cm).
• SPREAD 12in (30cm).

P. 'Blue Frost'
(Grandiflora)

P. Fantasy Series (mixed)

Habit Dwarf, compact, dense, weather-resistant annual.
Flowers Trumpet-shaped, from summer to autumn. Ivory, pink, red, blue, or salmon.
Leaves Oval. Mid- to dark green.
• HEIGHT 9–12in (23–30cm).
• SPREAD 9–12in (23–30cm).

P. Fantasy Series (mixed)
(Multiflora)

P. Carpet Series

Habit Dense, compact, spreading annuals.
Flowers Single, widely trumpet-shaped, borne from summer to autumn. White and shades of pink, red, purple, yellow, or orange.
Leaves Oval-shaped. Mid-green.
• HEIGHT 8–10in (20–25cm).
• SPREAD 12–36in (30–90cm).

P. Carpet Series
(Multiflora)

P. 'Brass Band'

Habit Spreading, wet weather-resistant, well-branched annual.
Flowers Single, to 2in (5cm) across, with ruffled margins, borne from summer to autumn. Creamy-yellow, with a darker center.
Leaves Oval. Mid-green.
• HEIGHT 10–12in (25–30cm).
• SPREAD 12in (30cm).

P. 'Brass Band'
(Multiflora)

Boraginaceae	

ANCHUSA CAPENSIS 'Blue Angel'

Habit Compact, upright biennial, may be grown as an annual. **Flowers** Saucer-shaped, to ⅜in (9mm) across, in open clusters, from summer. Ultramarine-blue. **Leaves** Narrowly lance-shaped, rough, bristly. Mid-green.
• NATIVE HABITAT Garden origin.
• CULTIVATION Grow in moist but well-drained, moderately fertile soil, in full sun. Good for bedding, borders, and containers.
• PROPAGATION Sow seed at 55–61°F (13–16°C) in late winter or early spring.

☼ ◊

Z 8–10

HEIGHT
8in (20cm)

SPREAD
8in (20cm)

Hydrophyllaceae	CALIFORNIAN BLUEBELL

PHACELIA CAMPANULARIA

Habit Upright, branching, aromatic annual. **Flowers** Upturned bell-shaped, to 1in (2.5cm) across, borne in loose heads, from late spring and summer. White or dark blue. **Leaves** Oval, toothed. Dark green.
• NATIVE HABITAT Southern California.
• CULTIVATION Grow in any fertile, well-drained soil, in sun. Good for a border or wildlife garden; the flowers are attractive to bees.
• PROPAGATION Sow seed *in situ* in spring or autumn.

☼ ◊

HEIGHT
6–12in
(15–30cm)

SPREAD
6in (15cm)

Solanaceae	

BROWALLIA SPECIOSA 'Vanja'

Habit Compact, bushy perennial. **Flowers** Saucer-shaped, 5-lobed, from summer. Deep blue, with a white eye. **Leaves** Oval. Mid-green.
• NATIVE HABITAT Garden origin.
• CULTIVATION Grow in soil-based potting mix, in full light; shade from hot sun. Used as bedding, or as a short-term house- or conservatory plant in cool climates. Water moderately and apply balanced fertilizer monthly.
• PROPAGATION Sow seed at 64°F (18°C) in early spring, or in late summer for winter flowers.

☼ ◊

Min 55°F
(13°C)

HEIGHT
to 10in
(25cm)

SPREAD
10in (25cm)

Boraginaceae	FORGET-ME-NOT

MYOSOTIS SYLVATICA 'Music'

Habit Vigorous, upright biennial. **Flowers** Saucer-shaped, ⅜–⅜in (9–10mm) across, in dense heads, from spring and early summer. Purplish-blue, with a yellow eye. **Leaves** Oval to lance-shaped. Bright green.
• NATIVE HABITAT Garden origin.
• CULTIVATION Grow in moderately fertile, moist but well-drained soil, in sun with mid-day shade, or in part-shade. Good for bedding.
• PROPAGATION Sow seed in containers in a cold frame, or in a seed bed, in early summer.

◑ ◊

Z 4–7

HEIGHT
10in (25cm)

SPREAD
10in (25cm)

Convolvulaceae	MORNING GLORY

CONVOLVULUS TRICOLOR
'Royal Ensign'

Habit Bushy annual. *Flowers* Funnel-shaped, from summer. Deep blue, with a white and yellow eye. *Leaves* Oval to lance-shaped. Dark green.
• NATIVE HABITAT Garden origin.
• CULTIVATION Grow in poor to moderately fertile, well-drained soil, in a warm, sunny site. Good for hanging baskets and sunny banks.
• PROPAGATION Sow seed *in situ* in mid-spring or autumn.
• OTHER NAME *C. minor* 'Royal Ensign'.

☀ ◊

HEIGHT
12in (30cm)

SPREAD
12in (30cm)

Compositae/Asteraceae	DUSTY MILLER

SENECIO CINERARIA 'Silver Dust'

Habit Bushy, evergreen shrub, grown as an annual. *Flowers* Daisy-like, borne in loose heads the second summer after sowing. Mustard-yellow. *Leaves* Deeply cut, lacy, densely hairy. White.
• NATIVE HABITAT Garden origin.
• CULTIVATION Grow in well-drained soil in sun. Ideal for creating massed foliage effects in bedding schemes.
• PROPAGATION By seed in spring at 66–75°F (19–24°C).
• OTHER NAME *Cineraria maritima* 'Silver Dust'.

☀ ◊

Z 7–9

HEIGHT
12in (30cm)

SPREAD
12in (30cm)

Compositae/Asteraceae	DUSTY MILLER

SENECIO CINERARIA 'Cirrus'

Habit Bushy, evergreen shrub, grown as an annual. *Flowers* Daisy-like, borne in loose heads in the second year after sowing. Mustard-yellow. *Leaves* Oval, toothed or lobed. White or silver-green.
• NATIVE HABITAT Garden origin.
• CULTIVATION Grow in well-drained soil in sun. Use for massed foliage effects in bedding schemes.
• PROPAGATION By seed in spring at 66–75°F (19–24°C).
• OTHER NAME *Cineraria maritima* 'Cirrus'.

☀ ◊

Z 7–9

HEIGHT
12in (30cm)

SPREAD
12in (30cm)

Dipsacaceae

SCABIOSA STELLATA 'Paper Moon'

Habit Upright, well-branched annual. *Flowers*
Solitary, hemispherical, with a pincushion-like
central dome of florets and larger marginal florets,
starting in summer. Creamy-pink. *Leaves* Oval to
lance-shaped, divided. Mid-green. *Fruits* Round
seedheads, to 3in (8cm) across, formed from
clustered, papery, cup-shaped bracts that enlarge
after flowering. Translucent, with green- and
maroon-centered bracts.
• NATIVE HABITAT Garden origin. Species from dry
meadows and rocky slopes, in southern Europe.

• CULTIVATION Grow in moderately fertile,
well-drained, neutral to alkaline soil, in a warm,
sunny site. The seedheads are ideal for cutting
and drying for use in winter arrangements.
Cut and air-dry by hanging upside down in
a well-ventilated place away from sunlight.
The species is well suited for a mixed, annual,
or wildflower border, where the flowers will
attract bees and butterflies.
• PROPAGATION Sow seed at 43–54°F (6–12°C)
in early spring, or *in situ* in mid-spring.

HEIGHT
to 18in
(45cm)

SPREAD
9in (23cm)

Gramineae/Poaceae	LESSER QUAKING GRASS

BRIZA MINOR

Habit Loosely tufted annual grass. **Flowers**
Oval spikelets, ⅕in (5mm) long, borne in slender-
stemmed, drooping clusters, from summer. Pale
green, often purple-tinted, ripening to straw-
yellow. **Leaves** Narrow, bristly. Pale green.
• NATIVE HABITAT Grasslands, Europe,
western Asia.
• CULTIVATION Grow in well-drained soil, in sun.
Seedheads are good for cutting, dying, and drying.
• PROPAGATION Sow seed *in situ* in spring
or autumn.

HEIGHT
18in (45cm)

SPREAD
10in (25cm)

Gramineae/Poaceae	CLOUD GRASS

AGROSTIS NEBULOSA

Habit Tufted annual grass. **Flowers** Tiny
spikelets, in whorled clusters, to 6in (15cm)
long, borne freely in summer. White.
Leaves Narrow, flat. Mid-green.
• NATIVE HABITAT Grasslands, Morocco, Iberia.
• CULTIVATION Grow in any well-drained soil,
in full sun. Flowerheads are good for cutting and
drying; cut and air dry before fully ripe. Suitable
for the front of a mixed or annual border. Deadhead to prevent self-sown seedlings.
• PROPAGATION Sow seed *in situ* in spring.

HEIGHT
14in (35cm)

SPREAD
8in (20cm)

Gramineae/Poaceae	GOLDEN TOP, TOOTHBRUSH GRASS

LAMARCKIA AUREA

Habit Loosely tufted annual grass. **Flowers**
Downswept spikelets, borne in dense, narrow,
one-sided clusters, to 2¾in (7cm) long, from
summer. Golden-yellow. **Leaves** Broadly
lance-shaped, flat, twisted. Bright green.
• NATIVE HABITAT Open ground, Mediterranean.
• CULTIVATION Grow in light, sandy, well-drained
soil, in sun. Good for a mixed or annual border,
and suitable for cutting and drying.
• PROPAGATION Sow seed *in situ* in succession
between early and late spring.

HEIGHT
12in (30cm)

SPREAD
10in (25cm)

Compositae/Asteraceae	

OSTEOSPERMUM 'Buttermilk'

Habit Upright, evergreen sub-shrub, grown as an annual. *Flowers* Daisy-like, 2in (5cm) across, from late spring to autumn. Primrose-yellow ray florets, white at the base, with a bronze-yellow underside. *Leaves* Lance-shaped. Mid-green.
• NATIVE HABITAT Garden origin.
• CULTIVATION Grow in light, well-drained soil, in a warm, sunny sheltered site. Suitable for a mixed or annual border.
• PROPAGATION By semi-ripe cuttings in late summer. Will not come true from seed.

☼ ◊

Z 8–10

HEIGHT
to 24in
(60cm)

SPREAD
24in (60cm)

Compositae/Asteraceae	AFRICAN DAISY, YELLOW AGERATUM

LONAS ANNUA

Habit Vigorous, bushy annual. *Flowers* Button-like, borne in dense, terminal heads, to 5in (12cm) across, from summer. Golden-yellow. *Leaves* Finely divided. Mid-green.
• NATIVE HABITAT Southwest Mediterranean.
• CULTIVATION Grow in a mixed or annual border, in any moderately fertile, well-drained soil, in full sun. Ideal for cutting and drying.
• PROPAGATION Sow seed in spring at 59–64°F (15–18°C).
• OTHER NAME *L. inodora.*

☼ ◊

HEIGHT
12–18in
(30–45cm)

SPREAD
9in (23cm)

Compositae/Asteraceae	POT MARIGOLD

CALENDULA OFFICINALIS 'Lemon Queen'

Habit Compact annual. *Flowers* Daisy-like, double, from summer to autumn. Lemon-yellow. *Leaves* Lance- to spoon-shaped. Bright green.
• NATIVE HABITAT Garden origin.
• CULTIVATION Grow in any well-drained soil, in sun. Good for cutting, bedding, and containers. Deadhead regularly. For plentiful cut flowers, pinch out the terminal bud to encourage laterals.
• PROPAGATION Sow seed *in situ* in spring or autumn.

☼ ◊

HEIGHT
to 18in
(45cm)

SPREAD
18in (45cm)

Loasaceae	BLAZING STAR

MENTZELIA LINDLEYI
Habit Upright, well-branched annual.
Flowers Night-scented, 5-petaled, 2–3½in
(5–9cm) across, borne in terminal clusters and
in the leaf axils, from summer. Golden-yellow.
Leaves Finely cut. Mid- to gray-green.
• NATIVE HABITAT Dry, sandy or rocky places,
California.
• CULTIVATION Grow in light, well-drained soil,
in full sun. Good for a mixed or annual border.
• PROPAGATION Sow seed *in situ* in spring.
• OTHER NAME *Bartonia aurea*.

☼ ◌

HEIGHT
6–28in
(15–70cm)

SPREAD
9in (23cm)

Compositae/Asteraceae	CREEPING ZINNIA

SANVITALIA PROCUMBENS
Habit Creeping, mat-forming annual. **Flowers**
Daisy-like, single, to ⅘in (2cm) across, from
summer to autumn. Yellow, with a black central
disk. **Leaves** Pointed, oval. Mid-green.
• NATIVE HABITAT Dry, rocky places, Mexico.
• CULTIVATION Grow in moderately fertile,
well-drained soil that is rich in organic matter,
in sun. Suitable for a mixed or annual border
or for hanging baskets and other containers.
• PROPAGATION Sow seed *in situ* in spring
or autumn.

☼ ◌

HEIGHT
to 8in
(20cm)

SPREAD
to 18in
(45cm)

Compositae/Asteraceae	

COREOPSIS GRANDIFLORA
'Early Sunrise'
Habit Clump-forming perennial, often grown as
an annual. **Flowers** Daisy-like, semi-double, to
2⅜in (6cm) across, from late spring to late summer.
Golden-yellow, flushed orange-yellow at the base.
Leaves Lance-shaped. Mid-green.
• NATIVE HABITAT Garden origin.
• CULTIVATION Grow in well-drained, fertile soil.
Good for a mixed or annual border, or for cutting.
• PROPAGATION Sow seed at 55–61°F (13–16°C)
in mid- to late winter.

☼ ◌

Z 6–9

HEIGHT
18in (45cm)

SPREAD
18in (45cm)

Compositae/Asteraceae	DAHLBERG DAISY, GOLDEN FLEECE

THYMOPHYLLA TENUILOBA

Habit Sturdy, well-branched annual.
Flowers Daisy-like, to ⅗in (1.5cm) across,
from spring to summer. Bright yellow. *Leaves*
Finely cut, fern-like, aromatic. Bright green.
• NATIVE HABITAT Dry slopes and prairies,
in Texas and Mexico.
• CULTIVATION Grow in light, well-drained soil,
in sun. Suitable for a mixed or annual border
or for hanging baskets and other containers.
• PROPAGATION Sow seed at 50–55°F (10–13°C)
in spring.

HEIGHT
12in (30cm)

SPREAD
12in (30cm)

Scrophulariaceae

CALCEOLARIA Anytime Series

Habit Compact biennials. *Flowers* Pouched,
slipper-like, borne 16 weeks after sowing.
Available in red or yellow, with bicolors.
Leaves Oval. Mid-green.
• NATIVE HABITAT Garden origin.
• CULTIVATION Grow in soil-based potting
mix, in bright, filtered light. Use as houseplants.
Water freely, and apply a balanced fertilizer
once a month.
• PROPAGATION Surface sow seed at 64°F (18°C)
at any time of year.

Z 8–10

HEIGHT
8in (20cm)

SPREAD
8in (20cm)

Compositae/Asteraceae

BIDENS FERULIFOLIA 'Golden Goddess'

Habit Short-lived perennial, grown as an annual.
Flowers Star-shaped, daisy-like, borne from mid-
summer to autumn. Golden-yellow, with a darker
yellow disk. *Leaves* Finely divided. Fresh green.
• NATIVE HABITAT Garden origin.
• CULTIVATION Grow in light, moderately fertile,
moist but well-drained soil, in sun. Suitable
for a mixed or annual border, gravel garden,
or for hanging baskets and other containers.
• PROPAGATION Sow seed at 55–64°F (13–18°C)
in spring.

Z 7–9

HEIGHT
12in (30cm)

SPREAD
12in (30cm)

Compositae/Asteraceae	TIDY TIPS

LAYIA PLATYGLOSSA

Habit Well-branched, fleshy-stemmed annual.
Flowers Daisy-like, to 2in (5cm) across, from
summer to autumn. Yellow with white tips,
around a deep golden-yellow disk.
Leaves Narrow, toothed, or cut. Gray-green.
• NATIVE HABITAT Meadows, California.
• CULTIVATION Grow in well-drained soil, in
a sunny site. Good for a mixed or annual border.
• PROPAGATION Sow seed *in situ* in spring
or autumn.
• OTHER NAME *L. elegans*.

HEIGHT
12–18in
(30–45cm)

SPREAD
10–12in
(25–30cm)

Compositae/Asteraceae	

GAZANIA 'Talent Yellow'

Habit Evergreen perennial, grown as an annual.
Flowers Solitary, daisy-like, 2⅜in (6cm) across,
from summer to autumn. Bright yellow.
Leaves Lance-shaped, felted. Mid-green.
• NATIVE HABITAT Garden origin.
• CULTIVATION Grow in light, sandy, well-
drained soil. Good for borders and containers.
One of the Talent Series.
• PROPAGATION Sow seed at 64–68°F (18–20°C)
in late winter or early spring. Also by basal
cuttings in late summer; overwinter under glass.

☀ ◊

Z 8–10

HEIGHT
10in (25cm)

SPREAD
10in (25cm)

Cruciferae/Brassicaceae	WALLFLOWER

ERYSIMUM CHEIRI 'Golden Bedder'

Habit Evergreen perennial, grown as a biennial.
Flowers Cross-shaped, fragrant, to 1in (2.5cm)
across, in short clusters, from spring. Golden-
yellow. *Leaves* Lance-shaped. Dark green.
• NATIVE HABITAT Garden origin.
• CULTIVATION Grow in fertile, well-drained,
alkaline soil, in sun. Good for spring bedding.
• PROPAGATION Sow seed in a seed bed between
late spring and early summer. One of the
Bedder Series.
• OTHER NAME *Cheiranthus cheiri* 'Golden Bedder'.

☀ ◊

Z 6–9

HEIGHT
9–12in
(23–30cm)

SPREAD
9in (23cm)

Cruciferae/Brassicaceae	WALLFLOWER

ERYSIMUM CHEIRI Fair Lady Series

Habit Evergreen perennials, grown as biennials.
Flowers Cross-shaped, fragrant, to 1in (2.5cm)
across, in short clusters, from spring. Pastel shades
of white, pink, salmon-pink, red, or yellow.
Leaves Lance-shaped. Dark green.
• NATIVE HABITAT Garden origin.
• CULTIVATION Grow in fertile, well-drained,
alkaline soil, in sun. Good for spring bedding.
• PROPAGATION Sow seed in a seed bed between
late spring and early summer.
• OTHER NAME *Cheiranthus cheiri* Fair Lady Series.

☀ ◊

Z 6–9

HEIGHT
12in (30cm)

SPREAD
10in (25cm)

Scrophulariaceae	

LINARIA RETICULATA 'Crown Jewels'

Habit Upright annual. *Flowers* Spurred,
irregularly 2-lipped, to ⅗in (1.5cm) long, in
tapering clusters, from late spring to summer.
Red, maroon, orange, or golden-yellow.
Leaves Narrow. Blue-green.
• NATIVE HABITAT Garden origin.
• CULTIVATION Grow in light, moderately fertile,
well-drained, preferably sandy soil, in sun.
Good as a filler in a mixed or herbaceous border.
• PROPAGATION Sow seed *in situ* in early spring.
May self-seed.

☀ ◊

HEIGHT
9in (23cm)

SPREAD
9in (23cm)

Amaranthaceae	PLUME COCKSCOMB

CELOSIA ARGENTEA 'Century Yellow'

Habit Vigorous, branching, bushy perennial, grown as an annual. *Flowers* Tiny, borne in dense, terminal, plume-like spikes, to 10in (25cm) long, from summer. Warm golden-yellow. *Leaves* Oval to lance-shaped. Pale green.
• NATIVE HABITAT Garden origin.
• CULTIVATION Grow in fertile, moist but well-drained soil, in a warm site in full sun, with shelter from strong winds. Suitable for summer bedding, and may also be grown as a short-term house- or greenhouse plant. The flowerheads are good for cutting and may be used in fresh or dried arrangements. Water thoroughly in prolonged dry periods. Under glass, use a soil-based potting mix. Provide good ventilation and admit full light, with some shade when in full bloom to prolong flowering. Water carefully and moderately and apply a balanced liquid fertilizer every two weeks when in full growth.
• PROPAGATION Sow seed at 64°F (18°C) between early and late spring.

Z 8–10

HEIGHT
18in (45cm)

SPREAD
12in (30cm)

PRIMULA

The genus *Primula* consists of some 400 species of fully hardy to frost-tender annuals, biennials, and perennials, some of which are evergreen. All have basal rosettes of leaves, and tubular, bell-shaped, or flat, primrose-like, flowers. The primulas that are grown as annuals and biennials include the half-hardy cultivars of *P. malacoides* and *P. obconica*, which are used primarily as houseplants. The most widely grown, however, are the hybrid primrose and polyanthus cultivars. Primrose cultivars bear short-stemmed flowers that nestle in the basal rosettes. Polyanthus cultivars, derived from *P. amoena*, *P. elatior*, *P. juliae*, *P. veris*, and *P. vulgaris*, produce flowers in long-stalked clusters on thick stems.

These two groups of cultivars both flower in spring or, if grown in a cold greenhouse, from winter to spring. Primrose and polyanthus cultivars are very diverse, and may be evergreen, semi-evergreen, or deciduous. They are also variable in hardiness, as some seed series are bred as house- or conservatory plants. Their cultivation requirements may be split into two groups, as follows:

Group 1 Grow in full sun or partial shade, in reliably moist but well-drained, moderately fertile soil.

Group 2 Grow in a cool greenhouse or as a houseplant, in a mix of 4 parts soil-based potting mix with one part each of grit and leaf mold. Admit bright filtered light. Water freely and apply a half-strength, balanced liquid fertilizer weekly when in growth.

Surface-sow seed in spring at 61°F (16°C). Set plants to be flowered outdoors in their flowering position in early autumn.

The plants tend to be susceptible to attacks by aphids, slugs, vine weevils, viruses, and grey mold (*Botrytis*).

P. OBCONICA
'Libre Mixed'
Habit Neat, rosette-forming perennial, grown as an annual.
Flowers Saucer-shaped, 1–2in (2.5–5cm) across, in whorls, from winter to spring. White, pink, red, blue, salmon, or apricot.
Leaves Coarse, oval, toothed. Mid-green.
• CULTIVATION 2.
• HEIGHT 12in (30cm).
• SPREAD 12in (30cm).

P. obconica
'Libre Mixed'

☼ ◑   Z 7–9

P. OBCONICA
'Appleblossom'
Habit Neat, rosette-forming perennial, grown as an annual.
Flowers Saucer-shaped, 1–2in (2.5–5cm) across, in whorls, from winter to spring. Pale pink, flushed salmon-pink.
Leaves Coarse, oval, toothed. Mid-green.
• CULTIVATION 2.
• HEIGHT 8in (20cm).
• SPREAD 10in (25cm).

P. obconica
'Appleblossom'

☼ ◑   Z 7–9

P. MALACOIDES
'Bright Eyes'
Habit Perennial, grown as an annual.
Flowers Single, ⅖in (1cm) across, in whorls, from winter to spring. White, pink, carmine, or purple, with yellow eye. Also in bicolors.
Leaves Oval, and downy. Pale green.
• CULTIVATION 2.
• HEIGHT 10in (25cm).
• SPREAD 8in (20cm).

P. malacoides
'Bright Eyes'

☼ ◑   Z 7–9

P. Cowichan Series
Habit Rosette-forming perennials, grown as biennials.
Flowers Saucer-shaped, 2in (5cm) across, velvety, borne from winter to spring. In red, purple, maroon, blue, or yellow.
Leaves Oval, strongly veined. Dark green.
• CULTIVATION 2.
• HEIGHT 12in (30cm).
• SPREAD 12in (30cm).

P. Cowichan Series
(Polyanthus)

☼ ◑   Z 5–9

P. Pacific Giants Mixed

Habit Rosette-forming, dwarf perennials, grown as biennials.
Flowers Saucer-shaped, borne freely from winter to spring. White, pink, red, blue, or yellow.
Leaves Oval. Mid-green.
• CULTIVATION 1.
• HEIGHT 6–12in (15–30cm).
• SPREAD 8in (20cm).

P. Pacific Giants Mixed
(Pacific Series)
(Polyanthus)
☼ ◊   Z 5–9

P. OBCONICA 'Cantata Lavender'

Habit Rosette-forming perennial, grown as an annual.
Flowers Saucer-shaped, 1in (2.5cm) across, in whorls, from winter to spring. White, pink, red, or lavender-blue.
Leaves Oval, coarse, toothed. Mid-green.
• CULTIVATION 2.
• HEIGHT 10in (25cm).
• SPREAD 10in (25cm).

P. obconica
'Cantata Lavender'
☼ ◊   Z 7–9

P. 'Dania'

Habit Rosette-forming perennial, grown as a biennial.
Flowers Saucer-shaped, 1in (2.5cm) across, borne in spring. Available in shades of pink, red, and gold, with some bicolors.
Leaves Lance-shaped, corrugated. Mid-green.
• CULTIVATION 2.
• HEIGHT 6in (15cm).
• SPREAD 8in (20cm).

P. 'Dania'
(Primrose)
☼ ◊   Z 7–9

P. Crescendo Series

Habit Rosette-forming perennials, grown as biennials.
Flowers Saucer-shaped, 1in (2.5cm) across, borne from winter to spring. Available in white, pink, red, yellow, or blue.
Leaves Oval, corrugated. Mid- to dark green.
• CULTIVATION 1 or 2.
• HEIGHT 6in (15cm).
• SPREAD 8in (20cm).

P. Crescendo Series
(Polyanthus)
☼ ◊   Z 7–9

P. Joker Series

Habit Rosette-forming perennials, grown as biennials.
Flowers Saucer-shaped, 1¼in (4.5cm) across, borne in spring. Varied colors, with a yellow eye. Also available in bicolors.
Leaves Lance-shaped, corrugated. Mid-green.
• CULTIVATION 2.
• HEIGHT 4in (10cm).
• SPREAD 8in (20cm).

P. Joker Series
(Primrose)
☼ ◊   Z 7–9

SALVIA

The *Salvia* genus consists of some 900 species of annuals, biennials, herbaceous evergreen perennials, and shrubs. *Salvia* plants bear upright, more or less interrupted spikes, or clusters, of 2-lipped flowers. The upper lip of each flower is erect and hooded, the lower lip more spreading. The flowers often have colorful tubular, bell- or funnel-shaped calyces, and conspicuous, leaf-like bracts.

The genus includes plants that are suitable for a diverse range of garden situations. They include cultivars of *S. coccinea* and *S. splendens*, which are, at best, short-lived as perennials, and are more usually grown as annuals. These cultivars flower freely and rapidly in their first year from seed, and provide brilliant color over long periods when used in bedding, as fillers in a mixed border, or in containers. Cultivars of the annual *S. viridis*, the annual clary, are suitable

for mixed borders, and are ideal for informal, cottage-garden style planting. They make good cut flowers that also dry well for winter arrangements. Cultivars and variants of *S. sclarea*, the biennial clary, are grown as biennials and bloom throughout summer into autumn, lending color to sunny, mixed, and herbaceous borders and other more informal situations.

Grow in light, moderately fertile, well-drained soil that is rich is organic matter, in full sun or light, dappled shade.

Sow seed of annuals in early to mid-spring at 64°F (18°C). Pinch out the growing tips when the young plants are 2–3in (5–8cm) tall, to encourage a bushy habit. Harden off and plant out when all danger of frost has passed. Sow seed of biennials in summer, *in situ*, or in containers in a cold frame. Plant out in their flowering site in autumn.

S. FARINACEA
'Alba'
Habit Upright, bushy, low-branching perennial, grown as an annual.
Flowers Tubular, hooded, 2-lipped, in long, dense, slender spikes, borne from summer to autumn. White.
Leaves Pointed, lance-shaped. Mid-green, with white, hairy underside.
• HEIGHT 24in (60cm).
• SPREAD 12in (30cm).

S. farinacea
'Alba'

 ☼ ◊   Z 8–9

S. COCCINEA
'Coral Nymph'
Habit Upright, bushy annual or perennial.
Flowers Hooded, 2-lipped, ⅘in (2cm) long, in slender, tiered spikes, borne from summer to autumn. Coral-pink.
Leaves Oval to heart-shaped, and hairy. Dark green.
• HEIGHT 16in (40cm).
• SPREAD 12in (30cm).

S. coccinea
'Coral Nymph'

 ☼ ◊   Z 8–9

S. SPLENDENS
Carabiniere Series
Habit Upright, bushy, early-flowering perennials, grown as annuals.
Flowers Hooded, 2-lipped, from summer to autumn. Pure white, and in single or mixed colors.
Leaves Oval, pointed, toothed. Dark green.
• HEIGHT 12in (30cm).
• SPREAD 10in (25cm).

S. splendens
Carabiniere Series

☼ ◊   Z 8–9

S. VIRIDIS
Habit Upright, bushy annual.
Flowers Tiny, enclosed in papery bracts, in whorled spikes, borne in summer. Pink to pale purple, with white, pink, or purple bracts.
Leaves Oval to paddle-shaped, hairy. Mid-green.
• OTHER NAME *S. horminum.*
• HEIGHT 20in (50cm).
• SPREAD 9in (23cm).

S. viridis
Annual clary

 ☼ ◊

S. SPLENDENS
Cleopatra Series
Habit Upright, bushy
perennials, grown
as annuals.
Flowers Hooded,
2-lipped, in dense
spikes, from summer
to autumn. White,
salmon-pink, red,
or purple.
Leaves Oval, pointed,
toothed. Fresh green.
• HEIGHT 12in (30cm).
• SPREAD 10in (25cm).

S. splendens
Cleopatra Series

 ☼ ◊   Z 8–9

S. SPLENDENS
'Carabiniere'
Habit Upright,
early-flowering, bushy
perennial, grown
as an annual.
Flowers Tubular,
hooded, 2-lipped, in
dense spikes, borne
from summer to
autumn. Scarlet.
Leaves Oval, pointed,
toothed. Dark green.
• HEIGHT 12in (30cm).
• SPREAD 10in (25cm).

S. splendens
'Carabiniere'
(Carabiniere Series)

☼ ◊   Z 8–9

S. SPLENDENS
Sizzler Series
Habit Upright,
bushy, early-flowering
perennials, grown
as annuals.
Flowers Hooded,
2-lipped, from summer
to autumn. White,
salmon, cerise, purple,
scarlet, or lavender-blue.
Leaves Oval, pointed,
toothed. Fresh green.
• HEIGHT 12in (30cm).
• SPREAD 10in (25cm).

S. splendens
Sizzler Series

☼ ◊   Z 8–9

S. VIRIDIS
'Claryssa'
Habit Compact, well-
branched, bushy annual.
Flowers Tiny, borne
in whorled spikes in
summer. Mixed or
single shades, enclosed
in white, rose-pink,
purple, or blue
papery bracts.
Leaves Oval to paddle-
shaped, hairy. Mid-green.
• HEIGHT 16in (40cm).
• SPREAD 9in (23cm).

S. viridis
'Claryssa'

☼ ◊

S. SPLENDENS
'Flare Path'
Habit Upright, bushy
perennial, grown as
an annual.
Flowers Hooded,
2-lipped, in dense
spikes, borne from
summer to autumn.
Scarlet.
Leaves Oval, pointed,
toothed. Fresh green.
• HEIGHT 12in (30cm).
• SPREAD 10–12in
(20–30cm).

S. splendens
'Flare Path'

☼ ◊   Z 8–9

S. SCLAREA var.
TURKESTANICA
Habit Branching
perennial or biennial.
Flowers Hooded,
2-lipped, spring to
summer. White,
flecked pink, with
lilac bracts on
pink stems.
Leaves Oval to narrow,
wrinkled, notched, or
toothed. Mid-green.
• HEIGHT 3ft (1m).
• SPREAD 12in (30cm).

S. sclarea var.
turkestanica

☼ ◊   Z 8–9

S. COCCINEA
'Lady in Red'
Habit Upright, bushy
annual or perennial.
Flowers Hooded,
2-lipped, ¾in (2cm)
long, in terminal, slender,
tiered spikes, borne
from summer to
autumn. Velvety-red.
Leaves Oval to heart-
shaped, and hairy.
Dark green.
• HEIGHT 16in (40cm).
• SPREAD 12in (30cm).

S. coccinea
'Lady in Red'

☼ ◊   Z 8–9

S. FARINACEA
'Victoria'
Habit Upright, bushy,
low-branching perennial,
grown as an annual.
Flowers Tubular,
hooded, 2-lipped, in
long, dense spikes,
from summer to
autumn. Deep blue.
Leaves Pointed, lance-
shaped. Mid-green
with white underside.
• HEIGHT 24in (60cm).
• SPREAD 12in (30cm).

S. farinacea
'Victoria'

☼ ◊   Z 8–9

VERBENA

A genus of some 250 species of annuals, perennials, and sub-shrubs, *Verbena* includes a large number of half-hardy, hybrid perennials, listed under *V.* x *hybrida*, that are best grown as annuals. These will not overwinter in frost-prone areas, and flower freely in their first year from seed. Cultivars of *V.* x *hybrida* are upright and bushy, or spreading and mat-forming, usually with rough, textured leaves. They are valued for their small, sometimes fragrant, saucer-shaped flowers, which grow up to 3in (8cm) or more across, in densely packed clusters. The flowers are available in a wide range of bright colors, and bloom throughout summer until the first frosts. *V.* x *hybrida* cultivars are ideal for summer bedding, edging, for an annual or mixed border, and for containers, including hanging baskets. The habit of *V.* x *hybrida* 'Imagination', which is sometimes found listed as

V. speciosa 'Imagination', is especially well suited to hanging baskets, and will spread to form a dense mound in open ground.

Grow in moist but well-drained, moderately fertile soil, in an open site in full sun. Water thoroughly during prolonged periods of warm, dry weather. In containers, use a soilless or soil-based potting mix with additional sharp sand. Water freely when in growth and apply a balanced liquid fertilizer regularly every 2–4 weeks.

Sow seed at 64–70°F (18–21°C) in late winter or early spring. Germination can be erratic and may take 14–21 days. Pinch out the growing tips of young plants to encourage a bushy habit. Harden off and plant out when danger of frost has passed.

Plants are susceptible to attacks from slugs, aphids, thrips, and leafhoppers, and may be affected by powdery mildew.

V. x *HYBRIDA*
**Novalis Series
(white)**
Habit Upright, bushy, compact perennial.
Flowers Long-tubed, saucer-shaped, to 3in (8cm) across, in rounded clusters, from summer to autumn. Pure white.
Leaves Oval to narrow, toothed, rough-textured. Mid-green.
• HEIGHT 10in (25cm).
• SPREAD 12in (30cm).

V. x *hybrida*
**Novalis Series
(white)**

☼ ◊   Z 8–9

V. x *HYBRIDA*
**'Peaches and
Cream'**
Habit Spreading, well-branched perennial.
Flowers Long-tubed, saucer-shaped, in clusters, 3in (8cm) wide, from summer to autumn. Orange-pink, creamy-yellow, or apricot.
Leaves Oval to narrow, rough. Mid-green.
• HEIGHT 18in (45cm).
• SPREAD 18in (45cm).

V. x *hybrida*
'Peaches and Cream'

☼ ◊   Z 8–9

V. x *HYBRIDA*
Romance Series
Habit Upright, bushy, compact perennials.
Flowers Long-tubed, saucer-shaped, borne in clusters, from summer to autumn. In shades of red, or blue-purple. Self-colored, with a white eye.
Leaves Oval to narrow, rough. Mid-green.
• HEIGHT 10in (25cm).
• SPREAD 12in (30cm).

V. x *hybrida*
Romance Series

☼ ◊   Z 8–9

V. x *HYBRIDA*
Sandy Series
Habit Upright, bushy, compact perennials.
Flowers Long-tubed, saucer-shaped, to 3in (8cm) wide, borne in clusters, from summer to autumn. White, rose-pink, magenta, or scarlet, some with a white eye.
Leaves Oval to narrow, rough. Mid-green.
• HEIGHT 10in (25cm).
• SPREAD 12in (30cm).

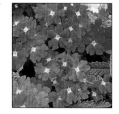

V. x *hybrida*
Sandy Series

☼ ◊   Z 8–9

V. × *HYBRIDA* 'Showtime'
Habit Upright, bushy, slow-growing perennial.
Flowers Long-tubed, saucer-shaped, borne in clusters, from summer to autumn. Available in a range of bright colors.
Leaves Oval to narrow, toothed, rough-textured. Mid-green.
• HEIGHT 10in (25cm).
• SPREAD 18in (45cm).

V. × *hybrida*
'Showtime'

☼ ◊   Z 8–9

V. × *HYBRIDA* 'Defiance'
Habit Upright, bushy, slow-growing perennial.
Flowers Long-tubed, saucer-shaped, in rounded clusters, borne from summer to autumn. Deep red, with a white eye.
Leaves Oval to narrow, toothed, rough-textured. Mid- to dark green.
• HEIGHT 8in (20cm).
• SPREAD 12in (30cm).

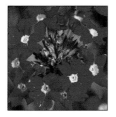

V. × *hybrida*
'Defiance'

☼ ◊   Z 8–9

V. × *HYBRIDA* 'Imagination'
Habit Mound-forming, spreading perennial.
Flowers Small, long-tubed, saucer-shaped, in long-stemmed clusters, from summer to autumn. Deep violet-blue.
Leaves Finely divided. Bright green.
• OTHER NAME
V. speciosa 'Imagination'.
• HEIGHT 12in (30cm).
• SPREAD 20in (50cm).

V. × *hybrida*
'Imagination'

☼ ◊   Z 8–9

V. × *HYBRIDA* 'Deep Blue with Eye'
Habit Upright, bushy, compact perennial.
Flowers Long-tubed, saucer-shaped, in rounded clusters, borne from summer to autumn. Blue, with a white eye.
Leaves Oval to narrow, toothed. Mid-green.
• HEIGHT 10in (25cm).
• SPREAD 12in (30cm).

V. × *hybrida*
'Deep Blue with Eye'
(Novalis Series)

☼ ◊   Z 8–9

Compositae/Asteraceae

OSTEOSPERMUM 'Salmon Queen'

Habit Upright, evergreen, sub-shrubby perennial, grown as an annual. *Flowers* Daisy-like, 2⅜in (6cm) across, borne freely from late spring to autumn. Available in pastel shades of salmon-pink or soft apricot-yellow, with a darker golden-brown central disk. *Leaves* Lance-shaped. Mid-green.
• NATIVE HABITAT Garden origin. The parent species occurs in grassland in southern Africa.
• CULTIVATION Grow in light, well-drained, moderately fertile soil, in a warm, sunny, sheltered site. Suitable for a mixed or annual border, for containers, for a dry, sunny bank, or the top of a dry-stone wall. The flowers are ideal for cutting. Deadhead regularly to prolong flowering. Plants will be truly perennial in areas with mild, frost-free winters.
• PROPAGATION By semi-ripe cuttings in late summer, as plants will not come true from seed. Overwinter young plants in frost-free conditions under glass, and set out in spring when danger of frost has passed.

☼ ◊

Z 8–10

HEIGHT
12in (30cm)

SPREAD
18in (45cm)

Papaveraceae	CALIFORNIA POPPY

ESCHSCHOLZIA CALIFORNICA
'Monarch Art Shades'

Habit Erect, mat-forming, well-branched annual.
Flowers Cup-shaped, semi-double or double,
2¼in (7cm) across, with frilled petals, from
summer. Cream, red, yellow, apricot, or orange.
Leaves Lance-shaped, finely cut. Grayish-green.
• NATIVE HABITAT Garden origin.
• CULTIVATION Grow in poor, light, well-
drained soil, in full sun. Good for cutting.
• PROPAGATION Sow seeds *in situ* in mid-
spring or autumn.

HEIGHT
12in (30cm)

SPREAD
6in (15cm)

Papaveraceae	CALIFORNIA POPPY

ESCHSCHOLZIA CALIFORNICA

Habit Mat-forming, well-branched annual.
Flowers Cup-shaped, single, 2¾in (7cm) across,
from summer. White, red, or yellow, but most
commonly available in orange. *Leaves* Lance-
shaped, finely cut. Grayish-green.
• NATIVE HABITAT Open grassland, from
Oregon to coastal California.
• CULTIVATION Grow in poor, light, well-
drained soil, in full sun. Good for cutting.
• PROPAGATION Sow seeds *in situ* in mid-
spring or autumn.

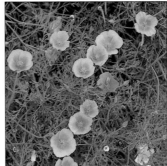

HEIGHT
12in (30cm)

SPREAD
6in (15cm)

Compositae/Asteraceae	FALSE SAFFRON

CARTHAMUS TINCTORIUS 'Goldtuft'

Habit Upright annual. *Flowers* Thistle-like, to
1⅝in (4cm) across, with tassel-like tufts of florets
in cupped, stiff bracts, borne in loose heads, from
summer. Golden-orange florets, with green bracts.
Leaves Oval or narrow, wavy-margined or
divided, spine-toothed. Grayish-green.
• NATIVE HABITAT Garden origin.
• CULTIVATION Grow in any light, well-drained
soil, in sun. Good for cutting and drying.
• PROPAGATION Sow seed at 50–59°F (10–15°C)
in spring.

HEIGHT
12–24in
(30–60cm)

SPREAD
12in (30cm)

Compositae/Asteraceae	MONARCH OF THE VELDT

ARCTOTIS FASTUOSA

Habit Spreading perennial, grown as an annual.
Flowers Daisy-like, from summer to autumn.
Orange, with a deep purple or black central disk.
Leaves Oval, deeply lobed, hairy. Silver-white.
• NATIVE HABITAT Dry stony soils. S. Africa.
• CULTIVATION Grow in light, moist but well-
drained soil, in a warm, sunny site. In cooler
climates, grow as a house- or conservatory plant.
• PROPAGATION Sow seed at 61–64°F (16–18°C)
in early spring. Also by stem cuttings at any time.
• OTHER NAME *Venidium fastuosum*.

Z 8–10

HEIGHT
12–24in
(30–60cm)

SPREAD
12in (30cm)

Compositae/Asteraceae	

URSINIA ANTHEMOIDES

Habit Bushy, upright annual. **Flowers** Daisy-like, solitary, to 2⅜in (6cm) across, from summer. Yellow-orange ray florets, zoned maroon or coppery purple beneath, around a purple-zoned disk. **Leaves** Finely cut, aromatic. Bright green.
• NATIVE HABITAT Dry savannah, S. Africa.
• CULTIVATION Grow in light, sandy, well-drained soil, in a warm, sunny site. Suitable as a filler in a mixed or herbaceous border. Good for cutting.
• PROPAGATION Sow seed at 55–64°F (13–18°C) in spring.

☀ ◊

HEIGHT
16in (40cm)

SPREAD
12in (30cm)

Cruciferae/Brassicaceae	WALLFLOWER

ERYSIMUM CHEIRI Bedder Series

Habit Compact, evergreen perennials, grown as biennials. **Flowers** Cross-shaped, fragrant, to 1in (2.5cm) across, in short clusters, from spring. Red, golden-yellow, primrose-yellow, or orange. **Leaves** Lance-shaped. Dark green.
• NATIVE HABITAT Garden origin.
• CULTIVATION Grow in fertile, well-drained, alkaline soil, in sun. Good for spring bedding.
• PROPAGATION Sow seed in a seed bed between late spring and early summer.
• OTHER NAME *Cheiranthus cheiri* Bedder Series.

☀ ◊

Z 6–9

HEIGHT
9–12in
(23–30cm)

SPREAD
10–12in
(25–30cm)

Amaranthaceae	

AMARANTHUS TRICOLOR 'Joseph's Coat'

Habit Bushy annual. **Flowers** Ornamentally insignificant, borne in clusters, from summer to early autumn. Red or green. **Leaves** Oval. Uppermost leaves, crimson and gold. Lower leaves, chocolate-brown, green, and yellow.
• NATIVE HABITAT Garden origin.
• CULTIVATION Grow in moist, fertile soil that is rich in organic matter, in a sheltered, sunny site. Ideal as bedding or as a short-term houseplant.
• PROPAGATION Sow seed at 68°F (20°C) in mid-spring.

☀ ◊

HEIGHT
to 18in
(45cm)

SPREAD
18in (45cm)

Scrophulariaceae	

CALCEOLARIA INTEGRIFOLIA 'Sunshine'

Habit Compact perennial, grown as a biennial.
Flowers Pouched, slipper-like, from summer.
Deep yellow. *Leaves* Lance-shaped. Mid-green.
• NATIVE HABITAT Garden origin.
• CULTIVATION Grow in light, slightly acid soil,
in sun or part-shade. Ideal for bedding or as
a houseplant. Under glass, grow in soil-based
potting mix, in bright, filtered light. Water freely.
• PROPAGATION By semi-ripe cuttings in
late summer.

Z 8–10

HEIGHT
8in (20cm)

SPREAD
8in (20cm)

Scrophulariaceae	

NEMESIA STRUMOSA Triumph Series

Habit Low-branching annuals. *Flowers*
Irregularly trumpet-shaped, 1in (2.5cm) across,
from mid- to late summer. Red, yellow, or
orange. *Leaves* Lance-shaped. Mid-green.
• NATIVE HABITAT Garden origin.
• CULTIVATION Grow in moderately fertile,
moist but well-drained, slightly acid soil, in
full sun. Good for bedding, for a mixed or
annual border, and for containers.
• PROPAGATION Sow seed at 59°F (15°C)
in spring.

HEIGHT
8in (20cm)

SPREAD
6in (15cm)

Tropaeolaceae	NASTURTIUM

TROPAEOLUM Alaska Series

Habit Compact, bushy annuals. *Flowers*
Funnel-shaped, single, to 2⅜in (6cm) across,
from summer to autumn. Cream, red, mahogany,
yellow, or orange. *Leaves* Rounded. Light green,
variegated creamy-white.
• NATIVE HABITAT Garden origin.
• CULTIVATION Grow in poor, light, well-drained
soil, in sun. Good for the front of a border and
for dry, sunny banks.
• PROPAGATION Sow seed at 55–61°F (13–16°C)
in early spring, or *in situ* in spring.

HEIGHT
12in (30cm)

SPREAD
18in (45cm)

Compositae/Asteraceae	POT MARIGOLD

CALENDULA OFFICINALIS 'Fiesta Gitana'

Habit Compact, bushy annual. *Flowers*
Daisy-like, double, to 4in (10cm) across, from
summer to autumn. Pastel yellow or orange.
Leaves Lance- to spoon-shaped. Bright green.
• NATIVE HABITAT Garden origin.
• CULTIVATION Grow in any well-drained soil,
in sun. Good for cutting, bedding, and
containers. Deadhead regularly.
• PROPAGATION Sow seed *in situ* in spring
or autumn.

HEIGHT
12in (30cm)

SPREAD
9in (23cm)

Compositae/Asteraceae	GLORIOSA DAISY

RUDBECKIA HIRTA 'Marmalade'

Habit Bushy perennial or biennial, grown as an annual. **Flowers** Daisy-like, from summer to autumn. Golden-orange, with a conical purple-brown disk. **Leaves** Oval to diamond-shaped. Mid-green.
• NATIVE HABITAT Garden origin.
• CULTIVATION Grow in fertile, moist, well-drained soil. Good for mixed borders or for cutting.
• PROPAGATION Sow seed at 61–64°F (16–18°C) in spring.
• OTHER NAME *R. gloriosa* 'Marmalade'.

☼ ◊

Z 3–7

HEIGHT
18in (45cm)

SPREAD
12in (30cm)

Papaveraceae	CALIFORNIA POPPY

ESCHSCHOLZIA CALIFORNICA (mixed)

Habit Mat-forming, well-branched annual. **Flowers** Cup-shaped, single, glossy, 3in (7cm) across, from summer. Shades of white, red, yellow, or orange. **Leaves** Lance-shaped, finely cut. Grayish-green.
• NATIVE HABITAT Open grassland, from Oregon to coastal California.
• CULTIVATION Grow in poor, light, well-drained soil, in full sun. Good for cutting.
• PROPAGATION Sow seeds *in situ* in mid-spring or autumn.

☼ ◊

HEIGHT
12in (30cm)

SPREAD
6in (15cm)

Cruciferae/Brassicaceae	WALLFLOWER

ERYSIMUM CHEIRI 'Orange Bedder'

Habit Compact, evergreen perennial, grown as a biennial. **Flowers** Cross-shaped, fragrant, in short clusters, from spring. Clear rich orange. **Leaves** Lance-shaped. Dark green.
• NATIVE HABITAT Garden origin.
• CULTIVATION Grow in fertile, well-drained, preferably alkaline soil, in sun. Good for spring bedding. One of the Bedder Series.
• PROPAGATION Sow seed in a seed bed between late spring and early summer.
• OTHER NAME *Cheiranthus cheiri* 'Orange Bedder'.

☼ ◊

Z 6–9

HEIGHT
9–12in
(23–30cm)

SPREAD
10–12in
(25–30cm)

Compositae/Asteraceae	

GAILLARDIA PULCHELLA 'Lollipops'

Habit Bushy, upright annual. **Flowers** Daisy-like, fully double, to 2in (5cm) across, from summer to autumn. Red and yellow. **Leaves** Lance-shaped. Gray-green.
• NATIVE HABITAT Garden origin.
• CULTIVATION Grow in fertile, well-drained soil, in sun. Good for a mixed or annual border, and as cut flowers. Deadhead regularly to prolong flowering.
• PROPAGATION Sow seed at 55–64°F (13–18°C) in early spring, or *in situ* in late spring.

☼ ◊

HEIGHT
12in (30cm)

SPREAD
12in (30cm)

Tropaeolaceae	NASTURTIUM

TROPAEOLUM Jewel Series
Habit Compact, bushy annuals. **Flowers**
Funnel-shaped, semi-double and double, from
early summer to autumn. Pink, scarlet, crimson,
or yellow. **Leaves** Rounded. Light green.
• NATIVE HABITAT Garden origin.
• CULTIVATION Grow in poor, light, well-drained
soil, in sun. Good for the front of a border and for
dry, sunny banks. Too rich a soil promotes leafy
growth which may obscure the flowers.
• PROPAGATION Sow seed at 55–61°F (13–16°C)
in early spring, or *in situ* in spring.

☀ ◊

HEIGHT
12in (30cm)

SPREAD
18in (45cm)

Compositae/Asteraceae	

BRACTEANTHA BRACTEATA
'Bright Bikini Mixed'
Habit Upright annual. **Flowers** Double, from
summer to autumn. White, pink, red, yellow,
or orange. **Leaves** Lance-shaped. Mid-green.
• NATIVE HABITAT Garden origin.
• CULTIVATION Grow in moist but well-drained,
moderately fertile soil, in full sun. Good for
cutting and drying, borders, and containers.
• PROPAGATION Sow seed at 64°F (18°C) in spring.
• OTHER NAME *Helichrysum bracteatum*
'Bright Bikini Mixed'.

☀ ◊

HEIGHT
12in (30cm)

SPREAD
12in (30cm)

Scrophulariaceae	

CALCEOLARIA 'Bright Bikinis'
Habit Compact biennials. **Flowers** Pouched,
slipper-like, in dense clusters, borne freely from
summer. Available in red, yellow, or orange.
Leaves Oval. Mid-green.
• NATIVE HABITAT Garden origin.
• CULTIVATION Grow in soil-based potting mix,
in bright, filtered light. Ideal as houseplants.
Water freely, and apply a balanced fertilizer
once every month.
• PROPAGATION Surface-sow seed at 64°F (18°C)
in late summer or spring.

☀ ◊

Z 8–10

HEIGHT
8in (20cm)

SPREAD
8in (20cm)

Onagraceae	

CLARKIA AMOENA Princess Series
(salmon)
Habit Slender, upright annual. **Flowers** Funnel-
shaped, with frilled, satiny petals, from summer.
Salmon-pink. **Leaves** Lance-shaped. Mid-green.
• NATIVE HABITAT Garden origin.
• CULTIVATION Grow in moist but well-drained,
moderately fertile soil, in sun or partial shade.
Ideal for cutting.
• PROPAGATION Sow *in situ* in spring or autumn.
• OTHER NAMES *Godetia amoena* Princess Series,
G. grandiflora Princess Series.

☀ ◊

HEIGHT
12in (30cm)

SPREAD
12in (30cm)

Cruciferae/Brassicaceae	WALLFLOWER

ERYSIMUM CHEIRI 'Fire King'

Habit Evergreen perennial, grown as a biennial.
Flowers Cross-shaped, fragrant, to 1in (2.5cm)
across, in short clusters, from spring. Fiery
orange-red. *Leaves* Lance-shaped. Dark green.
• NATIVE HABITAT Garden origin.
• CULTIVATION Grow in fertile, well-drained,
preferably alkaline soil, in sun. Ideally suited
for spring bedding. A reliable old cultivar.
• PROPAGATION Sow seed in a seed bed
between late spring and early summer.
• OTHER NAME *Cherianthus cheiri* 'Fire King'.

☼ ◊

Z 6–9

HEIGHT
15in (38cm)

SPREAD
12in (30cm)

Solanaceae	

CAPSICUM ANNUUM 'Holiday Time'

Habit Bushy, evergreen perennial, grown as
an annual. *Flowers* Star-shaped, from summer.
White or yellow. *Leaves* Oval. Mid-green. *Fruits*
Cone-shaped. Yellow, ripening to red in autumn.
• NATIVE HABITAT Garden origin.
• CULTIVATION Grow in fertile, well-drained soil
that is rich in organic matter, in full sun. Ideal
for window boxes and other containers, and as
a short-term house- or conservatory plant.
• PROPAGATION Sow seed at at 70°F (21°C) in
late winter.

☼ ◊

Z 8–10

HEIGHT
8–12in
(20–30cm)

SPREAD
8–12in
(20–30cm)

Solanaceae	

SOLANUM PSEUDOCAPSICUM 'Balloon'

Habit Evergreen shrub, grown as an annual.
Flowers Star-shaped, starting in summer. White.
Leaves Oval, wavy-margined. Dark green.
Fruits Round. Cream, ripening to orange.
• NATIVE HABITAT Garden origin.
• CULTIVATION In cool climates, grow as a
house- or conservatory plant in soilless or soil-
based potting mix, in indirect light. Use high-
potash fertilizer every 2 weeks. Water freely.
• PROPAGATION Sow seed at 64–68°F (18–20°C) in
spring. Also by semi-ripe cuttings in late summer.

☼ ◊

Z 8–10

HEIGHT
12in (30cm)

SPREAD
12–18in
(30–45cm)

Solanaceae	

SOLANUM PSEUDOCAPSICUM 'Red Giant'

Habit Evergreen shrub. *Flowers* Star-shaped,
starting in summer. *Leaves* Oval. Dark green.
Fruits Round, 1in (2.5cm) across. Orange-red.
• NATIVE HABITAT Garden origin.
• CULTIVATION In cool climates, grow as a
house- or conservatory plant in soilless or soil-
based potting mix, in indirect light. Use high-
potash fertilizer every 2 weeks. Water freely.
• PROPAGATION Sow seed at 64–68°F (18–20°C) in
spring. Also by semi-ripe cuttings in late summer.

☼ ◊

Z 8–10

HEIGHT
12in (30cm)

SPREAD
12in (30cm)

Amaranthaceae	PLUME COCKSCOMB

CELOSIA ARGENTEA
'Apricot Brandy'

Habit Bushy perennial, grown as an annual.
Flowers Tiny, in dense, terminal, plume-like spikes, to 10in (25cm) long, from summer. Deep orange. **Leaves** Oval to lance-shaped. Pale green.
• NATIVE HABITAT Garden origin.
• CULTIVATION Grow in fertile, moist but well-drained soil, in a warm, sheltered site. Suitable for summer bedding. Good for cutting and drying.
• PROPAGATION Sow seed at 64°F (18°C) between early and late spring.

☼ ◊

Z 8–10

HEIGHT
to 20in
(50cm)

SPREAD
12in (30cm)

Amaranthaceae	PLUME COCKSCOMB

CELOSIA ARGENTEA
'Fairy Fountains'

Habit Bushy perennial, grown as an annual.
Flowers Tiny, in plume-like spikes, to 6in (15cm) long, from summer. White, pink, red, or peach. **Leaves** Oval to lance-shaped. Pale green.
• NATIVE HABITAT Garden origin.
• CULTIVATION Grow in fertile, moist but well-drained soil, in a warm, sheltered site. Suitable for summer bedding. Good for cutting and drying.
• PROPAGATION Sow seed at 64°F (18°C) between early and late spring.

☼ ◊

Z 8–10

HEIGHT
16in (40cm)

SPREAD
12in (30cm)

Tropaeolaceae	NASTURTIUM

TROPAEOLUM
Whirlybird Series

Habit Compact, bushy annuals. **Flowers** Funnel-shaped, single to semi-double, from early summer to autumn. Cream, pink, scarlet, yellow, or orange. **Leaves** Rounded. Light green.
• NATIVE HABITAT Garden origin.
• CULTIVATION Grow in poor, light, well-drained soil, in sun. Good for the front of a border and for dry, sunny banks, and containers.
• PROPAGATION Sow seed at 55–61°F (13–16°C) in early spring, or *in situ* in spring.

☼ ◊

HEIGHT
10in (25cm)

SPREAD
14in (35cm)

Campanulaceae/ Lobeliaceae	

LOBELIA ERINUS 'Snowball'

Habit Bushy, compact perennial, grown as an annual. *Flowers* Tubular, 2-lipped, ⅜in (1cm) across, in loose clusters, borne from summer to autumn. Glistening white. *Leaves* Tiny, oval to grass-like, and glossy. Mid-green.
• NATIVE HABITAT Garden origin.
• CULTIVATION Grow in fertile, moist but well-drained soil, in sun or part-shade. Good for edging and containers.
• PROPAGATION Sow seed in late winter or early spring, at 55–64°F (13–18°C).

☼ ◊

Z 7–9

HEIGHT
6in (15cm)

SPREAD
6in (15cm)

Compositae/Asteraceae	FLOSS FLOWER

AGERATUM HOUSTONIANUM 'Hawaii White'

Habit Bushy, compact annual. *Flowers* Tiny, fluffy, in rounded plumes to 4in (10cm) across, from mid-summer to autumn. White. *Leaves* Oval, heart-shaped at the base, downy. Mid-green.
• NATIVE HABITAT Garden origin.
• CULTIVATION Grow in moist but well-drained soil. Good for bedding, edging, and containers.
• PROPAGATION Sow seed in early spring at 61–64°F (16–18°C), or sow in autumn, and overwinter young plants under glass at 50°F (10°C).

☼ ◊

HEIGHT
6in (15cm)

SPREAD
6–12in
(15–30cm)

Cruciferae/Brassicaceae	SWEET ALYSSUM

LOBULARIA MARITIMA 'Little Dorrit'

Habit Spreading, loosely branched annual. *Flowers* Small, scented, cross-shaped, in rounded clusters, 1in (2.5cm) or more across, borne in summer. White. *Leaves* Lance-shaped, sparsely hairy. Grayish-green.
• NATIVE HABITAT Garden origin.
• CULTIVATION Grows best in light soils. Ideal for edging, window boxes, and other containers.
• PROPAGATION Sow seed in early spring at 50–55°F (10–13°C), or *in situ* in late spring.
• OTHER NAME *Alyssum maritimum* 'Little Dorrit'.

☼ ◊

HEIGHT
4in (10cm)

SPREAD
8–10in
(20–30cm)

Boraginaceae	FORGET-ME-NOT

MYOSOTIS SYLVATICA 'Snowball'

Habit Rounded, compact biennial, or short-lived perennial. *Flowers* Small, saucer-shaped, ⅜in (9mm) across, in dense sprays, borne from spring to early summer. White, with a yellow eye. *Leaves* Oval or lance-shaped, and hairy. Mid-green.
• NATIVE HABITAT Garden origin.
• CULTIVATION Tolerates poor soil. Good in spring bedding, or wildflower and woodland gardens.
• PROPAGATION Sow seed *in situ* in spring, or sow in early summer in either a seed bed or containers in a cold frame.

☼ ◊

Z 7–9

HEIGHT
6in (15cm)

SPREAD
6in (15cm)

Cruciferae	VIOLET CRESS

IONOPSIDIUM ACAULE

Habit Compact, stemless annual. *Flowers* Small, scented, cross-shaped, borne in the leaf axils, from summer and early autumn. White with a blue flush, or violet. *Leaves* Rounded, oval, 3-lobed or entire, in basal rosettes. Mid-green.
• NATIVE HABITAT Portugal.
• CULTIVATION Grow in moist but well-drained soil in partial shade. May self-seed. Suitable for paving crevices, edging, and rock gardens.
• PROPAGATION Sow seed *in situ* in spring, summer and, in areas with mild winters, in autumn.

Z 7–9

HEIGHT
2–3in
(5–8cm)

SPREAD
1in (2.5cm)

Cruciferae/Brassicaceae	SWEET ALYSSUM

LOBULARIA MARITIMA
Easter Bonnet Series

Habit Very compact annuals. *Flowers* Scented, cross-shaped, in rounded clusters, from early summer to autumn. White, pink, or red-purple. *Leaves* Lance-shaped, hairy. Gray-green.
• NATIVE HABITAT Garden origin.
• CULTIVATION Ideal for edging and containers.
• PROPAGATION Sow seed in early spring at 50–55°F (10–13°C), or *in situ* in late spring.
• OTHER NAME *Alyssum maritimum*
Easter Bonnet Series.

HEIGHT
3–4in
(8–10cm)

SPREAD
4in (10cm)

Campanulaceae/ Lobeliaceae	

LOBELIA ERINUS 'Colour Cascade'

Habit Trailing perennial, grown as an annual. *Flowers* Tubular, 2-lipped, ⅜in (1cm) across, borne from summer to autumn. White, pink, carmine, red, violet, and blue, most with a white eye. *Leaves* Tiny, oval to grass-like. Mid-green.
• NATIVE HABITAT Garden origin.
• CULTIVATION Grow in fertile, moist but well-drained soil, in sun or part-shade. Good for hanging baskets and other containers.
• PROPAGATION Sow seed in late winter or early spring, at 55–64°F (13–18°C).

Z 7–9

HEIGHT
6in (15cm)

SPREAD
6in (15cm)

Compositae/Asteraceae	ENGLISH DAISY

BELLIS PERENNIS 'Goliath'

Habit Robust, rosette-forming perennial, grown as a biennial. *Flowers* Fully double, pompon-like, to 3in (8cm) across, borne from late winter to late summer. White, pink, red, and salmon. *Leaves* Lance- to spoon-shaped. Bright green.
• NATIVE HABITAT Garden origin.
• CULTIVATION Tolerates partial shade. Deadhead regularly. Suitable for bedding and edging.
• PROPAGATION Sow seed in a seed bed outdoors in early summer, or at 50–55°F (10–13°C) in early spring. Divide after flowering.

Z 4–9

HEIGHT
8in (20cm)

SPREAD
8in (20cm)

Compositae/Asteraceae	ENGLISH DAISY

BELLIS PERENNIS Carpet Series

Habit Compact, rosette-forming perennials, grown as biennials. *Flowers* Double, pompon-like, 1–2in (2.5–5cm) across, from late winter to late summer. White, pink, or red. *Leaves* Lance-shaped to spoon-shaped, glossy. Bright green.
• NATIVE HABITAT Garden origin.
• CULTIVATION Tolerates partial shade. Dead-head regularly. Suitable for bedding and edging.
• PROPAGATION Sow seed in a seed bed outdoors in early summer, or at 50–55°F (10–13°C) in early spring. Divide after flowering.

☀ ◊

Z 4–9

HEIGHT
6in (15cm)

SPREAD
6in (15cm)

Aizoaceae	

DOROTHEANTHUS BELLIDIFORMIS Magic Carpet Series

Habit Low-growing annuals. *Flowers* Solitary, daisy-like, to 1⅜in (4cm) across, from summer. White, cream, pink, purple, or orange.
Leaves Fleshy, oval to spoon-shaped. Light green.
• NATIVE HABITAT Garden origin.
• CULTIVATION Grow in poor, sharply drained soil.
• PROPAGATION Sow seed at 61–66°F (16–19°C) in late winter or early spring.
• OTHER NAME *Mesembryanthemum criniflorum* Magic Carpet Series.

☀ ◊

HEIGHT
6in (15cm)

SPREAD
12in (30cm)

Polemoniaceae	

PHLOX DRUMMONDII 'Bright Eyes'

Habit Compact, dense, free-flowering annual.
Flowers Saucer-shaped, 1in (2.5cm) across, from early summer to autumn. Pink with a contrasting eye, also available in a mixture of colors.
Leaves Narrowly lance-shaped to oval, stalkless. Mid-green.
• NATIVE HABITAT Garden origin.
• CULTIVATION Grow in fertile, well-drained soil, in sun. Ideal for bedding and edging.
• PROPAGATION Sow seed in early spring at 55–64°F (13–18°C) or *in situ* in spring.

☀ ◊

HEIGHT
4in (10cm)

SPREAD
8in (20cm)

Boraginaceae	FORGET-ME-NOT

MYOSOTIS SYLVATICA 'Victoria Rose'

Habit Rounded, compact biennial, or short-lived perennial. *Flowers* Small, saucer-shaped, ⅜in (9mm) across, from spring to early summer. Bright rose-pink, with a yellow eye.
Leaves Oval to lance-shaped, hairy. Mid-green.
• NATIVE HABITAT Garden origin.
• CULTIVATION Tolerates poor soil. Good for spring bedding and containers.
• PROPAGATION Sow seed *in situ* in spring, or in early summer in a seed bed or cold frame.

☀ ◊

Z 7–9

HEIGHT
4in (10cm)

SPREAD
4in (10cm)

Compositae/Asteraceae	ENGLISH DAISY

BELLIS PERENNIS 'Pomponette'

Habit Compact, rosette-forming perennial, grown as a biennial. *Flowers* Fully double, pompon-like, 1⅝in (4cm) across, with quilled petals, borne from late winter to late summer. White, pink, and red. *Leaves* Lance- to spoon-shaped. Bright green.
• NATIVE HABITAT Garden origin.
• CULTIVATION Suitable for bedding and edging. Tolerates partial shade. Deadhead regularly.
• PROPAGATION Sow seed in a seed bed outdoors in early summer, or at 50–55°F (10–13°C) in early spring. Divide after flowering.

☼ ◊

Z 4–9

HEIGHT
4–6in
(10–15cm)

SPREAD
4–6in
(10–15cm)

Polemoniaceae	

PHLOX DRUMMONDII 'Chanal'

Habit Compact, spreading, free-flowering annual. *Flowers* Saucer-shaped, 1in (2.5cm) across, in sprays, borne freely from summer to autumn. Clear, soft pink. *Leaves* Variable, ranging from oval to lance-shaped, stalkless. Mid-green.
• NATIVE HABITAT Garden origin.
• CULTIVATION Grow in fertile, well-drained soil, in sun. Well suited for bedding and edging.
• PROPAGATION Sow seed in early spring at 55–64°F (13–18°C).

☼ ◊

HEIGHT
6–8in
(15–20cm)

SPREAD
6–10in
(15–25cm)

Amaranthaceae	GLOBE AMARANTH

GOMPHRENA GLOBOSA 'Buddy'

Habit Bushy, upright annual. *Flowers* Tiny, in oval heads, to 1½in (3.5cm) across, borne on strong stems, from summer to autumn. Bright purple. *Leaves* Oval to paddle-shaped, densely hairy when young. Grayish-green.
• NATIVE HABITAT Garden origin.
• CULTIVATION Grow in moderately fertile, well-drained soil, in sun. Good for cutting and drying and for border edges.
• PROPAGATION Sow seed at 59–64°F (15–18°C) in early spring.

☼ ◊

HEIGHT
6in (15cm)

SPREAD
8in (20cm)

Cruciferae/Brassicaceae	SWEET ALYSSUM

LOBULARIA MARITIMA 'Wonderland Rose'

Habit Compact annual. *Flowers* Scented, cross-shaped, in rounded clusters, 1in (2.5cm) across, from early summer to autumn. Rose-pink. *Leaves* Lance-shaped, sparsely hairy. Gray-green.
• NATIVE HABITAT Garden origin.
• CULTIVATION Ideal for edging and containers.
• PROPAGATION Sow seed in early spring at 50–55°F (10–13°C), or *in situ* in late spring.
• OTHER NAME *Alyssum maritimum* 'Wonderland Rose'.

☼ ◊

HEIGHT
6in (15cm)

SPREAD
8in (20cm)

Polemoniaceae	

PHLOX DRUMMONDII Cecily Series

Habit Narrowly upright, free-flowering annuals.
Flowers Saucer-shaped, 1in (2.5cm) across,
borne from summer to autumn. Shades of white,
pink, red, purple, or blue, most with contrasting
centers. *Leaves* Narrowly lance-shaped to
oval, stalkless. Mid-green.
• NATIVE HABITAT Garden origin.
• CULTIVATION Grow in fertile, well-drained
soil, in sun. Ideal for bedding and edging.
• PROPAGATION Sow seed in early spring
at 55–64°F (13–18°C).

HEIGHT
6in (15cm)

SPREAD
4in (10cm)

Polemoniaceae	

PHLOX DRUMMONDII 'Sternenzauber'

Habit Compact, free-flowering annual. *Flowers*
Star-shaped, ⅘in (2cm) across, with pointed and
fringed petals, from summer to autumn. Many
shades of pink, including picotees. *Leaves*
Narrowly lance-shaped to oval. Pale green.
• NATIVE HABITAT Garden origin.
• CULTIVATION Grow in fertile, well-drained soil
in sun. Ideal for bedding, edging, and containers.
• PROPAGATION Sow seed in early spring at
55–64°F (13–18°C).
• OTHER NAME *P. drummondii* 'Twinkle'.

HEIGHT
6in (15cm)

SPREAD
4in (10cm)

Campanulaceae/ Lobeliaceae	

LOBELIA ERINUS 'Red Cascade'

Habit Trailing perennial, grown as an annual.
Flowers Tubular, 2-lipped, ⅜in (1cm) across,
from summer to autumn. Deep carmine-red to
purple-red, with a white eye. *Leaves* Tiny,
oval to grass-like. Mid-green.
• NATIVE HABITAT Garden origin.
• CULTIVATION Grow in fertile, moist but
well-drained soil, in sun or part-shade. Good
for hanging baskets and other containers.
• PROPAGATION Sow seed in late winter or
early spring, at 55–64°F (13–18°C).

HEIGHT
6in (15cm)

SPREAD
6in (15cm)

Portulacaceae	

PORTULACA GRANDIFLORA 'Cloudbeater'

Habit Fleshy, spreading annual. *Flowers* Cup-shaped, double, 1¾in (4.5cm) across, satin-textured, borne throughout summer. Magenta, with a yellow center. *Leaves* Cylindrical, fleshy. Bright green.
• NATIVE HABITAT Garden origin.
• CULTIVATION Grows best in poor, light, sandy soil. Good for window boxes and other containers, dry, sunny banks, and the tops of dry walls.
• PROPAGATION Sow seed at 55–64°F (13–18°C) in mid-spring.

HEIGHT
4–6in
(10–15cm)

SPREAD
6in (15cm)

Portulacaceae	

PORTULACA GRANDIFLORA Sundance Hybrids

Habit Spreading, semi-trailing annuals. *Flowers* Cup-shaped, semi-double or double, satiny, from summer to early autumn. White, red, yellow, or orange. *Leaves* Cylindrical, fleshy. Bright green.
• NATIVE HABITAT Garden origin.
• CULTIVATION Grows best in poor, light, sandy soil. Good for window boxes, dry, sunny banks, and the tops of dry walls.
• PROPAGATION Sow seed at 55–64°F (13–18°C) in mid-spring.

HEIGHT
6in (15cm)

SPREAD
6in (15cm)

Polemoniaceae	

PHLOX DRUMMONDII 'African Sunset'

Habit Compact, dense, free-flowering annual. *Flowers* Saucer-shaped, 1in (2.5cm) across, borne from early summer to autumn. Available in intense shades of red, with a white eye. *Leaves* Variable, from narrowly lance-shaped to oval, stalkless. Mid-green.
• NATIVE HABITAT Garden origin.
• CULTIVATION Grow in fertile, well-drained soil, in sun. Ideal for bedding and edging.
• PROPAGATION Sow seed in early spring at 55–64°F (13–18°C) or *in situ* in spring.

HEIGHT
4in (10cm)

SPREAD
8in (20cm)

VIOLA

The *Viola* genus comprises some 500 species of annuals, biennials, evergreen, semi-evergreen or deciduous perennials, and a few deciduous sub-shrubs.

The garden pansies described here are all cultivars of *V. x wittrockiana* and are the products of complex cross-breeding involving *V. altaica*, *V. cornuta*, *V. lutea*, and *V. tricolor*. Pansies have short-spurred flowers, with the lateral petals overlapping the upper and lower petals to give a rounded, flat-faced flower, 2⅜–4in (6–10cm) across. In some cultivars, the flowers are unmarked and self-colored, but, more often, they have dark hair-streaks, or blotches, on the lower petals that form the characteristic face-like markings. Although truly perennial and fully hardy, the garden cultivars are usually grown as biennials or annuals, because they tend to develop a leggy habit and produce fewer flowers with age.

Most pansies bloom from spring to early summer, but some flower from autumn to winter. A few, usually smaller-flowered, cultivars have been bred specially for winter- and early spring-flowering, and some of these, such as the Universal Series, can be used for summer or winter-flowering. Pansies are ideal for containers and for summer or winter bedding. They last well in water when cut, and are ideal for miniature arrangements.

Grow in fertile, moist, well-drained soil rich in organic matter, in sun or partial shade. Deadhead to prolong flowering.

Sow seed in containers in a cold frame, in late winter or early spring for summer-flowering, or in summer for winter-flowering.

Slugs, snails, and aphids may damage plants. Pansies may also be affected by powdery mildew, leaf spot, mosaic viruses, and rust.

V. 'Love Duet'
Habit Compact perennial grown as an annual or biennial.
Flowers To 2⅜in (6cm) across, borne in summer. Creamy-white, with a raspberry-pink to mahogany blotch.
Leaves Oval to heart-shaped, lobed, shiny. Mid-green.
• HEIGHT 6in (15cm).
• SPREAD 10in (25cm).

V. 'Love Duet'

☼ ◊   Z 7–9

V. Floral Dance Series
Habit Compact, grown as annuals or biennials.
Flowers To 2–2¾in (5–7cm) across, borne in winter to spring or summer. White, red, purple, blue, or yellow, with some bicolors.
Leaves Oval to heart-shaped. Mid-green.
• HEIGHT 6–9in (15–23cm).
• SPREAD 10in (25cm).

V. Floral Dance Series

☼ ◊   Z 7–9

V. Imperial Series
Habit Compact perennials grown as annuals or biennials.
Flowers To 2¾in (7cm) across, borne in winter to early spring, or summer. Varied colors.
Leaves Oval to heart-shaped, lobed, shiny. Mid-green.
• HEIGHT 6–9in (15–23cm).
• SPREAD 10in (25cm).

V. Imperial Series

☼ ◊   Z 7–9

V. 'Rippling Waters'
Habit Compact perennial grown as an annual or biennial.
Flowers To 2⅜in (6cm) across, borne in summer. Maroon, with white petal margins.
Leaves Oval to heart-shaped, lobed, shiny. Mid-green.
• HEIGHT 6–9in (15–23cm).
• SPREAD 10in (25cm).

V. 'Rippling Waters'

☼ ◊   Z 7–9

V. 'Roggli Giants'

Habit Bushy, vigorous, grown as annuals or biennials.
Flowers To 4in (10cm) across, borne from summer to autumn. Varied colors, most marked with dark blotches.
Leaves Oval to heart-shaped. Mid-green.
• HEIGHT 8in (20cm).
• SPREAD 8in (20cm).

V. 'Roggli Giants'

☼ ◊   Z 7–9

V. Joker Series

Habit Compact, grown as annuals or biennials.
Flowers To 2¾in (7cm) across, borne in summer. Bicolored, with marked faces, in mahogany, violet, pale blue, and gold.
Leaves Oval to heart-shaped. Mid-green.
• HEIGHT 6–9in (15–23cm).
• SPREAD 10in (25cm).

V. Joker Series

☼ ◊   Z 7–9

V. Princess Series

Habit Neat, very compact, grown as annuals or biennials.
Flowers To 2–2¾in (5–6cm) across, borne in spring and summer. Cream, purple, blue, or yellow, some bicolors.
Leaves Oval to heart-shaped. Mid-green.
• HEIGHT 5–8in (12–20cm).
• SPREAD 8in (20cm).

V. Princess Series

☼ ◊   Z 7–9

V. 'Azure Blue'

Habit Neat, very compact, grown as an annual or biennial.
Flowers To 2–2¾in (5–6cm) across, borne freely in spring. Azure-blue, with unmarked florets.
Leaves Oval to heart-shaped. Mid-green.
• HEIGHT 6–8in (15–20cm).
• SPREAD 8in (20cm).

V. 'Azure Blue'

☼ ◊   Z 7–9

V. Universal Series (blue)

Habit Compact, grown as an annual or biennial.
Flowers To 2¾in (7cm) across, borne from winter to early spring, or summer. Blue, some patterned bicolors.
Leaves Oval to heart-shaped. Mid-green.
• HEIGHT 6–9in (15–23cm).
• SPREAD 10in (25cm).

V. Universal Series (blue)

☼ ◊   Z 7–9

V. Crystal Bowl Series (primrose)

Habit Compact perennial, grown as an annual or biennial. Hot weather-resistant.
Flowers To 2⅜in (6cm) across, borne in summer. Warm, clear yellow.
Leaves Oval to heart-shaped, lobed, shiny. Mid-green.
• HEIGHT 6in (15cm).
• SPREAD 6in (15cm).

V. Crystal Bowl Series (primrose)

☼ ◊   Z 7–9

V. Crystal Bowl Series (yellow)

Habit Compact perennial, grown as an annual or biennial. Hot weather-resistant.
Flowers To 2⅜in (6cm) across, borne from summer. Yellow.
Leaves Oval to heart-shaped, lobed, shiny. Mid-green.
• HEIGHT 6in (15cm).
• SPREAD 6in (15cm).

V. Crystal Bowl Series (yellow)

☼ ◊   Z 7–9

V. Clear Crystals Series

Habit Compact, grown as annuals or biennials.
Flowers To 2in (5cm) across, borne freely throughout summer. Clear white, yellow, orange, red, or violet.
Leaves Oval to heart-shaped, lobed, shiny. Mid-green.
• HEIGHT 8in (20cm).
• SPREAD 8in (20cm).

V. Clear Crystals Series

☼ ◊   Z 7–9

V. Icequeen Series

Habit Compact, bushy, grown as annuals or biennials.
Flowers Neat, to 2¾in (7cm) across, borne from winter to early spring. Varied clear, bright colors, all with dark central blotches.
Leaves Oval to heart-shaped. Mid-green.
• HEIGHT 4½in (12cm).
• SPREAD 6in (15cm).

V. Icequeen Series

☼ ◊   Z 7–9

V. 'Super Chalon Giants'

Habit Bushy perennial, grown as an annual or biennial.
Flowers To 4in (10cm) across, with ruffled, marked, blotched petals, from summer to autumn. Deep colors, white, also some bicolors.
Leaves Oval to heart-shaped. Mid-green.
• HEIGHT 8in (20cm).
• SPREAD 8in (20cm).

V. 'Super Chalon Giants'

☼ ◊   Z 7–9

V. 'Redwing'

Habit Compact, grown as an annual or biennial.
Flowers To 2⅜–3in (6–8cm) across, with dark marks. Bicolored, in chocolate-brown and golden-yellow.
Leaves Oval to heart-shaped, lobed, glossy. Mid-green.
• HEIGHT 6–8in (15–20cm).
• SPREAD 8in (20cm).

V. 'Redwing'

☼ ◊   Z 7–9

V. Universal Series (yellow)

Habit Compact, grown as an annual or biennial.
Flowers To 2¾in (7cm) across, from winter to early spring, or summer. Yellow, some bicolors.
Leaves Oval to heart-shaped. Mid-green.
• HEIGHT 6–9in (15–23cm).
• SPREAD 10in (25cm).

V. Universal Series (yellow)

☼ ◊   Z 7–9

V. Universal Series (apricot)

Habit Compact, grown as an annual or biennial.
Flowers To 2¾in (7cm) across, from winter to early spring, or summer. Apricot, some bicolors.
Leaves Oval to heart-shaped. Mid-green.
• HEIGHT 6–9in (15–23cm).
• SPREAD 10in (25cm).

V. Universal Series (apricot)

☼ ◊   Z 7–9

V. 'Scarlet Clan'

Habit Compact, grown as an annual or biennial.
Flowers To 2⅜–3in (6–8cm) across, borne in summer. Orange-yellow, with a deep scarlet central blotch.
Leaves Oval to heart-shaped, lobed, glossy. Mid-green.
• HEIGHT 6–8in (15–20cm).
• SPREAD 8in (20cm).

V. 'Scarlet Clan'

☼ ◊   Z 7–9

V. 'Padparadja'

Habit Compact, grown as an annual or biennial.
Flowers To 2⅜–3in (6–8cm) across, borne in spring and summer. Intense, deep orange.
Leaves Oval to heart-shaped, lobed, glossy. Mid-green.
• HEIGHT 6in (15cm).
• SPREAD 6in (15cm).

V. 'Padparadja'

☼ ◊   Z 7–9

Campanulaceae	BLUE CALICO FLOWER

DOWNINGIA ELEGANS

Habit Fleshy, trailing or mat-forming annual.
Flowers Lobelia-like, 2-lipped, borne throughout summer. White, pink, purple, or blue, with a white eye. **Leaves** Lance-shaped. Mid-green.
• NATIVE HABITAT Damp ditches and seasonally wet areas, Washington State to California.
• CULTIVATION Grow in damp or well-drained soil, in sun or part-shade. Good for hanging baskets and other containers.
• PROPAGATION Sow seed in late winter at 55–61°F (13–16°C) or *in situ* in spring.

☀ ◊

HEIGHT
6in (15cm)

SPREAD
6in (15cm)

Crassulaceae	

SEDUM CAERULEUM

Habit Fleshy, branching, spreading annual.
Flowers Star-shaped, in plumes, borne throughout summer. Pale blue. **Leaves** Oval or spoon-shaped. Pale green, becoming red-flushed with age.
• NATIVE HABITAT Dry and rocky places, Corsica, Sardinia, Tunisia, and Algeria.
• CULTIVATION Grows best in poor, light soil. Good for dry banks and dry sunny borders. May self-seed.
• PROPAGATION Sow seed in early spring at 55–61°F (13–16°C) or *in situ* in spring.

☀ ◊

HEIGHT
4–6in
(10–15cm)

SPREAD
6in (15cm)

Campanulaceae/ Lobeliaceae	

LOBELIA ERINUS 'Sapphire'

Habit Trailing perennial, grown as an annual.
Flowers Tubular, 2-lipped, ⅜in (1cm) across, borne from summer to autumn. Bright sapphire-blue, with a white eye. **Leaves** Tiny, oval to grass-shaped. Mid-green.
• NATIVE HABITAT Garden origin.
• CULTIVATION Grow in fertile, moist but well-drained soil, in sun or part-shade. Good for hanging baskets and other containers.
• PROPAGATION Sow seed in late winter or early spring, at 55–64°F (13–18°C).

☀ ◊

HEIGHT
6in (15cm)

SPREAD
4–6in
(10–15cm)

Compositae/Asteraceae	FLOSS FLOWER

AGERATUM HOUSTONIANUM 'Blue Danube'

Habit Bushy, compact annual. **Flowers** Tiny, fluffy, in rounded clusters, from early summer to autumn. Lavender-blue. **Leaves** Oval, heart-shaped at the base, downy. Mid-green.
• NATIVE HABITAT Garden origin.
• CULTIVATION Grow in moist but well-drained soil. Good for bedding, edging, and containers.
• PROPAGATION Sow seed in early spring at 61–64°F (16–18°C), or sow in autumn and overwinter under glass at 50°F (10°C).

☀ ◊

HEIGHT
6–7½in
(15–18cm)

SPREAD
6–7½in
(15–18cm)

Cruciferae/Brassicaceae	

HELIOPHILA CORONOPIFOLIA

Habit Slender, branching annual.
Flowers Cross-shaped, 4-petaled, from spring to summer. White, pink, or pale to bright blue. **Leaves** Divided into narrow leaflets. Mid-green.
• NATIVE HABITAT Western Cape, S. Africa.
• CULTIVATION Grow in fertile, well-drained soil, in a sheltered site. Good for containers, and ideal for bedding.
• PROPAGATION Sow seed *in situ* between spring and early summer for successional flowering.
• OTHER NAME *H. longifolia.*

☼: ◊

HEIGHT
8in (20cm)

SPREAD
20in (50cm)

Boraginaceae	FORGET-ME-NOT

MYOSOTIS SYLVATICA 'Blue Ball'

Habit Rounded, compact biennial, or short-lived perennial. **Flowers** Small, saucer-shaped, ⅜in (9mm) across, in dense plumes, from spring to early summer. Azure-blue, with a yellow eye. **Leaves** Oval or lance-shaped, hairy. Mid-green.
• NATIVE HABITAT Garden origin.
• CULTIVATION Tolerates poor soil. Good in spring bedding, or wildflower and woodland gardens.
• PROPAGATION Sow seed *in situ* in spring. Alternatively, sow in early summer in a seed bed, or in containers in a cold frame.

☼: ◊

Z 7–9

HEIGHT
6in (15cm)

SPREAD
6in (15cm)

Compositae/Asteraceae	

FELICIA HETEROPHYLLA 'The Blues'

Habit Mat-forming annual. **Flowers** Solitary, daisy-like, ¾in (2cm) across, borne in summer. Pale blue, with blue disk florets. **Leaves** Lance-shaped, sometimes toothed. Gray-green.
• NATIVE HABITAT Garden origin. Species occurs in dry, sunny habitats in S. Africa.
• CULTIVATION Grow in light, well-drained soil, in sun. Tolerates poor soils. Good for bedding, window boxes, and other containers.
• PROPAGATION Sow seed at a temperature of 50–64°F (10–18°C) in spring.

☼: ◊

HEIGHT
4in (10cm)

SPREAD
12in (30cm)

Campanulaceae/ Lobeliaceae	

LOBELIA ERINUS 'Crystal Palace'

Habit Bushy, compact perennial, grown as an annual. **Flowers** Tubular, 2-lipped, ⅜in (1cm) across, in loose clusters, borne from summer to autumn. Deep blue. **Leaves** Tiny, oval to grass-like, glossy. Dark bronzed green.
• NATIVE HABITAT Garden origin.
• CULTIVATION Grow in fertile, moist but well-drained soil, in sun or partial shade. Good for edging and containers.
• PROPAGATION Sow seed in late winter or early spring, at 55–64°F (13–18°C).

☼: ◊

Z 7–9

HEIGHT
4in (10cm)

SPREAD
4–6in
(10–15cm)

Papaveraceae	CALIFORNIAN POPPY, CREAM CUPS

PLATYSTEMON CALIFORNICUS

Habit Spreading, well-branched annual.
Flowers Single, poppy-like, 1in (2.5cm) across, on slender stems, from summer. Creamy-yellow.
Leaves Narrow to lance-shaped, densely hairy. Gray-green.
• NATIVE HABITAT Grassland, chaparral, and desert margins, California, Arizona, and Utah.
• CULTIVATION Grow in poor, light soil, in full sun. Dislikes humid conditions. Good for a dry border or sunny bank.
• PROPAGATION Sow seed *in situ* in spring.

☀ ◊

HEIGHT
4–12in
(10–30cm)

SPREAD
9in (23cm)

Limnanthaceae	POACHED EGG PLANT

LIMNANTHES DOUGLASII

Habit Upright to spreading annual.
Flowers Scented, shallowly cup-shaped, 1in (2.5cm) across, borne freely throughout summer. White, with a yellow center. **Leaves** Fleshy, finely divided, and finely toothed. Bright yellow-green.
• NATIVE HABITAT Damp habitats, California to Oregon.
• CULTIVATION Grow in moist but well-drained soil. Good for a border front or edging. Self-sows freely.
• PROPAGATION Sow seed *in situ* in spring or autumn.

☀ ◊

HEIGHT
6in (15cm)

SPREAD
6in (15cm)

Compositae/Asteraceae	FEVERFEW

TANACETUM PARTHENIUM
'Golden Moss'

Habit Short-lived, carpet-forming perennial, grown as an annual. **Flowers** Daisy-like, to 1in (2.5cm) across, in dense clusters, borne in summer. White, with yellow disk florets. **Leaves** Moss-like, finely divided, aromatic. Yellow-green.
• NATIVE HABITAT Garden origin.
• CULTIVATION Grow in any well-drained soil. Good for a herb garden or edging. May self-seed.
• PROPAGATION Sow seed at 50–55°F (10–13°C) in late winter or early spring, or sow *in situ* in spring.

☀ ◊

Z 4–9

HEIGHT
4in (10cm)

SPREAD
to 12in
(30cm)

Papaveraceae	

ESCHSCHOLZIA CAESPITOSA

Habit Tufted annual. **Flowers** Fragrant, single, shallowly cup-shaped, 1⅕–2in (3–5cm) across, with 4 fine-textured petals, borne in summer. Bright yellow. **Leaves** Finely divided into thread-like segments. Mid-green.
• NATIVE HABITAT Open grasslands, central California.
• CULTIVATION Grows best in poor soils. Ideal for gravel plantings or in an annual border.
• PROPAGATION Sow seed *in situ* during mid-spring or early autumn.

☀ ◊

HEIGHT
6in (15cm)

SPREAD
6in (15cm)

Compositae/Asteraceae		Aizoaceae

CHRYSANTHEMUM MULTICAULE
'Moonlight'

Habit Bushy, freely branched annual.
Flowers Daisy-like, 1¾in (4.5cm) across,
borne throughout summer. Clear pale yellow.
Leaves Fleshy, coarsely toothed. Blue-gray.
• NATIVE HABITAT Garden origin.
• CULTIVATION Grow in well-drained,
moderately fertile soil, in sun. Good for bedding,
edging, window boxes, and other containers.
• PROPAGATION Sow seed in early spring at
55–61°F (13–16°C), or *in situ* in mid-spring.

DOROTHEANTHUS BELLIDIFORMIS
'Lunette'

Habit Low-growing annual. **Flowers** Solitary,
daisy-like, to 1⅜in (4cm) across, borne in summer.
Soft yellow with red center. **Leaves** Oval, spoon-
shaped, or cylindrical, and fleshy. Light green.
• NATIVE HABITAT Garden origin.
• CULTIVATION Grow in poor, sharply drained soil.
• PROPAGATION Sow seed at 61–66°F (16–19°C)
in late winter or early spring.
• OTHER NAMES *D. bellidiformis* 'Yellow Ice',
Mesembryanthemum criniflorum 'Yellow Ice'.

HEIGHT
4in (10cm)

SPREAD
12in (30cm)

HEIGHT
4–6in
(10–15cm)

SPREAD
12in (30cm)

Compositae/Asteraceae		Compositae/Asteraceae

LEUCANTHEMUM PALUDOSUM
'Show Star'

Habit Bushy annual. **Flowers** Daisy-like, to
1⅛in (3cm) across, borne throughout summer.
Bright yellow. **Leaves** Spoon-shaped, wavy-
margined, toothed. Mid-green.
• NATIVE HABITAT Garden origin.
• CULTIVATION Grow in moderately fertile soil,
in sun. Suitable for a mixed or annual border.
• PROPAGATION Sow seed *in situ* in spring.
• OTHER NAME *Chrysanthemum paludosum*
'Show Star'.

GAZANIA Chansonette Series

Habit Vigorous, evergreen perennials, grown
as annuals. **Flowers** Solitary, daisy-like, borne
in summer. Shades of pink, red, yellow, bronze,
or orange, often zoned in contrasting colors.
Leaves Narrow to spoon-shaped, glossy. Dark
green, with a white, silky, hairy underside.
• NATIVE HABITAT Garden origin.
• CULTIVATION Grow in light, sandy soil, in a
sheltered site, in sun. Good for coastal gardens.
• PROPAGATION Sow seed at 64–68°F (18–20°C)
in late winter or early spring.

HEIGHT
6in (15cm)

SPREAD
8in (20cm)

Z 7–9

HEIGHT
8in (20cm)

SPREAD
10in (25cm)

Compositae/Asteraceae	

GAZANIA 'Mini Star Tangerine'

Habit Compact, tuft-forming, evergreen perennial, grown as an annual. *Flowers* Solitary, daisy-like, borne freely from summer. White, bright pink, golden-yellow, beige, bronze, or orange. *Leaves* Narrow to spoon-shaped, glossy. Dark green, with a white, silky, hairy underside.
• NATIVE HABITAT Garden origin.
• CULTIVATION Grow in sandy, well-drained soil, in a sheltered site, in sun. Good in coastal gardens.
• PROPAGATION Sow seed at 64–68°F (18–20°C) in late winter or early spring.

☼ ◊

Z 7–9

HEIGHT
8in (20cm)

SPREAD
10in (25cm)

Scrophulariaceae	

MIMULUS × *HYBRIDUS* 'Calypso'

Habit Bushy, freely branched perennial, grown as an annual. *Flowers* Solitary, tubular, with flared mouths, 2in (5cm) across, borne in summer. Pink, burgundy-red, yellow, or orange, including self-colored, bicolored, and spotted flowers. *Leaves* Oval, toothed. Bright green.
• NATIVE HABITAT Garden origin.
• CULTIVATION Grow in sun or partial shade. Good for streamsides, bog gardens, and moist borders.
• PROPAGATION Sow seed in containers in a cold frame in autumn or spring.

☼ ◖

Z 7–9

HEIGHT
4½–9in
(12–23cm)

SPREAD
12in (30cm)

Scrophulariaceae	

MIMULUS × *HYBRIDUS*
Malibu Series (orange)

Habit Bushy, freely branched perennial, grown as an annual. *Flowers* Tubular, with flared mouths, 2in (5cm) across, borne in summer. Flame. *Leaves* Oval, toothed. Bright green.
• NATIVE HABITAT Garden origin.
• CULTIVATION Grows best in sun or partial shade. Good for streamsides, bog gardens, and moist borders. Ideal for bedding and hanging baskets.
• PROPAGATION Sow seed in containers in a cold frame in autumn or spring.

☼ ◖

Z 7–9

HEIGHT
6in (15cm)

SPREAD
to 12in
(30cm)

Compositae/Asteraceae	CREEPING ZINNIA

SANVITALIA PROCUMBENS
'Mandarin Orange'

Habit Compact, mat-forming, annual. *Flowers* Semi-double, daisy-like, ¾in (2cm) across, borne from summer to autumn. Bright orange. *Leaves* Oval, pointed. Mid-green.
• NATIVE HABITAT Garden origin. Species occurs in rocky places and dry river washes in Mexico.
• CULTIVATION Grow in moderately fertile soil that is rich in organic matter. Good for troughs, window boxes, hanging baskets, and other containers.
• PROPAGATION Sow *in situ* in autumn or spring.

☼ ◊

HEIGHT
6in (15cm)

SPREAD
14in (35cm)

How to Buy Annuals and Biennials

Annuals and biennials are some of the easiest plants to grow from seed. Buying seed generally offers the widest selection, although seed series are often available only as mixtures, rather than single colors. Seedlings and young plants are also widely available from nurseries and garden centers in spring and early summer. Although the range of cultivars is sometimes rather restricted, commercial growers can often obtain seed series in separate colors, which makes it easier to plan color-themed borders.

Buying bedding plants

Where no greenhouse is available to raise half-hardy annuals from seed, a practical option is to buy annuals or biennials as trays or blocks of young plants. In addition to saving on time and materials, young plants also provide an almost instant display of color when planted out in a garden border or in containers. For rapid establishment and good growth, it is important to select sturdy, well-branched young plants with short-noded shoots and healthy leaves. The roots should be well developed, but not pot-bound or constricted. If the roots are congested they are likely to be damaged when separating them to plant out, causing a severe check on the plants' growth and subsequent flowering. Avoid buying plants in dry potting mix, or with yellowed or diseased foliage, because although they will probably grow on, they establish less readily and may not flower as freely.

Half-hardy bedding plants are sold at various stages from seedling to flowering plant, and frequently appear in garden centers well before the date at which it is safe to plant them out. Before buying, ensure that you can provide suitable conditions for growing them on under cover until the danger of frost has passed. Young plants need to be hardened off, or gradually acclimatized, in a cold greenhouse or cold frame before setting out (see p.167). They are likely to have been produced in heated greenhouses,

---

BEDDING PLANTS

Choose plants (here, petunias) with vigorous, compact growth, and healthy green foliage. Reject any that are leggy (etiolated) or have yellowed or dead leaves (see inset).

POT-GROWN ANNUALS

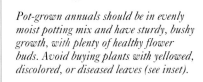

Pot-grown annuals should be in evenly moist potting mix and have sturdy, bushy growth, with plenty of healthy flower buds. Avoid buying plants with yellowed, discolored, or diseased leaves (see inset).

and a sudden change in environmental conditions, or exposure to frost or cold wind, will either kill them outright or else stunt the plants' growth. If plants are to be set out immediately after purchase, check with the supplier that they have been properly hardened off. Later in spring, as plants begin their flowering season, try to select plants with plenty of unopened flowerbuds. Once they are in full flower they will establish less readily, and may not flower so generously during the rest of the season.

Planting in containers

For an almost instant display of color in ornamental containers, select annuals or biennials that have been pot-grown or produced in modular plastic packs. Water the young plants thoroughly before planting, and allow to drain.

Plan the positioning of the plants carefully. Arrange trailing plants to cascade over the sides and front of the container and graduate taller plants to provide height at the back and center of the arrangement. Cover the base of the container with crocks (broken clay pots) to ensure free drainage, then fill half to three-quarters full with soil-based potting mix. Soilless mixes are useful for hanging baskets, since they are lighter in weight, but bear in mind that they can be difficult to re-wet if allowed to dry out, and will need supplementary feeding during the growing season.

Slide each plant gently from its pot, supporting the root ball with one hand. Tease out the roots carefully and set each plant in position. Aim to set the neck of each plant about ⅜in (1cm) below the container rim. Gently firm the compost around each plant and level off the surface. It is also important to check that there are no air pockets, especially at the sides and corners of the container. If any air pockets are found, fill them with moist potting mix. Finally, water in the plant thoroughly.

PLANTING IN CONTAINERS

1 *Cover the bottom of the container with crocks. Fill it half to three-quarters full with moist potting mix. Remove each plant gently from its pot.*

2 *Scoop back potting mix and set each plant (here,* Begonia, Lobelia, *and* Impatiens *cultivars) in position with the neck ⅜in (1cm) below the rim.*

3 *Firm the potting mix gently around each plant. Check for air pockets and fill with more moist potting mix if necessary. Level off the surface and water in thoroughly.*

SEEDS AND SEEDLINGS

SEED TAPE

SEED GEL

SEEDLINGS

Purchasing seeds and seedlings
Annuals may be raised from seedlings, or by the use of seed tapes or seed gel.

MARKING OUT ANNUAL BORDERS

1 *Make a planting plan, arranging plants in informal drifts by height, habit, and color. Mark out the outline of drifts on the soil with sand or grit.*

2 *Sow seed in drills within each drift, altering the direction of drills in adjacent drifts. Plants blend together as they grow and disguise the straight lines.*

Buying seeds

When buying seeds, check the packet for a packaging date to ensure that the contents are the current season's stock. For best results, always buy fresh seed that has been stored in cool, dry conditions. The viability of seeds varies greatly between species, but as a general rule, most begin to deteriorate after a year, especially if they become damp or warm. Seeds in sealed foil packets can last for several years, but once the seal has been broken, the seeds begin to deteriorate.

For most purposes, naturally pollinated (open-pollinated) seeds are perfectly satisfactory, although slight natural variations in color and habit can be expected. For plantings where vigor, uniformity of growth, and consistency of color are important, such as bedding schemes, choose F1 or F2 hybrids.

Pelleted and primed seeds

Some F1 or F2 hybrids are available in pelleted seeds, so named as they are individually coated with a nutritional and fungicidal paste to form a smooth pellet. Although slightly more expensive than untreated seeds, they can be space-sown at the recommended distance for the cultivar concerned, and so do not need wasteful thinning later. They must be watered thoroughly after sowing to ensure that water penetrates the seed coat evenly for germination to begin.

Primed seeds are treated so that they germinate immediately after sowing. This is particularly beneficial for the seeds of species and cultivars that do not germinate readily.

Seed tapes and gels

An effective way to sow seed is to use seed tape, a tissue-like strip of soluble material with seeds embedded in it. The tape is laid at the bottom of a drill and covered with a thin layer of soil. Seed gel kits may be purchased for fluid sowing. The seeds are suspended in a paste-like gel in a plastic bag and are then squeezed out along a prepared drill. Although initially more expensive than seed sown directly by hand, both these techniques ensure even and well-spaced seedlings that need little or no thinning later.

Pregerminating seed

Seeds may be pregerminated for an early start, particularly if cold soil will retard germination, risking rot. Store in a warm area, spaced out on damp paper towels. Keep moist until germinated, then sow in pots or outdoors. Seedling plugs are well-established plantlets grown in wedges of potting mix. The plantlets are ready to be planted up into individual pots or modular trays, and should be grown on at an appropriate temperature in good light until big enough to plant out. They are cheaper than larger bedding plants.

Storing seed

Packets often have more seed than is needed, and must be stored properly to ensure viability. Fold end of packet and seal before storing in a plastic container with a tight-fitting lid or in a resealable plastic bag. Place the container in the coldest part of the refrigerator. Most seeds will successfully freeze, as well.

Sowing methods

When and where to sow annuals and biennials is determined by when they are to flower, and the temperature needed for germination. Outdoors, seed may be sown broadcast or in drills. Broadcasting is useful for plants that develop deep tap roots that resent disturbance, such as *Gypsophila* and *Papaver*. Sowing in drills produces straight, regular rows of seedlings; this regimented appearance is lost when thinned. Sowing seed in informal drifts marked out in sand also creates a more natural arrangement. For both broadcasting and sowing in drills, prepare a seed bed by digging over the soil to a spade's depth. Rake to a fine tilth then firm gently with a tamper.

SOWING IN DRILLS

1 Prepare a seed bed by digging over to a spade's depth and raking to a fine tilth. Using a string line as a guide, make a furrow, 1in (2.5cm) deep, with a hoe.

2 Sow seed by hand, a few at a time, scattering them thinly and evenly along the length of the drill. Sow pelleted seed at its recommended spacing.

3 Rake the soil back over the drill, taking care not to dislodge the seed. Tamp the drill gently with the back of a rake. Label and water in thoroughly, using a watering can with a fine rose.

THINNING SEEDLINGS

1 *To thin individual seedlings (here, Consolida ajacis), press gently on either side of the seedling to be retained while pulling out unwanted seedlings.*

2 *To thin clumps of seedlings, lift them with plenty of soil around the roots. They can then be separated gently and re-planted at appropriate spacings.*

Most ordinary garden soils give good results, but do not sow annuals in very fertile soils, since these can produce excessive leafy growth at the expense of flowers. If the soil is very poor, apply a balanced granular fertilizer at a rate of $2oz/yd^2$ ($70g/m^2$). On germination, thin out seedlings to the recommended spacings for the plant concerned. Protect and support where necessary.

Sowing in containers

Pots, seed pans, trays, half trays, and modular packs are all suitable containers for seed sowing. Biodegradable pots are ideal for seedlings that resent root disturbance. All containers must be perfectly clean before sowing.

Fill the container with seed starting mix and level off. Tap container to remove air pockets, then firm with a tamper so that the soil surface is ⅜in (1cm) below the container rim. Water with a fine rose, or immerse container to its rim in a tray of water. Allow to drain for an hour. Sow seed thinly and evenly on the surface and cover to its own depth with a layer of sieved seed starting mix. To avoid damping-off problems on germination, spray with a commercial fungicide. Finally, cover container with both a sheet of glass and shade-cloth.

PROTECTING AND SUPPORTING SEEDLINGS

Tall or slim-stemmed annuals need the support of narrow twigs, pea sticks, or wire netting with a mesh size no greater than 1in (2.5cm). Supports should be slightly shorter than the plants' ultimate height, so that the plants grow through and disguise their supports when they reach maturity.

1 *Insert supports in soil as seedlings (here, Consolida ajacis) reach 2–2¼in (5–7cm) high.*

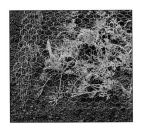

2 *Stretch wire netting over seedlings (here, Eschscholzia). Secure edges with sticks or pins.*

Hardy annuals

Plants categorized as hardy annuals germinate at a temperature of 45–55°F (7–13°C), and can be sown directly in their flowering site as soon as the soil reaches 45°F (7°C) in spring. Sowing in succession from spring to mid-summer ensures color throughout summer. Some hardy annuals, such as pot marigolds (*Calendula*) or poppies (*Papaver*), can be sown in autumn. They will overwinter safely as young plants for an earlier display the following season. In very cold or exposed areas, cloche protection should be provided as an insurance against winter losses.

Hardy biennials

The seeds of hardy biennials are sown in a seed bed outdoors between late spring and mid-summer. The exact timing depends on the speed of development of the plant in question. Forget-me-nots (*Myosotis*), for example, grow rapidly and are sown in mid-summer. Other hardy biennials, such as foxgloves (*Digitalis purpurea*), take longer to develop and are sown in late spring. The young plants are transferred to their flowering site in autumn, or in early spring the following year. Pinch out any flowerbuds that appear before winter, to avoid reduced flowering in the following season.

SOWING IN A SEED TRAY

1 *Fill a seed tray with seed starting mix, level off with the back of a tamper, and firm gently to about ⅖in (1cm) below the rim.*

2 *Sprinkle seeds thinly and evenly over the soil surface by tapping them out from a folded piece of paper.*

3 *Cover the seed with a layer of sieved seed starting mix to about the seeds' own depth. Label and water.*

4 *Spray the surface of the soil with fungicide and place a sheet of clear glass or polyethylene over the tray to maintain even humidity.*

5 *Shade the tray with cloth or a sheet of newspaper to protect from direct sunlight. Remove both shade-cloth and glass as soon as germination begins.*

PRICKING OUT INTO A PACK

1 When seedlings (here, Tagetes) are large enough to handle, tap container to loosen potting mix. Remove both seedlings and potting mix intact.

2 Separate seedlings carefully with a spoon. Handle only by their seed leaves and take care not to damage the roots. Retain potting mix around roots.

3 Place each root ball into a dibbled hole in the potting mix. Firm the potting mix around the roots with a dibble, level off, and water in carefully.

Half-hardy annuals and biennials

The germination temperature of half-hardy annuals and biennials is between 55–70°F (13–21°C). In warm climates, they may be sown *in situ*, or in a seed bed, in the same way as hardy annuals and biennials. In frost-prone areas, half-hardy annuals are sown in pots or trays under glass between late winter and early spring. Rapidly growing annuals, like marigolds (*Tagetes*), may also be sown *in situ* in mid-spring.

Half-hardy biennials are sown in containers between late spring and mid-summer. They should not be planted out until fully hardened off; half-hardy plants may tolerate cool conditions for short periods, but they are adversely affected by extreme cold. Tender annuals, such as begonias, will be killed or badly checked by exposure to low temperatures, so delay setting them out until weather conditions are warm and stable. The young plants must be overwintered in frost-free conditions in a frame or greenhouse, and set out in spring. Tender perennials grown as annuals, such as busy lizzies (*Impatiens*) and pelargoniums, are treated as for half-hardy annuals, but germinate best at 61–75°F (16–24°C). Consult the seed packet for specific temperatures.

Seeds with special requirements

A few seeds need special treatment to germinate. *Begonia, Impatiens,* and some other very fine seeds need light for germination. They are surface sown and not covered with potting mix. Most tender plants need constant temperatures to germinate; temperature fluctuation can cause failure. Primulas, which also need light to germinate, will fail at temperatures above 70°F (21°C). Some seeds, including pansies (*Viola* × *wittrockiana*), will only germinate in darkness. A number of hardy species, such as *Molucella*, need stratifying before they germinate freely. Place the seed pan in the bottom of the refrigerator for two weeks before bringing into warmth at 64–70°F (18–21°C).

Pricking out

Container-grown seedlings need to be transplanted, or pricked out, into larger containers to grow them on before planting out. If overcrowded, the seedlings become drawn and spindly and are likely to succumb to fungal diseases, such as damping-off. As soon as seedlings are large enough to handle, prick them out into individual 2⅜in (6cm) pots, modular containers, or at 1⅜–2in (4–5cm) spacings in trays. In order to avoid bruising the fragile stems and roots, it is important to handle them only by their seed leaves. Damaged tissue will not grow on successfully and is far more susceptible to fungal infections. Once seedlings have been pricked out, place them in a propagator or cover them with clear plastic for a few days while they re-establish. Do not allow the plastic to touch the leaves as this can lead to rotting off. Return the seedlings to their previous growing conditions until they are ready to be hardened off.

Hardening off

Half-hardy annuals raised in controlled growing conditions must be hardened off, or gradually acclimatized, to outdoor conditions before planting out.

HARDENING OFF

Polytunnel
If using a low polytunnel to harden off half-hardy annuals (here, Tagetes*), roll up sides to increase ventilation slowly.*

Cold frame
In a cold frame, ventilation is increased by opening the frame light progressively wider until it is finally removed.

PLANTING OUT INTO OPEN GROUND

1 *When plants are fully hardened off, (here,* Tagetes*) remove them from the container. Keep the root ball intact.*

2 *Place each plant in a hole large enough to accommodate the root ball, setting it at the same depth as it was in its container.*

3 *Gently push back the soil and firm around the roots so that there are no air pockets. Water in thoroughly with a fine rose.*

The aim is to wean plants from a warm, protected environment without exposing them to sudden, potentially damaging changes in conditions. About 6–7 weeks before planting outdoors, move the plants to a cooler part of the greenhouse for a week. Transfer to a closed cold frame or low polytunnel, and gradually admit more air, day by day, as weather conditions improve. Close the frame at night and, if frost threatens, insulate with burlap or old blankets. Remove the frame light for the last few days before planting out, but replace if frost is forecast.

Planting out

Prior to planting out, water the young plants thoroughly and allow to drain for an hour. Plant out into a prepared, weed-free bed or border. Remove the young plants from their containers carefully, to avoid damage to the root ball. Modular packs may be broken apart to free the root ball. Tap more substantial pots on a hard surface to loosen the potting mix. Invert the pot, and slide out the plant while supporting the root ball with a finger on either side of the main stem. If plants are in trays, slide out the contents in one piece, separate the plants by hand, and keep as much soil as possible around the roots. Set plants out at the same depth as they were in their containers. Firm soil around the roots gently, and water in thoroughly.

Planting out climbing annuals

Site climbing annuals where they can scramble naturally through a shrub or small tree, or train them against a fence, wall, or other support. If growing up a shrub or tree, position the climber at the perimeter of the canopy, on the sunniest side. Guide the leading shoots into the branches with slender canes. If a support is used to grow plants against a wall, set the plant 12in (30cm) from the wall base to enable the roots to obtain sufficient moisture. Insert cane pyramids before planting. Set the young plants just outside the canes, tying them in loosely.

Planting annuals to a design

Displaying annuals in formal patterns in beds and borders is a traditionally Victorian method of planting, although there is no reason why this technique

---

PLANTING OUT CLIMBING ANNUALS

Planting beside a host plant
Plant twining annuals (here, Ipomoea) *at least 9in (23cm) from the host's stem, and, if necessary, guide the leading shoot to the host's branches using slender canes.*

Planting against a cane support
Position the young plant (here, Thunbergia alata) *at the outside of the canes. Tie in the leading shoot loosely to the cane with soft twine, raffia, or sweet pea rings (inset).*

cannot be re-interpreted to create modern designs. Draw up a plan on paper, assemble all the bedding plants to be used, and, before starting to plant, check them off against the planting list. The plan shown here uses a large number of bedding plants, but a simpler design using only two to four different kinds of bedding can be equally effective. To check for spacing and to make any final adjustments that may be necessary before planting, initially set the plants out in their containers on top of the prepared bed. Keep a few plants in reserve as insurance against any failures.

PLANTING ANNUALS TO A DESIGN

1 *Mark out the design with string lines and sand, working from the center outwards or from back to front. Use planks or kneeler boards to avoid compacting the soil. Compacted soil inhibits drainage and adversely affects plant growth, which must be uniform and even, if the design is to be successful.*

2 *Plant out seedlings carefully, handling each individual as little as possible. Finish one section before moving on to the next.*

3 *As each section is completed, trim off any damaged, uneven, or straggly growth to keep each section even and compact.*

4 *Water thoroughly, section by section, so that the first plantings do not dry out before the entire planting is complete. Keep the bed well watered until plants are established. Remove discolored or damaged foliage as seen. Replace any failures as soon as possible with reserve plants to avoid any gaps in the design.*

ROUTINE CARE

Annuals have a relatively short lifespan and their requirements for routine maintenance are fairly basic. Tall annuals will need staking, to prevent them from blowing over, or toppling under the weight of their own flowers. Annuals need to be watered regularly during dry periods, especially if grown in containers, and deadheaded routinely to prolong their flowering period. If allowed to set seed early in the season, annuals will die prematurely as their life cycle will have been completed. Once they have finished their display at the end of the season, the plants should be disposed of, or added to the compost heap.

Providing support

Tall and slender-stemmed annuals in open ground need the support of wire netting or pea sticks, which should be inserted when the young plants reach a few inches in height (see p.164). Tall plants, like sunflowers (*Helianthus*), may need to be individually staked. At planting time, insert a cane for support where it will be least visible, tying in the main stem to the cane as growth proceeds.

Watering, weeding, and feeding

Once planted out, annuals and biennials need to be kept moist. Regular and thorough watering, using either a garden sprinkler or a watering can, may be necessary until well established. It is important to apply sufficient water to penetrate the soil deeply, as this encourages deep rooting. If only the surface layers of soil are wetted, the roots remain near the surface and become more susceptible to dry conditions. Once established, plants in the open ground usually need watering only during prolonged dry periods. However, bear in mind that if plants do not receive adequate water, they are likely to run to seed rapidly.

Plants in containers should be checked daily, and watered as often as necessary to keep the soil mix evenly moist but not waterlogged. When the weather is warm and dry, container-grown plants dry out very quickly and may need watering twice or more each day. Plants grown in plastic containers generally dry out less rapidly than in terracotta pots, so take care not to overwater.

SUPPORTING CLIMBERS

When planting climbers (here, Eccremocarpus scaber*) near a wall, tie them onto a wire netting. Tendril climbers may need initial guidance into their support. Scramblers will need tying onto the support with soft twine.*

SUPPORTING TALL ANNUALS

Tall annuals in pots (here, Salpiglossis*) can be supported by 3 or 4 canes, inserted into the soil mix around the pot rim. Twine soft string around canes. The plants will disguise the supports as they grow.*

Most annuals thrive in fairly poor soils, and seldom need additional feeding unless the soil is of very low fertility. Well-manured soils tend to produce rapid, abundant leaf growth with few flowers. In very poor soils, however, applying a fast-acting liquid fertilizer as flowerbuds develop will be beneficial.

Keep annuals and biennials weed-free to prevent competition for light, water, and soil nutrients.

Annuals as cut or dried flowers

Many annuals are ideal as fresh cut flowers for indoor decoration, and some may be dried for winter arrangements. Everlasting flowers, such as *Bracteantha*, are best cut when the flowers are half open. If allowed to open fully before cutting, they become overblown on drying. Suspend the annuals upside down in small bunches in a warm, airy, preferably dark place, as the colors will fade on exposure to strong light. The flowers of *Limonium sinuatum* should be fully open before drying, since they seldom open fully if cut in bud. Dip the cut stems of *Papaver croceum* in boiling water before arranging. This seals the cut ends, preventing the formation of air locks that block the uptake of water.

ANNUALS AS DRIED FLOWERS

1 *Cut flower stems (here,* Limonium sinuatum*) as near as possible to the basal rosette. If plants have leafy stems, strip leaves before tying in bundles of six.*

2 *Hang upside down in a warm, well-ventilated place, either in the dark or out of direct sun. Bright sunlight will fade the flowers' brilliant colors.*

MAINTAINING ANNUALS IN CONTAINERS

Plants in containers need little maintenance other than regular watering and occasional feeding. Deadhead to keep the display attractive, and as individual plants finish flowering, extract them from the container. Remove carefully, disturbing the roots of the other plants as little as possible. Replace with a later-maturing plant.

1 *Carefully extract plants that have finished flowering. Do not disturb the remaining plants.*

2 *Add fresh potting mix, and then fill any gaps with new plants to continue the display.*

DEADHEADING

To prolong the flowering period, cut off flowers (here, pansies) regularly as they fade, preferably before they begin to set seed. Using sharp scissors, pruners, or finger and thumb, remove the dead flower near the base of the stalk. This will encourage a fresh flush of blooms.

Deadheading

Regular deadheading of annuals has two main functions. Firstly, it improves the plant's appearance. Secondly, it prolongs the flowering season by preventing plants from setting seed. The plant's energy is then directed into producing a further flush of bloom.

Pinch off dead and fading flowers cleanly between finger and thumb, or use scissors and pruners for plants with tougher stems. If seed is needed for the following season, leave a few flowerheads in place at the end of the current flowering season. Do not deadhead plants that bear ornamental seedheads, such as honesty (*Lunaria annua*). A few annuals, such as poppies (*Papaver*), do not produce a new flush of bloom in response to deadheading.

Saving seeds

The seed of complex garden hybrids and cultivars will not come true, and their seed, if produced at all, is not worth saving. Many species, however, such as honesty (*Lunaria*), foxglove (*Digitalis*), and love-in-a mist (*Nigella*),

SAVING SEEDS

1 *Collect seedheads or capsules (here, Nigella) as they begin to ripen, but before they split. Place in a tray lined with newspaper or blotting paper and set in warm sun until dry.*

2 *When the seedhead is dry, shake out the seeds and, if necessary, separate them from the chaff. Transfer the seeds to a clean, dry, labeled envelope. Store in a dry place at a cool, even temperature.*

will produce identical offspring with perfectly acceptable levels of variation. Their seeds are easily collected and saved for sowing the following year. For best results, select seedheads from plants that have produced flowers of particularly good form and color.

Cut off the seedheads as they begin to turn brown, but before they split. Spread them on paper-lined trays and position in a warm, sunny, well-ventilated place until completely dry. Alternatively, bundle them together by their stems and hang them upside down with their heads in a clean paper bag. Extract the seed, clean off any chaff or debris, and transfer the seed to a clean, clearly labeled paper bag or envelope. Store in cool, dry conditions until ready for sowing the following spring.

Autumn clearance

At the end of the flowering season, dead, fading plants should be disposed of or transferred to the compost pile. If legal, it is best to burn rather than compost any diseased material, to avoid spreading the infection elsewhere in the garden. Perennials grown as annuals or biennials,

such as pansies (*Viola* x *wittrockiana*) or polyanthus, can be lifted and transferred to another part of the garden, where they may continue to bloom for several seasons. Hollyhocks (*Alcea rosea*) should be cut to the base after flowering, and will continue to produce flower spikes for several years. They do, however, lose vigor and flower quality with age. Hollyhocks are grown as biennials primarily because of their susceptibility to hollyhock rust (*Puccinia malvacearum*), which overwinters in the crown of the plant and re-infects the new growth in spring. Young plants succumb less readily, but it is good practice not to plant hollyhocks in the same soil and site year after year.

It is not worth re-planting wallflowers (*Erysimum*) or antirrhinums, as they rapidly become very woody or leggy and do not perform well after their first flowering season. Tender perennials, such as begonias and busy lizzies (*Impatiens*), can be lifted and potted up in late summer. Given adequate light and warmth, they will continue to bloom for many months in the home, greenhouse, or conservatory.

CUTTING DOWN SHORT-LIVED PERENNIALS

1 *Not all seedheads ripen at the same time. To prevent self-sown seedlings, cut back flowered stems before seedheads ripen fully.*

2 *Short-lived perennials, such as hollyhocks* (Alcea rosea), *produce flower spikes for several years if cut back after flowering.*

3 *Cut out each flowered stem at its base using a sharp pair of pruners. Do not damage new growth sprouting from the base.*

Sweet Peas

Lathyrus odoratus, commonly called sweet pea, is also deservedly known as the "queen of annuals." Sweet peas produce beautiful flowers over long periods, in a wide range of clear colors, but are perhaps best known for their characteristic sweet fragrance. They are ideal as cut flowers, and when well grown will provide fresh flowers daily over many weeks. The plants can be trained on wigwams, pillars, or canes to provide long and colorful displays. Sweet peas can also be grown in a cutting border, or among shrubs and perennials. They are indispensable when grown in cottage-style gardens, and also prove useful when grown in a potager, or vegetable garden, as they attract pollinating bees and other beneficial insects. Sweet peas can be grown either as bushes and allowed to develop naturally, or more commonly as cordons. Cordon-grown sweet peas produce top-quality, long-stemmed flowers and are ideal for cutting.

There are many different types of sweet pea. Among the tall cultivars, the best known are the Spencer types, with large flowers and frilled petals. Grandifloras, or old-fashioned sweet peas, have smaller but more intensely scented flowers. Dwarf sweet peas include variants that do not have tendrils, and are ideal for growing in window boxes and hanging baskets. They need little or no support when grown in open ground.

Sowing seed

Sweet pea seeds should be sown in mid-autumn, late winter, or early spring. Autumn-sown plants bloom earlier, but in frost-prone areas need cold frame protection over winter. To aid germination, nick seeds with a sharp knife before sowing, removing a small piece of seed coat opposite the eye. Seeds may be soaked before sowing as soon as they begin to swell. Sweet pea seeds are best sown in individual pots, with 2–3 seeds to a 2¼in (7cm) pot.

Old-fashioned Sweet Peas

Old-fashioned sweet peas were among the earliest cultivars of L. odoratus, *and are closer to the species than more modern cultivars. The flowers are smaller and more dainty than modern cultivars, with intense colors and a strong perfume.*

Dwarf Sweet Peas

Dwarf sweet peas grow to about 36in (90cm) tall and need little or no support. Some forms do not have tendrils. They are ideal for mixed or annual borders, and are also well suited for planting in tubs or other containers.

LATERAL 1. Located on or to the side of an axis or organ. 2. Side-shoot from the *stem* of a plant.

LEAF-MOLD Fibrous, flaky, organic material derived from decomposed leaves, used as an ingredient in potting media and as a soil improver or *mulch*.

LIP Prominent lower lobe on a flower, formed by one or more fused *petals* or *sepals*.

LOAM Well-structured, fertile soil that is moisture retentive but free draining.

MULCH Organic matter applied to the soil around plants to conserve moisture, protect roots from cold damage, reduce weed growth, and enrich the soil.

NEUTRAL (of soil) With a *pH* value of 7, the point at which soil is neither *acid* nor *alkaline*.

ORGANIC 1. Compounds containing carbon derived from decomposed plant or animal organisms. 2. Used loosely of *mulches*, soil improvers, and soil mixes that are derived from plant materials.

OVARY The part of the female portion of the *flower* containing *ovules* that will form the fruit.

OVULE The part of the *ovary* that develops into the *seed*.

PERENNIAL A plant that lives for at least three seasons.

PERFOLIATE Stalkless leaves, single or in opposite pairs, with the base united around the *stem*.

PETAL One portion of the usually showy and colored part of the *corolla*.

pH The scale by which the acidity or alkalinity of soil is measured. See also *acid*, *alkaline*, and *neutral*.

PLUME See *Spray*.

RAY FLORET One of the tiny *flowers* that together form the outer ring of flower petals in a composite *flowerhead*.

RHIZOME Horizontal, usually branching and fleshy *stem*, growing underground or, less often, at ground level.

ROSETTE A group of leaves that radiate from approximately the same point, often borne at ground level at the base of a very short *stem*.

SEED Ripened, fertilized *ovule*, containing a dormant embryo capable of developing into an adult plant.

SEED SERIES Name applied to a group of *cultivars* of annuals that share most of the same characteristics but differ from one another by one character (rarely more), usually color.

SEEDHEAD Any, usually dry, fruit that contains ripe *seeds*.

SEEDLING A young plant that has developed from a *seed*.

SELF-COLORED Describes a *flower* with a uniform color.

SELF-SEED To release viable *seed* which germinates around the parent to produce *seedlings*.

SEPAL Part of a *calyx*, usually insignificant, small, and green, but sometimes colored, showy, and *petal*-like.

SPECIES A category in plant classification, the rank below *genus*, containing closely related, very similar individual plants.

SPRAY A group of *flowers* or *flowerheads* on a single, branching *stem*.

SPUR A hollow projection from a *petal* that often yields nectar.

STEM The main axis of a plant, usually above ground and supporting leaves, *flowers*, and fruits. Sometimes referred to as a stalk.

STIGMA The part of the female portion of the *flower*, borne at the tip of the *style*, that receives pollen.

STRATIFY (Pre-chill) To expose *seed* to cold to break dormancy, either by sowing outdoors in winter or refrigerating before sowing.

STYLE The part of the *flower* on which the *stigma* is borne.

SUB-SHRUB Woody-based plant with soft, usually herbaceous *stems*.

TENDER Of a plant that is vulnerable to cold damage.

TERMINAL Located at the tip of a *stem*, shoot, or other organ.

TOOTH A small, marginal, often pointed lobe on a leaf, *calyx*, or *corolla*.

TRUE (of seedlings) Retaining the distinctive characteristics of the parent when raised from *seed*.

TUBERS Swollen food storage organ, usually underground, derived from a root or *stem*.

UPRIGHT (of habit) With vertical or semi-vertical main branches.

WHORL Circular arrangement of three or more *flowers*, leaves, or shoots, arising from the same point.

INDEX

Each genus name is shown in **bold** type, followed by a brief description. Species, varieties and subspecies are given in *italics;* cultivars are in roman type with single quotes. Common names appear in parentheses.

─────── A ───────

Abelmoschus
Frost-tender, hairy annuals and perennials, grown for their hibiscus-like flowers.
  moschatus Pacific Series 94

African daisy see *Dimorphotheca* and *Lonas annua*
African marigold see *Tagetes*

Ageratum (Floss flower)
Half-hardy annuals and biennials, grown for their clusters of rounded, brush-like flowerheads.
  houstonianum
    'Adriatic' 99
    'Bavaria' 99
    'Blue Danube' 155
    'Blue Mink' 113
    'Hawaii White' 146
    'Swing Pink' 182

Agrostemma (Corn cockle)
Cold-tolerant annuals bearing open, trumpet-shaped flowers. Seeds are tiny, rounded, dark brown, and toxic.
  coeli-rosa see *Silene coeli-rosa*
  githago
    'Milas' 33
    'Purple Queen' 45

Agrostis
Cold-tolerant annual and perennial grasses, some of which are important fodder crops or lawn grasses.
  nebulosa (Cloud grass) 126

Alcea (Hollyhock)
Fully hardy biennials and short-lived perennials, grown for their tall spikes of flowers.
  rosea 32
    'Chater's Double' 42
    Majorette Group 22
    Mixed 25

Alcea continued
    'Nigra' 49
    Summer Carnival Group 41

Alonsoa
Half-hardy perennials, grown as annuals, suitable for cut flowers.
  linearis (Mask flower) 73
  warscewiczii 40

Althaea rosea see *Alcea rosea*
Alyssum maritimum see *Lobularia maritima*

Amaranthus
Half-hardy annuals, grown for their dense clusters of tiny flowers or for their colorful foliage.
  caudatus (Love-lies-bleeding, Tassel flower) 43
  hypochondriacus (Prince's feather) 42
  tricolor 'Illumination' 97
    'Joseph's Coat' 140

Amberboa
Genus of upright annuals or biennials, with gray-green leaves and flowerheads with a thistle-like center, from spring to autumn.
  moschata (Sweet sultan) 64

Amblyopetalum caeruleum see *Tweedia caerulea*

Anchusa
Cold-tolerant annuals, biennials, and perennials, some of which are evergreen, mostly bearing blue flowers.
  capensis 'Blue Angel' 123

Annual clary see *Salvia viridis*
Annual phlox see *Phlox drummondii*

Anoda
Half-hardy annuals, perennials, and sub-shrubs, grown for their mallow-like flowers borne over long periods from summer to autumn.
  cristata
    'Opal Cup' 48
    'Silver Cup' 57

Antirrhinum (Snapdragon)
Fully to half-hardy annuals, perennials, and semi-evergreen sub-shrubs, producing flowers

Antirrhinum continued
from spring through to autumn.
    'Bells' 85
    Coronette Series 84
    Floral Carpet Series 85
    Hyacinth-flowered Series 85
    Madame Butterfly Series 85
    'Magic Carpet Mixed' 84
    Princess Series 85
    Royal Carpet Series 85
    Sonnet Series 84
    Tahiti Series 84
    'Trumpet Serenade' 85

Apple of Peru see *Nicandra physalodes*

Arctotis
Cold-tolerant annuals and perennials, grown for their flowerheads and foliage.
  fastuosa (Monarch of the Veldt) 139
    'Zulu Prince' 81
    Harlequin Hybrids 'Torch' 75
  venusta (Blue-eyed African daisy) 19

Argemone
Fully to half-hardy annuals and perennials, most of which are best treated as annuals.
  grandiflora 19
  mexicana (Devil's fig, Prickly poppy) 65

Atriplex
Genus of cold-tolerant annuals, perennials, and evergreen or semi-evergreen shrubs, grown for their foliage.
  hortensis var. *rubra* 43

─────── B ───────

Baby blue-eyes see *Nemophila menziesii*
Bartonia aurea see *Mentzelia lindleyi*
Basket flower see *Centaurea americana*

Bassia
Half-hardy perennials and annuals, grown for their feathery foliage and autumn tints.
  scoparia f. *trichophylla* (Burning bush, Summer cypress) 61

Beard grass see *Polypogon monspeliensis*

T

ACKNOWLEDGMENTS

Key: t=top; b=bottom; r=right; l=left; c=center; cra=center right above; cla=center left above; crb=center right below; clb=center left below

The publishers would like to thank the following for their kind permission to reproduce the photographs:

A-Z Botanical Collection 19bl, 22tr, 31cl, 70cr, 93cl, 115br / Robert J Erwin 41bl / P Etchells 88cr / Robert W Greig 122cl / Matt Johnston 39l / Anthony Menzies Shaw 156l / T G J Rayner 47br / Dan Sams 41r, 155cl / Heather Angel 119tr / Gillian Beckett 21bl;

Pat Brindley 28r, 29b, 38cl, 46br, 63cl, 75cl, 91cl, 91bl, 99cl, 126bl, 155cr, 157cr;

Eric Crichton 81cr, 83l, 92br, 132bl, 142br;

Garden Matters 148cl / Jeremy Hoare 140r;

Garden Picture Library 10, 12, 13t / Chris Burrows 133tl / Brian Carter 31tr, 99br, 111cr, 134br, 139l / Christopher Gallagher 27cl / John Glover 26cl, 108cl, 153cra;

John Glover 53tl, 132cr;

Derek Gould 117crb, 124tr, 159cr;

Holt Studios International 56r, 82br;

Andrew Lawson 2, 5, 65cr, 66tl, 71br, 84br, 85br, 123cr, 127tr, 145l, 147br, 154cra, 159bl;

Photo Flora 60cl, 60bl, 66bl;

Photos Horticultural 20, 22br, 24br, 27b, 30l, 30br, 40bl, 54cr, 55cl, 65tl, 67l, 70bl, 75r, 81cl, 82l, 84cr, 87tr, 89tr, 105tr, 111bl, 113br, 117clb, 118cl, 122tl, 127l, 128r, 149bl;

Plant Pictures World Wide 24bl, 45bl, 73cl, 81br, 83cr, 85tl, 88l, 91br, 105b, 130br, 146br;

Howard Rice 24tr, 25l, 26bl, 26br, 29cl, 31b, 32r, 36l, 36br, 37l, 37cr, 37br, 39br, 40br, 41cl, 43br, 45cl, 46cr, 48cr, 48bl, 48br, 49cl, 49cr, 49bl, 51tl, 52b, 54cl, 54br, 57, 58cr,

59cr, 60br, 61l, 61tr, 62bl, 65br, 69cr, 69bl, 71cl, 71cr, 78r, 80bl, 83br, 85cra, 87cr, 87b, 93br, 96cl, 96cr, 96bl, 100cl, 100br, 101crb, 102r, 103tl, 104r, 105cl, 107cl, 108bl, 108r, 110cl, 110br, 111cl, 116cl, 116bl, 116br, 117tl, 117cla, 117bl, 119cl, 119cr, 119br, 120cr, 120br, 122tr, 122bl, 123br, 126r, 129cl, 129cr, 129br, 133cl, 133cr, 133b, 135tr, 136br, 138, 139bl, 140bl, 145br, 146cl, 146cr, 147cr, 147bl, 148br, 149cr, 150r, 151cl, 154br, 158cl, 158cr, 159cl;

Harry Smith Collection 11, 19tl, 19br, 21tl, 21tr, 22l, 28l, 29tl, 29tr, 39cr, 40cl, 44cl, 44cr, 44bl, 44br, 47cl, 47cr, 47bl, 48cl, 51tr, 52tl, 53tr, 53cl, 53cr, 53b, 58cl, 58bl, 59l, 62r, 63bl, 63r, 64bl, 67tr, 68cl, 74bl, 74r, 79cr, 79br, 85bl, 87tl, 88br, 89cr, 94cl, 94bl, 94br, 98cl, 101br, 105cr, 107br, 109cl, 109bl, 113cl, 115cr, 119tl, 119bl, 120tr, 121tl, 121tr, 122br, 123bl, 126tl, 129bl, 130cr, 130bl, 133tr, 135cra, 137b, 141cl, 142bl, 143cr, 143br, 144cr, 144br, 147cl, 148bl, 152cl, 152cr, 153tr, 154tr, 156cl, 156cr;

Sutton Seeds 87cl, 132cl;

Thompson and Morgan 91cr, 157cl;

Unwins Seeds Ltd. 66br, 90tr, 100cr, 109cr, 119tl, 120cl, 152br;

Tom Wright 13b

Abbreviations

C	centigrade
in	inch, inches
cm	centimeter
m	meter
cv.	cultivar
mm	millimeter
F	Fahrenheit
oz	ounce
f.	forma
sp.	species
ft	foot, feet
subsp.	subspecies
g	gram
var.	variant

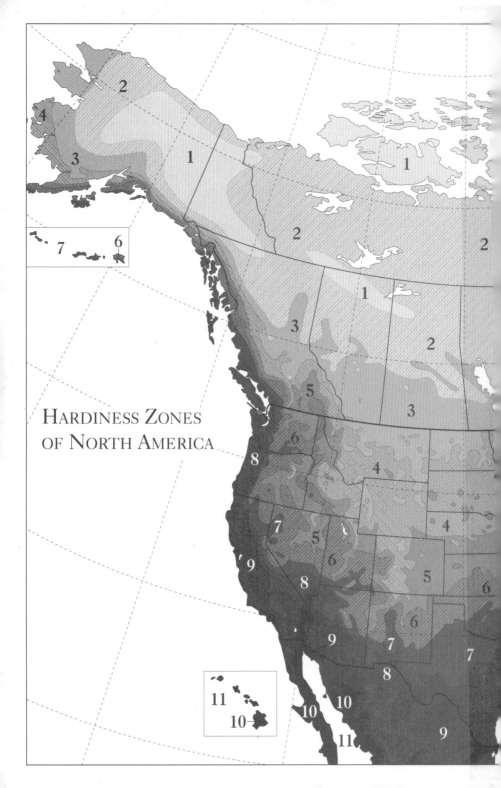

HARDINESS ZONES
OF NORTH AMERICA